Inter-linkages

UNU Policy Perspectives

In its series of *UNU Policy Perspectives*, the United Nations University Press publishes studies that are directly policy related yet based on solid scholarly research and analysis. Its objective is to provide timely expert information and insight on current issues and thereby to promote the useful application of knowledge.

This book was prepared under a joint project of the UNU Institute of Advanced Studies (UNU/IAS), Multilateralism and Sustainable Development Programme (MSD), and the Global Environment Information Center (GEIC).

Inter-linkages:

The Kyoto Protocol and the International Trade and Investment Regimes

EDITED BY W. BRADNEE CHAMBERS

**United Nations
University Press**

TOKYO · NEW YORK · PARIS

United Nations University Press
The United Nations University, 53-70, Jingumae 5-chome, Shibuya-ku, Tokyo, 150-8925, Japan
Tel: +81-3-3499-2811 Fax: +81-3-3406-7345
E-mail: sales@hq.unu.edu http://www.unu.edu

United Nations University Office in North America
2 United Nations Plaza, Room DC2-1462-70, New York, NY 10017, USA
Tel: +1-212-963-6387 Fax: +1-212-371-9454
E-mail: unuona@igc.apc.org

United Nations University Press is the publishing division of the United Nations University.

Cover design by Joyce C. Weston

Printed in the United States of America

UNUP-1040
ISBN 92-808-1040-5

Library of Congress Cataloging-in-Publication Data

Inter-linkages : The Kyoto Protocol and the international trade and investment regimes / Edited by W. Bradnee Chambers.
    p. cm.
Includes bibliographical references and index.
  ISBN 92-808-1040-5
1. Global warming—Government policy—Economic aspects.
2. Greenhouse gas mitigation—Government policy—Economic aspects. 3. United Nations Framework Convention on Climate Change (1992). Protocols, etc., 1997 Dec. 11 I. Chambers, Bradnee W.
  QC981.8.G56 I55 2001
  363.738'74526—dc21   2001000718

CONTENTS

TABLES

FIGURES

FOREWORD

This book – *Interlinkages: The Kyoto Protocol and the International Trade and Investment Regime* – reflects the core mission of the United Nations University Institute of Advanced Studies (UNU/IAS). In April 1996, the UN Secretary-General inaugurated the UNU/IAS as an in-house community of scholars established to vigorously pursue knowledge at the intersection between societal and natural systems. The programmatic theme of the IAS was created to be dynamic and flexible, focusing on finding creative solutions to the pressing global issues arising at this nexus. As an overarching theme, the IAS adopted the concept of *Eco-restructuring*, an approach to sustainable development that envisions shifting technological and societal systems towards a greater equity between developing and developed countries, between humankind and the environment, and between current and future generations. An integral component of the IAS *Eco-restructuring* dynamic involves the examination of global institutions, regimes, values, and policies relating to sustainable development. These issues are dealt with under the programmatic sub-theme of *Multilateralism and Sustainable Development (MSD)*. Within this programme, in-depth theoretical research is combined with relevant policy studies and the formulation of practical policy options. A strong capacity-building component that seeks to enhance the participation of policy actors in global environmental negotiations has also been built into the programme.

This book was also the result of a joint project with Global Environment Information Centre (GEIC), an initiative of the UNU and the Japanese Environment Agency, GEIC was established on 29 October 1996, and focuses on providing information to the Major Groups identified in Agenda 21 – mostly the small civil groups and individuals.

GEIC has a commitment to better involve civil groups and people in environmental issues, and undertakes studies and activities that can better involve NGOs and other grassroots organizations in international and national environmental processes. GEIC also undertakes activities that involve packaging information for use and consumption by non-experts. In this way, perhaps, the term *Peoples' Think Tank* may be an easy way for people to learn about and understand GEIC.

In terms of dissemination, GEIC is concerned with promoting the nexus between information development and environment. It works to find ways in which the Internet may be useful to people in contemplating environmental issues. On other fronts, GEIC publishes EarthWrap, a small newsletter (and homepage) that aims to disseminate information to the major groups of Agenda 21 and get people involved in environmental issues.

W. Bradnee Chambers

ACKNOWLEDGEMENTS

This book was prepared with the assistance of many people. First and foremost I would like to thank Jerry Velasquez, Programme Co-ordinator of the Global Environment Information Center (GEIC) and the project leader of the joint research initiative that has led to the conclusion of this volume. Without his professionalism and energy this research would not have been possible.

I wish to express my appreciation to those participating in the brainstorming sessions that led to the initiation of this project. From the first session held at the UNU/IAS with the PhD Fellows and Research Associates, I would like to thank Glen Paoletto who helped in putting together the proposal and conceptualizing the project. From the Bonn session held as a Special Event during a UNFCCC Subsidiary Meeting, I would like to thank the many participants, particularly Heike Schroeder who was of great assistance in organizing the meeting and Gary Sampson for his advice and support.

In putting together this manuscript I would like to thank the staff and associates from the UNU Centre, UNU/IAS, and GEIC. This includes Ms Lynn Rutherford and Shona Dodds who assisted in the editing, Ms Miho Komiyama who continues to lend invaluable support to the IAS Multilateralism and Sustainable Development Programme (MSD), and Ms Yoko Kobayashi from GEIC, who worked long hours assisting Jerry and me throughout this project.

I would also like to express my gratitude to the Senior UNU Faculty Members for supporting this project. Dr Juha Uitto, Senior Programme Officer of the UNU Environment and Sustainable Development Programme, who saw the potential for collaboration between the UNU Centre, GEIC, and UNU/IAS, gave his continual guidance, encouragement, and support.

Lastly, I would like to thank Professor Tarcisio Della Senta, whose vision and drive continues to inspire the researchers and staff at the UNU/IAS.

W. Bradnee Chambers

LIST OF ABBREVIATIONS AND ACRONYMS

ADR	Alternative dispute settlement
AIJ	Activities Implemented Jointly
AIPN	Association of International Petroleum Negotiators
BASEL	Basel Convention
BOT	Build, Operate, and Transfer
CBD	Convention on Biodiversity
CCAP	Center for Clean Air Policy
CDM	Clean development mechanism
CDMJV	Clean development mechanism joint venture
CDMJVA	Clean Development Mechanism Joint Venture Agreement
CEC	Commission of the European Communities
CER	Certified emission reductions
CITES	Convention on the International Trade in Endangered Species of Wild Fauna and Flora
CO_2	Carbon dioxide
COP	Conference of the Parties
CTE	Committee on Trade and Environment
DSU	Dispute Settlement Understanding
EC	European Commission
EIT	Economies in transition
EMEP	Co-operative Programme for Monitoring and Evaluation of the Long-Range Transmission of Air Pollutants in Europe
ERT	Emission-reduction target
ERU	Emission-reduction unit
ET	Emissions trading
ETC	Emission-trading contract

ETS	Emissions-trading system
EU	European Union
FCCC	Framework Convention on Climate Change
FDI	Foreign Direct Investment
GATS	General Agreement on Trade in Services
GATT	General Agreement on Tariffs and Trade
GEF	Global Environment Facility
GEIC	Global Environmental Information Center
GHG	Greenhouse gas
ICC	International Chamber of Commerce
ICCAT	International Commission for the Conservation of Atlantic Tuna
ICJ	International Court of Justice
IFF	Intergovernmental Forum on Forests
IFI	International financial institution
IGO	Intergovernmental organization
IPF	Intergovernmental Panel on Forests
IPPC	Intergovernmental Panel on Climate Change
ISO	International Standards Agreement
ITTO	International Tropical Timber Organization
JI	Joint implementation
JOA	Joint Operating Agreement
JVA	Joint Venture Agreement
KP	Kyoto Protocol
LRTAP	Long-range transboundary air pollution
MAI	Multilateral Agreement on Investment
MCP	Multilateral consultative process
MDB	Multilateral development bank
MEA	Multilateral Environmental Agreement
MFN	Most favoured nation
MMT	Methylcyclopentadienyl manganese tricarbonyl

MOP	Meeting of the Parties (to the Protocol)
MRA	Mutual recognition agreement
NAAEC	North American Agreement on Environmental Co-operation
NAFTA	North American Free Trade Agreement
NCP	Non-compliance procedure
NGO	Non-governmental organization
NT	National treatment
ODA	Overseas Development Assistance
ODS	Ozone-depleting substances
OECD	Organization for Economic Co-operation and Development
PAAs	Parts of assigned amount
PAMs	Policies and measures
PPM	Process and production method
QELR	Quantified emission-limitation reduction
QELROs	Quantified emission-limitation reduction objectives
SBI	Subsidiary Body for Implementation
SBSTA	Subsidiary Body for Scientific and Technological Advice
SCM	Subsidies and countervailing measures
SO_2	Sulphur dioxide
SPS	Sanitary and Phytosanitary (GATT 1994)
TBT	Technical Barriers to Trade Agreement (GATT 1994)
TREM	Trade-related environmental measure
TRIM	Trade-related investment measure
UNCITRAL	United Nations Commission on International Trade Law
UNCTAD	United Nations Conference on Trade and Development

UNDP	United Nations Development Programme
UNEP	United Nations Environment Programme
UNFCCC	United Nations Framework Convention on Climate Change
UNIDO	United Nations Industrial Development Organization
UNU	United Nations University
UNU/IAS	United Nations Institute of Advanced Studies
USEPA	United States Environmental Protection Agency
VOC	Protocol Concerning the Control of Emissions of Volatile Organic Compounds or Their Transboundary Fluxes
WTO	World Trade Organization

Introduction

W. BRADNEE CHAMBERS

This collection of essays and discussion papers originates in research carried out by three divisions of the United Nations University (UNU) – the UNU Environment and Sustainable Development Programme, the Global Environment Information Center (GEIC), and the UNU Institute of Advanced Studies (UNU/IAS). These three divisions have pooled their resources and expertise and combined them with those of a network of scholars and institutions to produce this volume on climate change, one of the most pressing global issues of our time. In conducting this research, the UNU has sought not to repeat research on current trends of climate change undertaken by a host of institutions but to look ahead strategically to advanced issues that are of a suppositional nature. The volume also contributes to the work programme that the UNU has set out on the issue of interlinkages among multilateral environmental agreements and other multilateral regimes.

The eight papers presented in this volume are written with the intent of depicting interlinkages pertaining to the climate-change regime and the international trade and investment regimes. These interlinkages are discussed and interpreted within the context of the growing body of international law and policy in many different fields. By the use of hypothetical examples, cross-linkages among international laws and their respective provisions (i.e. areas of over-lap, present and future inconsistencies, contradictions, and/or positive synergies) are here identified and analysed. This is done in an effort to anticipate and, if possible, to assist in solving some of the problems that are bound to attend the difficult process of facilitating the continuing construction and further evolution of a coherent and integrated body of international law.

Ultimately, the goal of the volume is to move the makers of climate change and other international policies and laws to consider the interlinkages more deeply and comprehensively, within a broader context, and from this to make more informed decisions.

The initiative to create this volume of papers began with the simple recognition of the need for a strong and effective regime to protect the earth's climate. This was followed by the realization that the accomplishment of the task of creating such a regime will take not only the vision and the cooperation of the parties, which has been made manifest in the Kyoto Protocol, but also a large public awareness. This awareness, to have an effect, must entail wide international and multidisciplinary understanding and recognition of the climate-change issue, on the part of policy makers and ordinary people alike. The human community at large must acquire, on the one hand, an appreciation of the comprehensiveness of the climate-change problem and, on the other, a realization of the vast socio-economic impact that the Climate Change Convention and the Kyoto Protocol could and must have, to be effective.

The cross-cutting nature of the climate-change regime gives it the potential to affect not only technology, industry, and lifestyle but also the very regimes that regulate and manage virtually every aspect of these areas. In other words, both the form and the content of the Climate Change Convention are capable of affecting the form and content of other multilateral regimes, such as trade and investment. The challenge, therefore, when such regimes of law have jurisdictional overlaps (whether territorial or conceptual), is to design legal architectures to accommodate, understand, and interface in mutually supportive ways. Unfortunately, because of the complexity of the issues involved and the protracted nature of the international legis-

lative process, international treaties and agreements are often negotiated by specialized ministries or by functional organizations in
relative isolation from the forums in which other international
agreements are being made. This segregation of policy making by
topic, sector, or territory, leads to treaties that incidentally overlap,
come into conflict with, or inadvertently override the normative assumptions, principles, or tenets of other treaties. Therefore, unless an
international agreement is struck by negotiators with full knowledge
of other related (or potentially related) agreements, its appropriate-
ness and effectiveness are likely to be dubious. Thus, the creation of
an effective agreement on climate change depends not only on the
growing public perception of its importance, as described above, but
also on the shared belief by law and policy makers in every area of
international affairs that the Climate Change Convention and the
Kyoto Protocol must be perceived in a far wider context than that of
just the "environment" in its conventional sense. The "environment"
of the Kyoto Protocol includes international laws on trade, development, transportation, and other aspects.

Makers of international policy and law are currently overwhelmed
by the sheer diversity and number of international agreements and
negotiations on their political agendas. Given the plethora of urgent
international negotiations and of multilateral activity related to law
and policy, the obvious need for policy coherence, treaty compatibility, and capitalization on the synergistic potential of complementary aspects of related treaties is correspondingly greater.

In the light of the tremendous importance of effective laws on
climate change to sustainability and to the welfare of future generations, the makers of international laws and policies must take
these needs seriously and make an earnest effort to find the means of
fulfilling them.

In an attempt to address the two needs described above – on the
one hand for a greater awareness of the importance and of the
sweeping potential impact of climate change, and on the other hand
for a broader view of the context of law on climate change in general
– the UNU has undertaken this volume, approaching the study by
examining the manner in which the Climate Change Convention

and its recently negotiated Kyoto Protocol mesh and interact with
the international trade and investment regimes. These include aspects of the international trade and investment regime – the World
Trade Organization (WTO), the North American Free Trade
Agreement (NAFTA), the European Union (EU), and the proposed
Multilateral Agreement on Investment (MAI) – and private contractual regimes and standard forms – the United Nations Commission on International Trade Law (UNCITRAL).

The first part of the book lays the foundation for tackling the
issues that are dealt with in greater specificity later in the volume.
Since the Kyoto Protocol is still in a unfinished state and the actual
details will not be known until the final outcome of the Conference
of the Parties (COP) negotiations, it is important to establish certain
criteria for the substantive discussion contained in later parts of the
monograph. In the first chapter, Joanna Depledge sets out the unresolved issues from Kyoto and what can be expected in future COP
negotiations. Chapter 2 goes into greater detail on the outstanding
issues of particular relevance to the four regimes that are later examined. In this chapter, Laura Campbell describes the potential role
of non-state actors or, as the Protocol describes, legal entities. It is
thought that any future Protocol negotiation anticipates a greater
role for these actors. This expanding role of non-state actors is of
particular importance to chapter 8, which is to link the Protocol's
provisions effectively to those of the international investment regime.

Chapter 3 examines non-compliance, one of the most essential
components for the successful implementation of the Kyoto Protocol. In this chapter Catherine Redgwell addresses the issues of non-
compliance by first drawing upon legal conceptual models. She then
applies her observations and conclusions to the actual Protocol in
order to establish what provisions should be included in a final
agreement. The chapter also examines, to a limited extent, the compliance issues related to the flexible mechanisms of the Protocol. In
this regard, the chapter provides a basis for the rest of the discussion
in the book, as well as an interesting contrast to the proposal (discussed later in chapter 9) to use standard form contracts and existing
legal formulas for governing these flexible mechanisms.

Chapters 4–7 investigate the relationship of the Protocol to international trade regimes, particularly that of the WTO but to some extent also those of the NAFTA and the EU. Chapter 4, by Gary Sampson, former Director of the Trade and Environment Division of the World Trade Organization (WTO), presents an overview of the relationship of WTO *vis-à-vis* multilateral environmental agreements (MEAs). It describes some of the proposals made by members of the Committee on Trade and Environment (CTE) concerning possible inconsistencies between the WTO and MEAs. The chapter also emphasizes the need for policy coherence between the two regimes and argues that this can be attained if MEAs such as the Kyoto Protocol are made effective agreements that can solve disputes within their own frameworks. Chapter 5 explores some of the potential conflicts between trade law and climate regimes, respectively. It looks at both the non-trade-related provisions of the Protocol, such as the policies and measures, and the trade-related environmental measures (TREMs) to determine if any incompatibilities with trade law exist. In addition, it investigates the relationship of the Protocol to the NAFTA and EU. The chapter also touches on the shortcomings of the Vienna Convention on the Law of Treaties with respect to the issue of incompatible provisions of the Kyoto Protocol and the international trade regime. Chapter 6, by Zhong Xiang Zhang, deals more precisely with some of the concerns raised by chapters 4 and 5 on emissions trading. Chapter 7, by Jacob Werksman, continues the book's focus on emissions trading, but offers an alternative view to previous chapters in that it argues that emission allowances are neither goods nor services for the purpose of the WTO. It concludes, however, that the way in which the allowances are allocated and used may affect trade and therefore must remain sensitive to WTO disciplines of non-discrimination.

In chapter 8, Jacob Werksman and Claudia Santoro delve into the interrelationship between the Kyoto Protocol and the proposed Multilateral Agreement on Investment (MAI). This is, perhaps, the most speculative of the chapters, as it compares two agreements that are not fully negotiated: on one side, the details of the Protocol's investment rules for joint implementation and the clean development mechanism (CDM) remain at their infant stage; on the other, the question of whether the MAI will be adopted is far from answered. However, given the time-frame of the Protocol's commitment period, which does not start until 2008, there is plenty of time for resumption of interest in an MAI in one form or another before the next phase of the emissions-control programme of the climate-change regime. Even if the MAI is not ratified, the negotiating text of the MAI is largely based upon models of the already adopted bilateral and transnational investment treaties; although the paper does explore these in detail, with the exception of some references made to NAFTA provisions on investment, the connections to these other investment treaties and the implications of these connections can be easily discerned. The analysis by Jacob Werksman and Claudia Santoro of the MAI and the Kyoto Protocol is ground-breaking and its implications should be considered by not only the Parties negotiating the Kyoto Protocol but also the negotiators of any future MAI.

The final chapter (9) deals with private investment rules. Moving beyond the previous discussion, which focuses on incompatibilities and conflicts, it turns instead to an analysis of potential synergies and positive linkages between the climate regime and the existing "standard form rules" of the UNCITRAL. In this chapter it is observed that certain standard forms that the Parties could draw upon to conclude contracts on the CDM already exist. These suggested forms have inbuilt dispute-settlement mechanisms, such as mandatory arbitration or a clause indicating in advance the procedure for resolving conflicts among the contracting parties. This could be an alternative policy option for the climate-change parties, which are faced with designing a compliance system for the Protocol but must also consider special requirements for compliance at the level of the flexible mechanisms which involve state/state, state/legal-individual, or legal-individual/legal-individual relationships. According to Worika and colleagues, some existing standard forms are suitable for this purpose as long as they are "properly drafted to reflect the substance of the agreement." Interestingly, the paper outlines ideal standardized agreements that could be used for the CDM.

1

From Kyoto to Buenos Aires and Beyond

JOANNA DEPLEDGE

In May 1992, over 150 governments decided that climate change was a serious threat. In response, they adopted the UN Framework Convention on Climate Change (UNFCCC), with the ultimate objective of stabilizing greenhouse-gas concentrations in the atmosphere at a "safe" level. The Convention has now been ratified by over 176 Parties (as of October 1998) and it is nearing universal membership.

The Convention calls on developed countries, the so-called Annex I Parties, to return their emissions to 1990 levels by 2000. When countries adopted the Convention, however, they knew that these commitments would not be sufficient to meet its objective. Therefore, at the first Conference of the Parties (COP) to the Convention (March 1995, Berlin), negotiations were launched to agree on stronger commitments for developed countries by the third COP. Intensive and difficult negotiations took place over 31 months and these were finally concluded at COP 3 in Kyoto on 11 December 1997, when the Kyoto Protocol to the UNFCCC was eventually adopted by consensus.

When the Kyoto Protocol was adopted in the early morning, after almost 72 hours of round-the-clock negotiations, most of those present were too exhausted to comprehend fully what had just been agreed. Since then, much time and effort has been expended by all those involved in the process to try to make sense of the Kyoto Protocol puzzle and to understand its implications. An important step in this direction was taken at the fourth Conference of the Parties (COP 4) in Buenos Aires (2–14 November 1998) where, less than a year after Kyoto, Parties devised a so-called "Buenos Aires Plan of Action," including work programmes on the key unresolved elements of the Kyoto Protocol. The next important milestone on the road to the implementation of the Kyoto Protocol will be the sixth Conference of the Parties (COP 6), scheduled to be held in late 2000; COP 6 is the deadline, set at COP 4, for decisions for be taken on many key issues.

Climate change: The issues

Climate change has particular features that render it a unique environmental problem and one which poses some of the greatest challenges for our current structures of governance:

1. It is one of the very few truly global problems in terms of both causes and impacts. Tackling climate change therefore requires global cooperation.
2. The stakes are high – even under optimistic scenarios, the impacts of climate change will be significant and irreversible; under some scenarios, and for some regions, the impacts will be catastrophic.
3. Long time-scales are involved; politicians must therefore act on a problem, the worst effects of which will not be felt until after the end of their term in office and not by present voters but by their grandchildren.
4. Climate change has important equity implications: the bulk of the problem has been caused by those countries that will be the least affected by it.

Further challenges presented by climate change are its linkages to other issue areas and therefore to other international agreements.

Potential conflicts between international action to tackle climate change and trade agreements, such as under the World Trade Organization (WTO), have been the subject of particular attention. In this context, it is important to remember that climate change and, therefore, the UNFCCC and the Kyoto Protocol, concern economics and development as much as they do the environment. Addressing climate change will require important changes to economic systems to move them towards a lower carbon path; the precise aim of the Kyoto Protocol is to change the pattern of "business as usual." Such shifts in economic structures may, in turn, have repercussions on international trade in a number of ways. What those effects might be, and how they would be linked to the WTO, are as yet uncertain.

The Kyoto Protocol

The challenges for governments posed by climate change mean that the adoption of the Kyoto Protocol was a remarkable achievement. The negotiations overcame a multitude of obstacles to forge a "package deal" that struck a delicate balance between the widely diverging positions of Parties. The key now is to maintain and strengthen that balance.

It may help to make sense of this "package deal" if the Protocol is broken down into six parts:

1. emission commitments for Annex I Parties
2. mechanisms for implementation
3. mechanisms for credibility
4. mechanisms for review
5. advancing the existing Convention commitments for all parties
6. institutions and introductory and final clauses.

The centrepiece of the Kyoto Protocol is, of course, its legally binding emission commitments for Annex I Parties which, assuming compliance, will together lead to a reduction in emissions from 1990 levels for that group of parties of around 5.2 per cent.

Another way of looking at this target is to compare it with "business-as-usual" projections. The reduction in Annex I Party emissions due to Protocol commitments below what they would otherwise have been around 2010 is over 20 per cent. Assuming compliance, this will be the key achievement of the Protocol – to have reversed the historical upward trend in emissions in the industrialized world over the past 150 years.

Unfinished business

When negotiators emerged from the exhaustion and excitement of Kyoto, they began to realize just how much the negotiations had left unresolved and how many questions had been pushed back to future meetings. In hindsight, this large burden of unfinished business was inevitable: the practical complexity of some of the issues at stake (e.g. emissions trading) meant that their details could never have been ironed out during the negotiations leading up to Kyoto, whilst the differences among Parties also meant that consensus could be forged only by deferring some of the most difficult decisions to future negotiations.

Two key elements of "unfinished business" which have charted the road from Kyoto to Buenos Aires and beyond are (a) mechanisms for implementation and (b) mechanisms for credibility.

Mechanisms for implementation

The Protocol contains four mechanisms through which Parties can implement their emission commitments: these are domestic policies and measures (Article 2) and three so-called "flexibility mechanisms" – "joint implementation" (Article 6), the clean development mechanism (CDM; Article 12), and emissions trading (Article 17).

The focus on the flexibility mechanisms has largely overshadowed Article 2 on domestic policies and measures. It would be unwise to dismiss this Article, however, as it contains some important provisions that could be built on in the future. Building on Article 2 has already emerged as an area of debate at COP 4. The provisions in the Article to promote cooperation amongst Parties in the mitigation of climate change is likely to become a "hook" to ensure that the industrialized countries implement the policies necessary to spur real changes towards less carbon-intensive production and consumption patterns.

For the time being, however, it is still the flexibility mechanisms that have attracted the most attention – and, indeed, controversy – since Kyoto. To some extent, this is because little in-depth discussion of their details took place during the Protocol negotiations. For example, most Parties did not see the text on the CDM until 48 hours before it was adopted.

The three flexibility mechanisms share some common features:

1. All the mechanisms involve action "*offshore*." The Protocol, however, links such "offshore" activities to the implementation of domestic policies and measures by requiring use of the flexibility mechanisms to be supplemental to domestic emission reduction action (the terminology used in the case of the CDM is slightly different).

2. The mechanisms provide new opportunities to *engage the private sector* in emission-reducing activities.

3. All have *integral linkages* with each other, and with the other Protocol articles, particularly the "mechanisms for credibility."

4. As *project-based mechanisms*, there are certain issues that are common to both joint implementation and the CDM. These include determination of baselines, processes for verification and certification, and the relationship with projects under the Convention's pilot phase of Activities Implemented Jointly (AIJ).

As well as the commonalities between them, each mechanism comes with its own specific issues to resolve.

The CDM is perhaps the most innovative of the mechanisms – it certainly was the greatest surprise in Kyoto. Its early starting date in 2000 places added pressure on negotiators. Some particularly difficult questions for future negotiations will centre around the amount of the "adaptation levy" and the eligibility of projects involving carbon "sinks."

Emissions trading is probably the most politically controversial mechanism. The most difficult set of issues is the concern of some developing countries that establishing an emissions-trading system will confer "rights to emit" on the Annex I Parties. Such concerns over the principle and equity implications of emissions trading were left pending from Kyoto and will need to be addressed in the design of an acceptable emissions-trading system.

Clearly, many issues have yet to be resolved, concerning both the principle and the practice of the mechanisms. The fate of the flexibility mechanisms is as yet uncertain and the stakes are high: if they are poorly designed, the mechanisms could become dangerous loopholes undermining the credibility of the Protocol; if well designed, however, they could provide an unprecedented opportunity to reduce emissions in an economically and environmentally effective manner and to engage the private sector in this effort.

Credibility mechanisms

The fate of the flexibility mechanisms depends to a large extent on a less well known set of provisions in the Protocol, the "credibility mechanisms." These include provisions relating to measurement and reporting, monitoring and verification, and non-compliance. Negotiators sought to include these provisions in the Protocol to give meaning and credibility to the legally binding nature of the Protocol's emission commitments; once again, however, their details remain to be elaborated.

Article 5, for example, together with decision 2/CP.3, requires Annex I Parties to set up "national systems" for their greenhouse-gas inventories based on common methodologies, thus increasing comparability and transparency.

Articles 7 and 8 establish that Annex I Parties must provide supplementary information on the actions they are taking to meet their commitments under the Protocol and that this information will be reviewed by expert review teams. Guidelines for the reporting of information and the expert reviews will be developed at the first COP serving as the meeting of the Parties to the Protocol (COP/MOP 1) after the Protocol's entry into force. These provisions promise to lead to a considerable strengthening of the corresponding procedures under the Convention.

Under Article 18, procedures and mechanisms to determine and address cases of non-compliance are also to be agreed at COP/MOP 1. The eventual shape of these non-compliance procedures and mechanisms will be important in determining whether the Protocol has any "teeth" and how sharp those teeth are. Debates on non-compliance promise to match those on the flexibility mechanisms over the next few years.

With the exception of non-compliance, the credibility mechanisms do not have the same visibility or high profile as the flexibility mechanisms; they are less media friendly. However, it will be important for the full set of credibility mechanisms to be elaborated in tandem with the flexibility mechanisms if the environmental and economic effectiveness of the Protocol is to be secured.

Prompt-start provisions

The architects of the Kyoto Protocol sought to compensate for the large volume of unfinished business left over from COP 3 by deciding on a "prompt start" process to close the remaining gaps in the Protocol.

This process was launched by decision 1/CP.3, which highlighted five Protocol provisions requiring further work and placed these on the agenda for COP 4. These provisions include work on the flexibility mechanisms and on land-use change and forestry, another key issue requiring work beyond COP 3.

The Protocol also identifies a number of important tasks to be carried out by the first COP/MOP. As previously mentioned, these mostly concern the credibility mechanisms (e.g. design of a compliance system and guidelines for national communication and reviews). Work on these complex issues will, of course, need to begin well before entry into force of the Protocol and preferably in tandem with the flexibility mechanisms. Recognizing this, decision 1/CP.3 provided a mandate to Parties to begin work on the tasks for COP/MOP 1 as soon as possible. Preparations for COP/MOP 1 therefore also appeared on the agenda for COP 4.

COP 4: Charting the road ahead

In the run-up to COP 4, many Parties had sought to lower expectations that Buenos Aires would be a rerun of Kyoto and result in a similarly high-profile outcome. The main goal of the conference, and the indicator of its success, was billed as forging a work programme for the future implementation of the Kyoto Protocol. This was certainly an important goal as, before being able to ratify the Protocol, many Parties need to have a clearer idea of its eventual shape and, in particular, of how the flexibility mechanisms will function. In order to ensure the early entry into force of the Protocol, COP 4 therefore needed to launch the "prompt start" process for work on the Protocol's unfinished business and to set clear deadlines for its completion.

In the event, although COP 4 was essentially a "process" session lacking the drama of Kyoto, negotiations proved to be equally tough. Parties had to face up to the "invisible brackets" in the Protocol – the difficult issues that had been deferred to future negotiations so that the Kyoto Protocol could be adopted. As in Kyoto, this COP ended with all-night negotiations that ran more than 12 hours over schedule. The outcome was a so-called "Buenos Aires Plan of Action," consisting of a set of decisions that chart the road ahead for both Convention work and the future implementation of the Protocol. The two main decisions regarding the key Protocol issues were as follows:

1. *Decision 7/CP.4*, entitled "work programme on mechanisms of the Kyoto Protocol," sets out a process for working on the operational details of the mechanisms, including the organization of technical workshops. It establishes a deadline for decisions at COP 6 and explicitly places priority on the CDM. Annexed to the work programme is a long list of 142 elements to be considered as part of this process. Just as the work programme itself marks a significant step towards the design of fully functioning flexibility mechanisms, the list and its many internally contradictory points shows just how many obstacles may still lie ahead.

2. *Decision 8/CP.4*, on preparations for COP/MOP 1, launches work on the various issues requiring action by the first COP/MOP, including the credibility mechanisms. As in the case of the flexibility mechanisms, decision 8/CP.4 sets a deadline of COP 6 for decisions on guidelines for reporting information under the Protocol, for expert reviews and for national systems for greenhouse-gas inventories.

   A key element of decision 8/CP.4 is the start of a process to build on the Protocol's framework compliance provisions. COP 4 revealed considerable support among Parties for moving ahead on the design of a compliance mechanism as a matter of priority. This is reflected in the detail of the decision, which calls for a joint working group to be set up to consider the issue at the next session of the subsidiary bodies (31 May to 11 June 1999).

   As a further complement to the offshore, flexibility mechanisms, decision 8/CP.4 also instigated work to enhance cooperation on domestic policies and measures, albeit at the analytical level. It called for a report to be prepared on "best practices" in policies and measures and for a workshop to be held on this issue.

These two sets of decisions – one on the flexibility mechanisms, the other focusing on the credibility mechanisms – together lay the foundations for a balanced approach to work on the Kyoto Protocol, which augurs well for its eventual economic and environmental effectiveness.

Conclusions

COP 4 was a crossroads which defined the road ahead for the inter-governmental climate-change process. It was at this conference that Parties were finally able to digest and come to terms with the Kyoto Protocol outcome. Sceptics have claimed that all COP 4 achieved was "to decide what to decide," but this is to misrepresent the significance of the Conference. Parties took the important step of un-ravelling the many loose threads from Kyoto and ordering them in a coherent and workable way. They addressed, head on, the key issues in the Protocol requiring further work and devised programmes, with clear deadlines, for conducting that work. The road to COP 6 will see a challenging process of in-depth analysis and detailed technical work.

The Kyoto Protocol, however, is not the final word in the climate-change story. If we are to avert the worst effects of climate change, the commitments of the Annex I Parties will need to be strengthened and, eventually, emission commitments will need to be ex-tended to a wider group of Parties.

There is reason, however, to be optimistic. It is little more than a decade ago that the problem of climate change was first placed on the agenda of the UN General Assembly at its forty-third session in 1988. The international community has come a long way in tackling climate change since then: in 1988, few countries had even greenhouse-gas inventories, let alone targets to reduce those greenhouse gases. Addressing climate change is clearly a long-term process. The Kyoto Protocol, however, with its legally binding emission targets and review mechanisms to strengthen those targets in the future, has laid the foundations for a truly effective international response to the problem.

2

The Role of the Private Sector and Other Non-state Actors in Implementation of the Kyoto Protocol

Laura B. Campbell

Introduction

The Kyoto Protocol to the United Nations Framework Convention on Climate Change reflects its drafters' understanding that changes in the global economy — globalization of markets, emerging global governance in the areas of trade and services, privatization and internationalization of the energy sector, and the ascending role of the private sector — are changing the context in which environmental problems must be addressed. As a result, the Kyoto Protocol represents a new generation of environmental treaties negotiated in an age of globalization and is aimed at influencing important economic activities such as energy production and foreign investment in order to minimize their impacts on the environment. The potential economic effects of the Protocol are so far-reaching that it is sometimes referred to as an economic instrument disguised as an environmental agreement. The Protocol is also precedent setting in its specific inclusion of non-state actors in its implementation provisions, reflecting a recognition that they are critical to the success of this economics-based treaty.

The Kyoto Protocol contains three mechanisms allowing for international implementation, which are aimed at achieving the environmental goals of the treaty by affecting market-based activities. These mechanisms are related to (1) greenhouse-gas (GHG) emissions trading, (2) joint implementation (JI), and (3) the clean development mechanism (CDM). Each of these mechanisms specifically includes provisions relating to the participation of non-state actors in its implementation.

Although the Kyoto Protocol authorized Annex B (industrialized) countries to utilize these mechanisms in order to meet their assigned GHG-emission limits set forth in Article 3, it did not specify the rules and guidelines for the implementation of the mechanisms but deferred these issues to subsequent meetings of the Parties. Similarly, the Protocol did not define the role of the private sector and other non-state actors in implementing the mechanisms. The Parties to the Climate Change Convention began informal discussions on elaboration of rules governing the implementation of the mechanisms shortly after the Protocol was adopted and have continued to negotiate these issues at the Fourth and Fifth Conferences of the Parties (COP 4 and COP 5, respectively). Achieving consensus on the details of the mechanisms will be a primary focus of the Sixth Conference of the Parties (COP 6), which is scheduled for November 2000.

The purpose of this chapter is to examine the roles to be played by various non-state actors in implementing the Protocol, particularly in the context of the mechanisms for international implementation noted above. In exploring the potential roles of non-state actors, this chapter discusses (1) economic trends and developments that influenced the structure of the Kyoto Protocol, (2) the Protocol mechanisms – emissions trading, JI, and the CDM – and the legal basis for participation of non-state actors in carrying out these mechanisms, and (3) the key non-state actors involved in implementation of the Protocol by means of the mechanisms and some examples of activities already undertaken by these actors, including the private sector, non-governmental organizations (NGOs), intergovernmental organizations (IGOs), and multilateral development banks (MDBs).

Economic trends and developments that influenced negotiation of the Kyoto Protocol

Globalization

Globalization – the rapid integration of economies worldwide through trade, financial flows, transport, technology transfers, and cross-cultural flows – is occurring at an increasingly rapid pace. According to the World Trade Organization (WTO), global trade in products and services exceeded US$5 $\times$ 10^{12} in 1998. Over the same period, the World Bank estimated the amount of foreign direct investment at more than US$240 billion ($240 $\times$ 10^9).

While much more work needs to be done to assess all the impacts of globalization on the environment, it was clear by the time of the negotiation of the Kyoto Protocol that changes in the global economy had altered the context in which environmental problems such as climate change had to be addressed. Economic globalization; the emergence of the WTO as an institution of global governance in the areas of trade and services; the increasing power of the private sector, particularly multinational corporations; and competitiveness concerns had all resulted in the diminution of national sovereignty and of the capacity of states to provide effective environmental governance. Ensuring the effectiveness of the Protocol required its drafters to take into account the realities of globalization, including the relationship between trade, investment, and the environment.

As environmental treaties such as the Kyoto Protocol have developed in a manner that increasingly addresses international economic activities, the range of issues covered by economic regimes has also expanded. The multilateral trade regime, for example, has evolved from a post-World War II tariff-reduction scheme into a far more comprehensive set of agreements administered by the WTO governing trade in services, non-tariff trade barriers, agriculture, food safety, and intellectual property rights. The modalities and details for operation of the mechanisms as well as the national policies and measures taken to implement the Protocol will be subject to scrutiny for compliance with international trade rules and raise the possibility of controversy over the competing priorities of the climate change and international trade regimes.

Overseas Development Assistance (ODA) versus private capital transfers

The overwhelming shift toward private capital transfers compared with official Overseas Development Assistance (ODA) underscores the diminishing role of national governments in a global economy as well as the importance of engaging the private sector on environmental issues. In 1990, private investment in the developing world totalled US$44 billion; by 1995 this figure had climbed to US$167 billion while ODA had fallen to a total of US$59 billion. The move away from ODA-financed development toward privately driven economic expansion means that the private sector must play a major role in implementing the Kyoto Protocol in order to ensure its effectiveness.

Energy-sector reform

As developing nations grow, many are moving away from centrally planned, state-owned electric utilities toward privately owned and operated generation, transmission, and distribution companies in order to reduce public debt, to improve accountability and transparency, and to enhance customer service. Both developed and developing countries have pursued four basic types of reform in the energy sector. First, in the process of commercialization, governments have removed subsidies and preferential fiscal policies but retained ownership of electric utilities. In many cases, commercialization has preceded privatization, which can entail purchase of electricity from private sources, sale of facilities to private firms, and independent regulation. Additionally, a number of countries are restructuring the energy sector by breaking up utilities into individual firms that independently provide services related to power generation, transmission, distribution, and sales to customers. Reforms in the energy sector may also include creating competition for whole-sale and retail power.

Largely as a result of these reforms, private energy companies have become increasingly multinational, with rising levels of foreign direct investment in the energy sector of both developed and developing countries. Private companies are subject to competition and market pressures which are expected to result in more economically efficient energy production and supply but which, without effective policy intervention on the national and international level, are not likely to be climate friendly.

For example, if coal and other fossil fuels are the cheapest sources of energy, it is not likely that that the private sector will invest in fuels and technology generating less carbon dioxide in the absence of policy interventions and incentives. Developing effective rules for implementation of programmes under the Protocol's provisions on JI and the CDM could do a great deal to promote more climate-friendly foreign direct investment in the energy sector, by providing incentives for investment based on environmental factors in addition to business-as-usual economic considerations.

The legal basis: Key provisions of the Kyoto Protocol relating to the involvement of non-state actors in the implementation of the mechanisms

The Kyoto Protocol provides both implicit and explicit support for the involvement of the private sector and other non-state actors in its implementation, and particularly in implementation of the flexibility mechanisms. Since the majority of the activities that cause climate change are carried out by private entities, it is obvious that engaging the private sector in minimizing the environmental impacts of these activities will be crucial in achieving the Protocol's environmental objectives. As noted above, in many countries electric power is increasingly supplied by private companies; likewise, design and manufacture of consumer products is a private-sector activity.

The Kyoto Protocol breaks new ground in specifically including non-state actors within key implementation provisions. The Protocol authorizes the involvement of the private sector and other non-state actors in the workings of the mechanisms for international implementation: (1) Article 6 states that parties shall have the power to authorize "legal entities" to participate in JI; (2) Article 17 stipulates that participation in the CDM may involve "private and/or public entities." Consistent with its overall emphasis on economic issues, by including non-state actors within the flexibility mechanisms the Protocol recognizes that national governments, constrained by political concerns, are not necessarily the most efficient cost-minimizing agents.

Development of the flexibility mechanisms: Pilot phase for activities implemented jointly

The United Nations Framework Convention on Climate Change (UNFCCC), signed at the Earth Summit in 1992, established a pilot phase for Activities Implemented Jointly (AIJ). The term AIJ was used to refer to offshore activities to reduce GHG emissions, in general, to meet the reduction obligation of the home country. During the years following entry into force of the UNFCCC, a limited number of AIJ projects were carried out, primarily on a bilateral basis but also under the auspices of intergovernmental organizations such as the World Bank. These activities provided valuable experience for policy makers in formulating the provisions concerning JI contained in the Kyoto Protocol.

Greenhouse-gas emissions trading

Article 6 of the Kyoto Protocol provides for GHG emissions trading among Annex I (developed) countries. The overall purpose of this provision is to enable countries to meet their commitments under Article 3 in a manner which minimizes the overall cost of emission reductions by allowing potentially cheaper reductions in GHG emissions in one developed country to be traded against more expensive reductions in the home country. Article 12 allows developed countries to meet "part of" their Article 3 commitments by carrying out projects in developing countries which result in greater than business-as-usual reductions in GHG emissions, thereby generating certified emission reductions.

Article 6 of the Kyoto Protocol states:

1. For the purpose of meeting its commitments under Article 3, any Party included in Annex I may transfer to, or acquire from, any other such Party emission reduction units resulting from projects aimed at reducing anthropogenic emissions by sources or enhancing anthropogenic removals by sinks of greenhouse gases in any sector of the economy, provided that:
   (a) Any such project has the approval of the Parties involved;
   (b) Any such project provides a reduction in emissions by sources, or an enhancement of removals by sinks, that is additional to any that would otherwise occur;
   (c) It does not acquire any emission reduction units if it is not in compliance with its obligations under Articles 5 and 7; and
   (d) The acquisition of emission reduction units shall be supplemental to domestic actions for the purposes of meeting commitments under Article 3.

Many issues concerning implementation of Article 6 were not resolved at the time of adoption of the Protocol, such as the bases for approval of projects by the Parties, the definition of "additional" in subparagraph 1 (b), and the meaning of "supplemental to domestic actions" in subparagraph 1 (d). Paragraph 2 of Article 6 indicates that issues such as these would be resolved in the process elaborating further guidelines on implementation prior to the First Meeting of the Parties to the Protocol.

Paragraph 3 of Article 6 also states that:

A Party included in Annex I may authorize *legal entities* to participate, under its responsibility, in actions leading to the generation, transfer or acquisition under this Article of emission reduction units.

Recognizing that many issues needed to be resolved before an emissions trading scheme could be operational, the Protocol states in Article 17:

The Conference of the Parties shall define the relevant principles, modalities, rules and guidelines, in particular for verification, reporting and accountability for emissions trading. . . .

While it is clear that the term "legal entities" in Article 6 refers to non-state actors, further guidance from the Parties is needed to provide more specificity concerning the type of participation envisioned by the Parties and which entities would have a role. One of the ongoing tasks of Conference of the Parties to the Climate Change Convention under Article 17 has been the development of rules and guidelines for emissions trading and the role of non-state actors included within the term "legal entities." It is anticipated that these guidelines will be adopted at COP 6.

Joint implementation

Article 3, which provides for JI among Annex I (developed) countries, is closely related to Article 6. Paragraph 1 of Article 3 concerns JI and creates a legal basis for carrying out activities outside a country's borders in order to meet its national emission commitments. Paragraphs 10–13 provide a basis for recalculation of a Party's obligations by means of emissions trading.

Article 3, paragraph 1 of the Protocol states:

The Parties included in Annex 1 shall *individually or jointly*, ensure that their aggregate anthropogenic carbon dioxide equivalent emissions of the greenhouse gases listed in Annex A do not exceed their assigned amounts, calculated pursuant to their quantified emission limitation and reduction commitments inscribed in Annex B and in accordance with the provisions of this Article, with a view to reducing their overall emissions of such gases by at least 5 per cent below 1990 levels in the commitment period 2008 to 2012.

As noted above, Paragraphs 10 and 11 provide a mechanism for calculating the Parties' emissions-limitation and -reduction obligations under a JI scenario involving the transfer of "emission reduction units" (ERUs). Paragraph 10 states:

> Any emission reduction units, or any part of an assigned amount, which a Party acquires from another Party in accordance with the provisions of Article 6 or of Article 17 shall be added to assigned amount for the acquiring Party.

Paragraph 11 states:

> Any emission reduction units, or any part of any assigned amount, which a Party transfers to another Party in accordance with provisions of Article 6 or 17 shall be subtracted from the assigned amount for the transferring Party.

Along with the programme on emissions trading envisioned by Article 6, the detailed guidelines for carrying out a JI programme were not elaborated when the Protocol was adopted, and are expected to be completed by COP 6. As discussed in the earlier section on restructuring of the energy sector, assigning an appropriate role to non-state actors, particularly the private sector and NGOs, will be critical in achieving successful implementation of a JI scheme. Some of the activities that have already been undertaken by non-state actors in carrying out JI projects on an interim basis are discussed later in this chapter (pp. 27–38).

Clean development mechanism

Article 12 establishes the CDM, a scheme for encouraging Annex I countries to carry out emission-reduction projects in developing countries by providing credit for "certified emission reductions" which can be used to meet the Annex I countries' commitments under Article 3. Importantly, paragraph 2 of Article 12 articulates the dual purpose of the CDM – achieving sustainable development consistent with climate protection in developing countries and assisting developed countries in meeting their commitments under Article 3. Article 12, paragraph 2 states:

The purpose of the clean development mechanism shall be to assist Parties not included in Annex I in achieving sustainable development and in contributing to the ultimate objective of the Convention, and to assist Parties included in Annex I in achieving compliance with their quantified emission limitation and reduction commitments under Article 3.

In achieving the dual purposes of the CDM noted above, projects must also meet two criteria listed in Article 12, Paragraph 3:

(a) Parties not included in Annex I will benefit from project activities resulting in certified emission reductions, and

(b) Parties included in Annex I may use the certified emission reductions accruing from such project activities to contribute to compliance with part of their quantified emission limitation and reduction commitments under Article 3, as determined by the Conference of the Parties serving as the meeting of the Parties to this Protocol.

Paragraph 4 indicates that the CDM "shall be subject to the authority and guidance of the Conference of the Parties serving as the meeting of the Parties to this Protocol and be supervised by an executive board." Defining the make-up and detailed role of the executive board may also involve assigning a role to non-state actors such as NGOs and IGOs.

As noted above and stated in Article 17, the Conference of the Parties to the Climate Change Convention is expected to define "the relevant principles, modalities, rules and guidelines, in particular for verification, reporting and accountability for emissions trading." Again, while the Protocol authorized emissions trading as a mechanism under which Annex I countries can receive credit for emission reductions for both JI and CDM activities, the specifics of how these interrelated programmes will function remains to be elaborated. With respect to the potential roles for non-state actors, a number of provisions contained in Article 12 require actions which may be most effectively executed by non-governmental bodies or international organizations, particularly those related to ensuring transparency and accountability.

Roles for non-state actors and examples of activities undertaken by non-state actors

Private sector

There are several reasons why the private sector could be motivated to participate in activities related to JI, emissions trading, and the CDM. First, in order to achieve their emission-reduction commitments under the Kyoto Protocol, many national governments will allocate rights to emit GHGs among industrial sources responsible for the emissions. Consequently, the private sector will be required to achieve reductions and, if allowed to do so, may choose to meet some of their obligations by carrying out JI and CDM projects or by purchasing emission credits.

Second, private entities, motivated by profit, may seek to become involved in the newly emerging markets and services needed to implement the flexibility mechanisms. For example, the international emissions-trading scheme would require the development of monitoring equipment in order to obtain accurate inventories of emissions. Because it is likely that the value of emission credits will be influenced by the reliability of the project's measurement procedures and technology, there will be an incentive for companies to develop instruments for measurement. The private sector could also engage in the development of climate-friendly technologies and sequestration methods that aid private firms or countries in meeting their GHG emission limits.

Because private entities possess detailed information about their own emissions, technological options, and costs, they are in the best position to determine accurately the most cost-effective abatement schemes for their own companies, including the possibility of emissions trading. In addition, allowing private entities to participate directly in an international emissions-trading programme would increase the number of actors involved in the trading scheme, thereby increasing competition and stimulating greater cross-border capital flows.

New opportunities for private brokering agencies and the international insurance industry also exist within the international emissions-trading market. Brokering agencies could aid in developing forums for emission trading by identifying projects, matching partners, auditing and certifying emission offsets, and tracking emission trades. The growth of the international insurance industry may also occur as a result of the implementation of these flexibility mechanisms, as companies may seek to limit investment and political risk by use of insurance.

Although major business opportunities exist under the Protocol, few companies have taken early action in adopting the flexibility mechanisms to reduce their emissions. Because the Kyoto Protocol has not been ratified, and no national emission limitations are currently effective, there is uncertainty as to whether emission reductions achieved as a result of voluntary actions on the part of the private sector will ultimately be applied in determining if a company has met mandatory reduction requirements in the future. Some companies have chosen to take early action even in the face of uncertainty over the effect of these actions on future emission-reduction requirements. For example, BP Amoco and Monsanto have undertaken GHG emission-abatement schemes and adopted pilot emission-trading programmes. Such early action could lead to a competitive advantage when the Protocol enters into force.

BP Amoco's intra-firm emissions-trading scheme

To the extent that corporations within Annex I countries are subject to national emission limitations, these corporations may have an interest in trading GHG emission credits among their various subsidiaries or branches. Such intra-firm trading could occur between branches located within an Annex I country or between branches in different countries. In collaboration with the Environmental Defense Fund, BP Amoco has implemented such an intra-firm trading programme among its 12 multinational business units. With its overall company target to reduce GHG emissions to 10 per cent below 1990 levels by 2010, BP Amoco allocated emission rights to each business unit for 1999 through 2003.

Under the proposed programme, compliance will be measured on an annual basis, and any unused emission rights may be used for future commitments. Business units that are able to reduce emissions to below their assigned limits may be able to sell these excess allocations to another business unit, thereby allowing each branch to determine a cost-effective means of meeting their emissions commitment. An independent third party will be responsible for verifying emission baselines and reductions, and a broker within BP Amoco's trading arm will register all trades.

By the middle of 2000, BP Amoco aims to expand the programme to include all its activities. Trading began in September 1998 and approximately 50,000 tons of carbon dioxide had been traded by early 1999. In 1998, the company also reported that its emissions were 1 per cent lower than 1990 levels. BP Amoco also plans to share these results with other private entities.

Monsanto: Emissions trading using carbon-sequestration projects

Monsanto, a multinational company specializing in research and technology development in the areas of agriculture, pharmaceuticals, and food products, has also been involved in developing an international emissions-trading system. Under this trading scheme, the private sector would be able to purchase verifiable carbon-emission credits from farmers who sequester carbon through conservation tillage or other sequestration methods. Conservation tillage eliminates ploughing, which exposes the soil to air and releases carbon. To encourage farmers to avoid ploughing, Monsanto has established this emissions-trading programme and has developed products and farming methods that promote sequestration of carbon.

Non-governmental organizations (NGOs)

Non-governmental organizations (NGOs) could potentially play a number of important roles in the implementation of the flexibility mechanisms. In addition to the language in Articles 6 and 12 discussed above, Article 13 subparagraph 4 (i) of the Protocol specifically requires the COP, in implementing the Protocol, to:

... seek and utilize, where appropriate, the services and co-
operations of, and information provided by, competent international organizations and intergovernmental and non-governmental organizations.

By including this language, the Parties recognized the importance of
non-state actors and NGOs specifically in the Protocol's effective
implementation.

Some of the potential roles for NGOs relate to verification, enforcement, expertise, and public education, particularly in implementation
of the mechanisms. The use of NGOs in implementing the mechanisms offers both economic and political advantages.

In order to ensure that self-reported data of actual emission reductions from participants in the mechanisms are accurate, independent verification could be performed by NGOs. The verification
process is critical for both parties to a transaction under the mechanisms. To avoid the possibility of either the host country or the investing agent inflating the carbon emissions from a baseline scenario
or the actual GHG-emission reductions derived from the project,
careful monitoring and verification will be necessary. Verification
would involve confirming that the estimated GHG abatement had
actually occurred and ascertaining whether "additional" reductions
took place which would not have occurred under a business-as-usual
scenario.

In a verification role, NGOs could perform independent assessments and monitoring of individual sources. NGOs could also conduct on-site inspections or indirect inspections of collected data. In
examining collected data, NGOs would need to consider technical
information concerning baseline calculations, data relating to actual
emissions, and the projected estimates of GHG abatement.

Verification by independent NGOs could serve as one element of a
cost-efficient compliance mechanism, making violations by private
and governmental parties transparent to the public and investing
parties. On the basis of information submitted by individual investors and the monitored data, NGOs would be able to detect whether

GHG reductions had actually been achieved, and they could make their findings available to the public. Under some circumstances, NGOs could initiate legal action against public and private entities on behalf of the environment. Of course, the effectiveness and fairness of this type of compliance mechanism would depend greatly upon the expertise and legitimacy of these NGOs. To be effective, NGOs must have the capacity to perform complicated, technical evaluations, and they must have access to important information from public and private firms. Furthermore, the validity of assessments performed by NGOs hinges on these groups being "relatively impermeable to 'capture' by the industries they were certifying."

Aside from acting as an agent for enforcement, NGOs could also share their expertise with both developing countries and countries with economies in transition in the implementation of the flexibility mechanisms. With respect to capacity building in non Annex I countries and countries with economies in transition, NGOs could assist in building a climate-related infrastructure, such as developing the institutions needed to perform monitoring, reporting, and verification. They could also ensure that these countries have the capacity to request technology and projects that would help them attain sustainable development. NGOs, for example, could perform the environmental and socio-economic assessments needed to advise developing countries in identifying projects that would encourage the transfer of energy-efficient technologies and result in long-term economic and environmental benefits that are consistent with national goals.

NGOs that specialize in environmental law could also provide legal assistance to developing countries relating to the drafting of ERU-acquisition contracts and competitive-bidding documents. These legal NGOs could assist developing countries in establishing a domestic regulatory framework that would encourage other countries and private entities to invest in JI and CDM projects within their country.

For both developed and developing countries, the use of NGOs in the implementation of the flexibility mechanisms could provide both economic and political advantages. In terms of the economic advantages, verification by NGOs could counteract the tendency of participants in CDM and JI projects to overestimate emission reductions, thereby promoting a credible and stable emission market. Additionally, a credible market encourages further investment and trust by private and public entities. At the same time, private firms could gain knowledge in energy-efficient, cost-saving technologies. NGOs could work with private businesses in developing programmes and technology that balance economic and environmental concerns.

Perhaps the most important aspect of the involvement of NGOs in the implementation of the mechanisms could be to confer additional "legitimacy and transnationalism" in enhancing the transparency of activities conducted under these mechanisms. The promotion of transparency by NGOs could be valuable in revealing violations and encouraging compliance with the Protocol's commitments. Under certain circumstances, NGOs may even be in a position to bring legal actions as a way of encouraging compliance among participants. Essentially, NGOs would promote transparency by performing independent assessments and monitoring of individual sources in order to ensure that there are no distortions in official, self-reported data of actual emission offsets.

In addition to these roles, NGOs could work with private businesses in developing programmes and technology that balance economic and environmental concerns. They could also provide certification of emission offsets, even specializing in sector-specific, JI, or CDM certifications.

Intergovernmental organizations (IGOs)

As with the private sector and NGOs, the authority for the involvement of intergovernmental organizations in the flexibility mechanisms discussed in this chapter arises primarily from language in Articles 6, 12, and 13 of the Kyoto Protocol. Paragraph 5 of Article 12 states that "Emissions reductions resulting from each project activity shall be certified by operational entities to be designated by the Conference of the Parties serving as the meeting of the Parties to this Protocol ..." and also refers to the participation of "public entities" in CDM activities more generally in Paragraph 9.

United Nations Conference on Trade and Development (UNCTAD)

UNCTAD has proposed playing a role as an intermediary in international trading of certified emission-reduction credits. Along with the Earth Council, UNCTAD has agreed to form the first independent international verifier of company emissions reports, the International Emissions Trading Association. Before the formal market authorized by the Protocol comes into existence, UNCTAD and the Earth Council intend to solicit membership from the private sector, enabling these private entities to trade among themselves. In addition to brokering emission trades, UNCTAD and the Earth Council would help its members to identify emission-offset projects.

Although the Protocol does not specify the procedure for verification and certification, UNCTAD could analyse the reports and data submitted by individual firms as to actual emissions and could compare this information with the estimated, baseline data. UNCTAD could also perform audits and on-site inspections to verify emissions from projects. As to certification, UNCTAD could be responsible for converting GHG reductions achieved through JI or CDM projects into credits capable of being traded or transferred.

UNCTAD's role in this trading scheme has been criticized by many organizations. Many oppose the verification of emission offsets by an entity that participates in the trading and creating of credits. Acting under both of these rules, UNCTAD would have to be aware of a potential conflict of interest that could result in a tendency to establish a framework that might overestimate emission reductions from projects.

United Nations Commission on International Trade Law (UNCITRAL)

For both government-sponsored and private-sector activities carried out under either a JI scheme or the CDM, project contracts could serve as an important means of ensuring compliance with the rules of the mechanisms as well as with the overall goals of the Kyoto Protocol. By requiring incorporation of environmental guarantees into the contractual arrangements between private parties or between governmental entities and private parties, the Conference of the Parties could create a highly effective means of enforcing the provisions of the Protocol. Indeed, during COP 5 some options for providing legal assistance to developing countries in drafting intergovernmental and private contracts were put forward. UNCITRAL could play a role in drafting model agreements for this purpose.

To achieve compliance with the Protocol and fulfil the expectations of both contracting parties, a standard agreement for JI and CDM projects might include a number of provisions. At a minimum, UNCITRAL will need to provide guidance on how to draft language in defining the amount of emission reductions to be delivered and how emissions will be measured, verified, certified, and shared. The Protocol also sets forth some supplementary principles that should be addressed in standard JI and CDM contracts, such as a provision that requires "real, measurable, and long term" reductions which are "additional to any that would occur in the absence of the certified project activity."

For both government-sponsored and private sector activities carried out under JI and the CDM, there will be a compelling need for guidance in drafting standard contractual language. Some of the advantages in creating standard contractual guidelines would include the reduction of negotiation costs, the facilitation of financing, and the minimization of exploitation due to unequal bargaining power between the parties. UNCITRAL could play an important role in contributing standard, contractual language that is consistent with specific provisions of the Protocol, achieves the environmental and economic objectives of the Protocol, and ensures compliance by private entities, to which the Protocol does not apply directly.

If JI and CDM projects are carried out by private entities, contracts between these entities must be agreed to. As noted above, private firms are not signatories to the Protocol and have made no direct legal obligations under it; it is, therefore, very important that private contracts are structured to be consistent with the provisions and goals of the Protocol. Private actors' compliance with the over-arching goals of the Protocol is essential, not only to achieve real emission reductions but also for the benefit of the companies themselves. UNCITRAL could provide suggestions on specific contractual language that would ensure that projects conducted by private parties are in accordance with the Protocol and subject to the legal commitments of the parties' respective governments.

To achieve compliance with the objectives of the Protocol, private contracts, for example, could contain provisions relating to an independent third-party verification, ensuring that contracts accurately assess the amount of anticipated reductions. As mentioned earlier, this type of system would promote transparency and encourage compliance with the goals of the Protocol.

In addition to provisions relating to transparency, private contracts should include enforcement and penalty arrangements in the event that the estimated reductions are not actually attained by the project or that objectives of the Protocol are not fulfilled. In the event that a project fails to meet its estimated reductions, a private contract should indicate which party will be liable. With respect to non compliance with the Protocol, UNCITRAL could also recommend contract provisions relating to dispute settlement and applicable law.

The Protocol also provides that emission reductions resulting from CDM projects must be "real, measurable, and [have] long-term benefits related to the mitigation of climate change." To this end, contracts will have to present a timetable during which emission reductions will take place and be measured, to detail procedures for monitoring, and to explain methods for updating estimates of emission reductions. This provision may require that contracts contain procedures for conducting environmental-impact assessments.

Just as contracts for the CDM may have to enumerate how the project will produce real, measurable, and long-term reductions, CDM contracts may also have to detail how the project will result in sustainable development. In specifying how the latter result will be achieved, contracts should include language concerning the non-GHG environmental impacts of the project. Contracts, for instance, could specify how projects promote technology transfer and encourage energy efficiency in developing countries that will lead to long-term environmental improvements.

In addition to the sustainable-development objectives of the CDM mechanism, the Protocol also provides that "a share of the proceeds from certified project activities is used to cover administrative expenses as well as to assist developing country parties that are particularly vulnerable to the adverse effects of climate change to meet the costs of adaptation." In accordance with this provision, CDM contracts should designate the amount of proceeds allocated to cover assistance to developing countries for adaptation to climate change.

Multilateral development banks (MDBs)

Multilateral developments could play an important role in the implementation of the mechanisms by absorbing some of the risk associated with early use of emerging mechanisms, as well as reducing transaction costs. MDBs, and particularly the World Bank, could provide information-related services, capacity-building services, and risk-management services. With respect to information-related services, MDBs and other international financial institutions (IFIs) could act as brokers, matching firms seeking emissions credits with groups seeking funding for GHG-reduction activities. In this capacity, IFIs could lessen the costs of seeking partners and provide market recognition to smaller companies and obscure projects in developing countries. In addition, these organizations could use their expertise in identifying projects suitable for investment, assessing the potential environmental benefits and ERUs generated from the CDM or JI project. IFIs would also be able to help developing countries choose projects that would result in sustainable development.

IFIs could also aid in establishing the national infrastructure necessary for developing countries and for countries with economies in transition to participate in JI and CDM. Through capacity building, IFIs could invest in monitoring technology; provide legal assistance in making appropriate changes to the law in order to facilitate CDM and JI projects; establish a system for regulating and tracking emission sales; create a reporting, verification, and certification protocol; and assist in communication and cooperation between countries.

As risk managers, IFIs could also create funds in which capital for emission-reduction projects would be pooled together, and dividends could be paid in the form of ERUs. Once results from projects were established and firms could be sure that emission offsets were actually attained, it is likely that investors would be increasingly willing to place their resources into the project. Funds could further reduce risks associated with CDM and JI through the use of a reserve, which would contain excess emission offsets beyond the amount actually sold to investors in order to cover investments should the actual emissions fall short of the estimated emissions.

The World Bank has been involved in disseminating information and research to the Convention Secretariat and then to the Parties to the Convention concerning the guidelines, modalities, and procedures for the mechanisms in Article 6 and Article 12. Authorized by the UNFCCC, the Bank has undertaken the AIJ programme, which, as noted above, has served as a pilot phase for JI projects. While, currently, investors do not receive emission-reduction credits, this programme has furnished valuable information for the structure of similar market-based mechanisms, particularly in the areas of data concerning baseline and additionality assessment, criteria for project selection, and reporting methods. To date, the Bank has established AIJ programmes in Mexico, Poland, Burkina Faso, and India.

In June, 1997, the World Bank also proposed to undertake the Global Carbon Initiative. Under this initiative, projects already financed through the Bank's conventional operating funds would be pooled and modified to generate GHG-reduction credits for investors. Funds would come from the government or private-sector entities seeking to achieve their emission limits under the Protocol.

Consistent with Protocol, the Bank would ensure that emissions from the project would be certified by the CDM, or a third party approved by the CDM. The Bank would essentially operate as a trustee over the carbon fund, disbursing funds for emission-reduction projects in client countries and distributing credits generated by the project to investors. The amount of credits distributed to investors would be based upon the size of their contribution to the fund.

The fund is intended to attract both private and public capital because the Bank has an established pipeline of projects which could be converted to provide GHG-emission credits; thus, the early start-up costs of searching for partners and establishing the credibility of projects could be minimized. Through the fund, the Bank could further reduce transaction costs by employing various schemes to mitigate insurance costs. For instance, the Bank could require buyers and sellers of emission credits to enter into carbon performance contracts in which the seller would agree to provide a specific amount of credits to the buyer in exchange for payments at certain intervals. Should the actual emission offsets fall short of those projected, the payment would be adjusted accordingly. The Fund could also create a reserve of credits to bedistributed to investors if the project fails to deliver the offsets.

Consistent with the provisions of the Protocol relating to CDM, the World Bank intends to ensure that the Fund will promote equitable sharing of cost savings and benefits between both countries. To achieve the CDM's sustainable-development goal, the Bank could also assist developing countries in choosing projects that are in the national interest; helping countries to examine the costs and benefits of baseline assessment tools; developing measurement, reporting, and verification infrastructures; and evaluating environment-friendly technology.

Conclusions

The Kyoto Protocol, negotiated in an era of economic globalization, is precedent setting in its specific inclusion of non-state actors in its implementation provisions. Ensuring the effectiveness of the Protocol requires that a variety of non-state actors be constructively engaged in its implementation, including the private sector, NGOs, inter-governmental organizations, and international financial institutions.

Bibliography

Anonymous. "Climate Change: Association For Making Emission Trades Proposed by U.N. Group, Earth Council." *CHEM (BNA)* 22 (2 October): 1070, 1998.

Anonymous. "Climate Change: Emission Marketing Association Opposes U.N. Proposal For Private Trading Group." *ER (BNA)* 29 (23 October): 1234, 1998.

BP Amoco. "Environmental and Social Report 1998" (visited 11 June 1999). ⟨http://www.bpamoco.org/Reports/hse/⟩.

Center for Clean Air Policy. "Setting Priorities for the Implementation of the Kyoto Agreement: Making Flexibility Mechanisms Work." Washington, DC: Center for Clean Air Policy, February 1998.

Center for Clean Air Policy. "The Clean Development Mechanism: How Do We Get There From Here?" Center for Clean Air Policy, September, 1998.

Di Leva, Charles E. "International Environmental Law and Development." *Georgetown Journal of International Environmental Law Review* 10: 501, 1998.

Esty, Daniel and Brad Gentry. *Economic Globalization and the Environment.* OECD: Paris, 1997.

"Kyoto Protocol to the UN Framework Convention on Climate Change," 10 December 1997, *International Legal Materials* 37: 22.

Giorgetti, Chiara. "The Role of Nongovernmental Organizations in the Climate Change Negotiations." *Colo. J. Int'l Environmental Law and Policy* 9 (Winter): 115–121, 1998.

Goldberg, Donald M. and Glenn M. Wiser. "Rethinking the JI Pilot Phase: A Call For Independent Evaluation and a Legal Framework." *Widener Law Symposium Journal* 3: 385, 1998.

Hanafi, Alex G. "Joint Implementation: Legal and Institutional Issues for an Effective International Program to Combat Climate Change." *Harvard Environmental Law Review* 22: 441, 1998.

Hecht, Joy and Brett Orlando. "Can the Kyoto Protocol Support Biodiversity Conservation? Legal and Financial Challenges." *Environmental Law Reporter* 28: 105–108 (September): 1998.

Hydrocarbon Online. Mobil Executive Lambasts the Kyoto Protocol. 28 September 1998, ⟨http://news.hydrocarbon/industry-news/ 19980928-6886.html⟩.

Joshua, Frank T. *et al.* "Greenhouse Gas Emissions Trading: Defining the Principles, Modalities, Rules and Guidelines for Verification, Reporting, and Accountability." Geneva: UNCTAD, August, 1998.

Kozloff, Keith. "Electricity Sector Reform in Developing Countries: Implications for Renewable Energy." Research Report Series, *Research Report No. 2*, March 1998. Renewable Energy Policy Project, Washington, DC.

Kosloff, Laura H. "Linking Climate Change Mitigation with Sustainable Economic Development: A Status Report." *Widener Law Symposium Journal* 3 (Fall): 351, 1998.

Llobet, Gabriela. "'Trust But Verify': Verification in the Joint Implementation Regime." *George Washington Journal of International Law and Economics* 31: 233, 242–243, 1997–1998.

Monsanto. Monsanto Position on Climate Change (visited 11 June 1999). ⟨http://www.monsanto.com/monsanto/m...nter/ background/ClimateChange.html⟩.

Thomas, Charles. "Explaining BP Amoco's Pilot CO_2 Emissions Trading System." BP Amoco, January 1999 (memorandum).

Wiener, Jonathan. Designing Markets for International Greenhouse Gas Control, Resources for the Future. Oct. 1997.

Worika, Ibibia Lucky *et al.* "Contractual Aspects of Implementing the Clean Development Mechanism and Other Flexibility Mechanisms Under the Kyoto Protocol." Centre for Energy, Petroleum, & Mineral Law & Policy, 30 August 1998.

World Bank. "AIJ Program Brief" (visited 11 June 1999). ⟨http://www-esd.worldbank.org/aij/brief.htm⟩. Washington, DC: World Bank.

World Bank. "Global Climate Change: The Prototype Carbon Fund" (visited 11 June 1999). ⟨http://www-esd.worldbank.org/cc/⟩. Washington, DC: World Bank.

World Bank. "Lessons for the World Bank for the Kyoto Mechanisms: A Review of World Bank Reports." April, 1999. Washington, DC: World Bank.

World Resources Institute. *Safe Climate, Sound Business: An Action Agenda.* Washington DC: WRI, 1998.

Zacaroli, Alec. "Climate Change: Companies Should Act Soon or Risk Competitive Disadvantage, Official Says." *Environmental Reporter* 29: 1792, 1999.

3

Non-Compliance Procedures and the Climate Change Convention[1]

CATHERINE REDGWELL

Introduction

A number of recent environmental treaties, including the 1997 Kyoto Protocol to the 1992 United Nations Framework Convention on Climate Change (UNFCCC), have adopted a non-compliance procedure (NCP) to address failure by Contracting Parties fully to implement their treaty obligations. Recourse to such procedures is evidence of a growing awareness that traditional rules of international law concerned with material breach of treaty obligations and with state responsibility are inappropriate to address problems of environmental treaty implementation.[2] It is the purpose of this chapter to set forth some of the issues that will need to be addressed in establishing an NCP under the Climate Change Convention, in particular in connection with the application of such procedures to the mechanisms for achieving the substantive commitments undertaken by developed States under the Kyoto Protocol.[3] Before the Climate Change Convention and the Protocol are considered, the concept of NCP and the development of such procedures in contemporary international environmental law is traced.[4]

What are "non-compliance procedures" (NCPs)?

Essentially, NCPs embody procedures established under multilateral treaties to meet the following objectives:

1. To provide positive encouragement to Contracting Parties to comply with their treaty obligations.

2. To provide a multilateral forum for dispute resolution/avoidance.

3. In the event of non-compliance, to provide a "softer," less legalistic mechanism than offered by traditional dispute-settlement procedures under international law. NCPs generally apply a less rigid test by which compliance is measured and the first object is to obtain a return to full compliance by the "defaulting" state, rather than impose a sanction for non-compliance or award compensation to an injured party.

4. To provide for internal resolution of disputes, without recourse to external adjudicators or institutions.

5. To facilitate access, since NCPs may typically be invoked by, *inter alia*, one Party, and are therefore not dependent upon common agreement; thus, unlike traditional dispute-settlement mechanisms, NCPs need not be consent-based.

From these objectives, it may be seen that NCPs are concerned both with facilitating compliance by Contracting Parties with their Convention obligations, and with providing a "softer system" for addressing non-compliance by a Contracting Party than is currently afforded by traditional dispute-settlement procedures under international law. In the latter context, NCPs may be viewed as an international form of alternative dispute settlement (ADR),[5] long employed in municipal legal systems to resolve conflicts arising in longer-term legal relationships. The use of NCPs at the international level is thus a recognition of the relational character of certain international treaties and the need to ensure both continuing participation and the fulfilment of generally non-reciprocal treaty obligations designed to ensure the achievement of common goals. Accordingly, NCPs are less confrontational and generally less legalistic and are designed to assist the defaulting State in returning to compliance, not necessarily to incriminate for non-compliance.[6] This is reflected in a trend away from provisions relying solely on "dispute settlement," a phenomenon observable not just in the environmental sphere, towards the addition of provisions addressing "assessment,"[7] "monitoring,"[8] "verification,"[9] "verification of compliance,"[10] "implementation,"[11] and "considering progress made in the implementation" of the Convention.[12] Many of the perceived advantages of an NCP are reflected in the rationale for the multilateral consultative process set forth in Article 13 of the Climate Change Convention.[13]

The dual nature of NCPs is also a reflection of the various reasons for non-compliance by states with their international obligations, which may range from the free rider exploiting the economic advantage derived from non-compliance[14] to an inability to meet treaty obligations because of their high cost or a lack of capacity, e.g. lack of relevant technology or expertise.[15] An NCP needs both to reduce/eliminate the economic benefit to be derived from non-compliance and to facilitate compliance where obstacles relating to lack of capacity, particularly for developing states, are identifiable.

The goal of NCPs is therefore distinguishable from traditional rules on state responsibility, since the object is to ensure a return to full compliance with treaty obligations rather than to require compensation by the defaulting state for the harm caused to another state or states for breach of an international obligation. The latter point highlights a further negative feature of traditional dispute-settlement mechanisms in the environmental context – namely, that environmental damage has generally already occurred. Moreover, in the climate-change context, the effects of non-compliance may be "subtle and cumulative," with the full effects manifest only over a considerable time. In common with other transfrontier environmental problems, it may also be difficult to attribute particular harm to the actions or omissions of one state or several states. This enhances the need for a NCP that places the emphasis on prevention rather than on remedying harm caused.

Although they are not confined to the environmental context, it is none the less clear that NCPs have a particularly important role to play in that context because of the distinctive character of environmental treaty obligations. A number of factors may be identified: the pace, magnitude, and irreversibility of environmental problems; the essentially non-reciprocal nature of the treaty obligations which renders enforcement *inter partes* ineffective; the failure to operationalize traditional rules on state liability and responsibility; the ability to measure compliance against quantifiable targets; and the necessity for national implementation to render international environmental obligations effective.[16] Perhaps the best-known existing NCP is that established under the 1987 Montreal Protocol to the 1985 Vienna Convention on the Protection of the Ozone Layer ("Ozone Convention").[17] This was the first multilateral environmental treaty to go beyond reporting and dispute-settlement provisions in providing for a non-compliance procedure.[18] While Article 11 of the Convention provides for traditional dispute settlement, Article 8 of the Protocol envisages an NCP, which has subsequently been developed by meetings of the Parties.[19] The procedure was finalized at the Fourth Meeting of the Parties (MOP) in London in 1992. A pivotal role is played by a ten-member Implementation Committee.[20] Early issues included data reporting to establish important baselines for assessing compliance with quantitative and temporal obligations (targets and timetables).[21]

Monitoring and compliance are essential bedfellows.[22] There is little point in adopting a compliance mechanism without the capability to gather information relevant to a determination whether treaty obligations are being met. This is part of an integrated process that has been termed "implementation control." This can take place in incremental stages, i.e. monitoring and information gathering preceding the development of non compliance mechanism(s). A good example of this process is the 1979 Geneva Convention on Long-Range Transboundary Air Pollution[23] (LRTAP), which has seen data collected under the EMEP Programme[24] form the basis for an assessment of the first sulphur-emissions protocol in 1985[25] and led to agreement on a tightened emission-reduction schedule in the second sulphur protocol in 1994 with a non-compliance mechanism.[26] Of course, the obligation to report is itself a concrete obligation, non-compliance with which may be subject to an NCP.

If such information gathering and reporting is viewed as part of a broader compliance-information system, the question remains of what response is made, if any, to identified problems of non-implementation by Parties. In the absence of a non-compliance mechanism, non-implementation can be addressed only (in formal legal terms at any rate) as a dispute between contracting Parties, dealt with – if at all – under traditional dispute-settlement mechanisms. This is the present position under the 1992 Convention on Biological Diversity – it is the Parties themselves who inspect reports, with any alleged non-implementation a matter for dispute settlement under Article 27 of the Convention. Other recent environmental treaties go further – these include the 1987 Montreal Protocol; the 1991 Protocol Concerning the Control of Emissions of Volatile Organic Compounds or their Transboundary Fluxes (VOC) and 1994 Sulphur Protocols to the 1979 LRTAP Treaty;[27] the 1992 Convention for the Protection of the Marine Environment of the North-East Atlantic;[28] and, of course, the 1997 Kyoto Protocol, all of which envisage a separate mechanism for compliance being established. The Parties to the 1989 Basel Convention on the Transboundary Movement of Hazardous Wastes and their Disposal are also considering an NCP.[29] Of these examples, only the NCP under the Montreal Protocol is fully operationalized.

Without concrete obligations, and the monitoring of implementation/compliance with those obligations, it is not practicable to speak of non-compliance mechanisms. This is seen clearly in the climate-change context, which has proceeded from general commitments without specific timetables and targets to agreement upon such specific commitments with attention turned to the implementation thereof and to compliance control.[30] The 1987 Montreal Protocol, the 1994 Second Sulphur Protocol, and the 1997 Kyoto Protocol suggest a new cycle of strengthening compliance systems gradually, and in step with the strengthening of commitments.[31]

The FCCC[32]

The traditional dispute-settlement approach is present in Article 14, which adopts an approach that conceptualizes disputes as arising between two or more Contracting Parties in connection with the interpretation or application of the Convention. If ever activated, the traditional hierarchy of peaceful dispute-settlement mechanisms would apply, ranging from negotiation and third-party mediation or good offices, through to arbitration or submission of the dispute to the International Court of Justice. Under Article 14, recourse to negotiation or other means of peaceful settlement is obligatory,[33] with either Party able to request creation of a conciliation commission in the event that negotiation is unsuccessful; however, the awards of the commission are recommendatory only.[34] This bilateral dispute-settlement route is considered to be complementary to the Article 13 process.[35]

Article 13, on the other hand, is a good example of the trend away from total reliance on traditional dispute-settlement methods in recent multilateral environmental agreements noted above. It establishes a multilateral consultative process (MCP) for resolution of questions concerning the implementation of the Convention. Little detail is contained in Article 13; thus, the first meeting of the COP established an Ad Hoc Group on Article 13 to operationalize the MCP.[36] The sixth and final session of this Group was held in Bonn in June 1998, where its work was completed in anticipation of COP 4.[37] It has adopted the framework for an MCP which must now be considered at COP 4, including the resolution of the matters left unresolved in the Committee.[38] Annex II to the Group's Report on its sixth session[39] contains the terms of reference for the MCP, including the proposal for a standing Multilateral Consultative Committee to be established to consider questions of implementation referred to it by Contracting Parties or by the COP as a whole.[40] This will clearly encompass the commitments contained in Articles 4–6 and 12 of the Convention. Of particular note is the objective of the process, set forth in Paragraph 2, and the mandate of the proposed standing Multilateral Consultative Committee, set forth primarily in Paragraph 6:[41]

2. The objective of the process is to resolve questions regarding the implementation of the Convention, by:

   (a) Providing advice on assistance to Parties to overcome difficulties encountered in their implementation of the Convention;

   (b) Promoting understanding of the Convention;

   (c) Preventing disputes from arising.[42]

6. The Committee shall, upon a request received in accordance with paragraph 5, consider questions regarding the implementation of the Convention in consultation with the Party or Parties concerned and, in light of the nature of the question, provide the appropriate assistance in relation to difficulties encountered in the course of implementation, by:

   (a) Clarifying and resolving the questions;

   (b) Providing advice and recommendations on the procurement of technical and financial resources for the resolution of these difficulties;

   (c) Providing advice on the compilation and communication of information.

In earlier sessions the Group has emphasized the advisory rather than supervisory nature of the MCP, further distancing the process from a more rigorous form of NCP. This is clearly reflected in the language of Paragraph 6 which is strongly facilitative: "appropriate assistance," "clarifying and resolving," "providing advice and recommendations," and "providing advice." The advisory nature of the MCP is further enforced by the link between Paragraphs 6 and 12. Under Paragraph 12, the Committee may make "[r]ecommendations regarding cooperation between the Party or Parties concerned and the other Parties to further the objectives of the Convention", and "[m]easures that the Committee deems suitable to be taken by the Party or Parties concerned for the effective implementation of the Convention." Whilst specific outcome is not expressed in mandatory terms ("may"), Paragraph 12 is mandatory in the requirement that the outcome of the Committee's deliberations must be consistent with its mandate in Paragraph 6.[43]

The MCP is without prejudice to the dispute settlement provisions of Article 14, the latter applying, *mutatis mutandis*, to the Protocol.[44] There is no internal "exhaustion of local remedies rule" in operation. However, there is some doubt whether Article 14 will ever be invoked in a traditional dispute settlement;[45] indeed, one of the reasons for including Article 13 was the perception that traditional dispute settlement would have a very limited role to play under the Convention where the likely nature of disputes would not be amenable to such procedure. None the less, the relationship between the two requires some clarification. Some states favoured the automatic suspension of Article 13 when Article 14 is invoked, but in the event this is not the approach of Paragraph 4 of the terms of reference of the MCP, which stresses that the process is both separate from and without prejudice to the provisions of Article 14 of the FCCC. Whilst this addresses the procedural hierarchy of the Article 13 and 14 processes, it may not wholly cover the substantive interaction of disputes arising under Article 13 and Article 14 procedures. For example, the "without prejudice" argument might be difficult to maintain where non-conforming behaviour has been condoned under an Article 13 mechanism but an Article 14 dispute none the less arises in connection with that act or omission. Though it is beyond the scope of this chapter fully to explore the issue, condonation of behaviour in technical breach of the treaty could give rise to acquiescence and estoppel arguments being maintained against the complaining state.

NCP under the 1997 Kyoto Protocol

The application of the Article 13 MCP to the Protocol[46] is an issue left undetermined by the Protocol itself. Article 16 of the latter provides that the COP serving as a meeting of the Parties to the Protocol shall "as soon as practicable" consider such application, with or without modification.[47] If the Article 13 MCP were so extended, the Protocol expressly provides that such procedure would operate without prejudice to the NCP under the Protocol (which in turn is without prejudice to the dispute-settlement provisions of

Article 14 FCCC). What is clear is the determination to distinguish a specific NCP under the Protocol from *both* the dispute settlement provisions of Article 14 of the Convention/Protocol *and* the MCP of Article 13 (if extended to the Protocol).[48]

It is Article 18 of the Protocol that expressly refers to non-compliance in the following terms:

> The Conference of the Parties serving as the meeting of the Parties to this Protocol shall, at its first session, approve appropriate and effective procedures and mechanisms to determine and to address cases of non-compliance with the provisions of this Protocol, including through the development of an indicative list of consequences, taking into account the cause, type, degree and frequency of non-compliance. Any procedures and mechanisms under the Article entailing binding consequences shall be adopted by means of an amendment to this Protocol.[49]

Owing to the politically sensitive nature of NCPs — in particular, binding consequences flowing from a determination of non-compliance — it is not surprising that decision on any such characteristics will require the stringent treaty-amendment procedures of the Protocol to be followed.[50] Establishing this significant procedural hurdle to the adoption of binding consequences for non-compliance is, in part, a reaction against the dynamic development of the Montreal Protocol NCP unfettered by such further requirement of treaty amendment but subject rather to the decision-making rules of the COP.[51] There is a clear reluctance to provide a "blank cheque" for binding non-compliance consequences to the COP, even as the supreme body of the Convention.

The design of a future NCP under the Protocol will entail both institutional and functional aspects: what is the procedure designed to achieve, and which organ(s) will be responsible for it? A special body will need to be established, probably a standing committee of legal, economic, and technical experts (or generalists with access to a roster of experts). Moreover, the relationship between this body and the existing Convention bodies will require careful definition. Experience has shown that the development of an NCP can take some time. How, then, will the NCP be operationalized pending the entry into force of the Protocol? This is particularly problematic, given that the key features of the flexibility mechanisms under the Protocol have also yet to be determined.

In fact, these matters have already been raised in the Subsidiary Body for Scientific and Technological Advice (SBSTA) and the Subsidiary Body for Implementation (SBI) which have met since the adoption of the Kyoto Protocol (Bonn, June 1998). Included on the agenda of each body was consideration of suggested elements for a work programme to operationalize the mechanisms under the Kyoto Protocol[52] – in particular, joint implementation (JI), the Clean Development Mechanism (CDM), and emissions trading.[53] Compliance is identified as one of the outstanding issues under each of these mechanisms, addressed in turn below.

Mechanisms under the Kyoto Protocol

Joint implementation by Annex I parties

Under Article 6 of the Protocol, Annex I countries may acquire "emission-reduction permits" resulting from projects with other Annex I Parties aimed at reducing emissions or enhancing natural carbon sinks.[54] Such JI is, however, expressly stated to be supplemental to domestic action to curb greenhouse-gas (GHG) emissions; thus, it is not possible for Annex I Parties wholly to meet their Article 3 reduction commitments via this route. Nor is it possible to buy up emission-reduction units (ERUs) to meet Article 3 commitments where a question of implementation has arisen in the course of the expert review of annual inventories.[55] Key elements of JI remain to be addressed by the first meeting of the COP serving as a meeting of the Parties to the Protocol, most notably guidelines on implementation, including verification and reporting procedures. The extent to which ERUs may be utilized as "supplemental to domestic actions" also requires clarification, given concerns that the flexibility of Article 6 may be used to avoid meeting Article 3 commitments through domestic measures. Not least, this raises competition concerns, with the "burden on business" perceived to be less where an Annex I Party relies extensively on ERUs in meeting Article 3 commitments.

Where JI is pursued, Article 4 provides that a failure to achieve joint emission-reduction targets (ERTs) does not absolve Parties from the obligation to meet their own ERTs which are obliged to be set forth in the agreement.[56] This simplifies the application of an NCP to the JI process where there has been a failure to achieve targets, and provides additional incentive for reaching the targets set forth in the JI agreement. Whilst implementation may be joint, responsibility for non-compliance with targets is still that of the individual State.

The verification and reporting criteria which are to be established at the Meeting of the Parties to the Protocol (MOP) 1 (or as soon as practicable thereafter) could give rise to non-compliance thresholds, as could the extent to which JI is supplemental to domestic implementation measures. The additionality requirement of Article 6 (1) (b) provides a further benchmark for the application of an NCP.

The clean development mechanism

Article 12 of the Protocol establishes the CDM, the purpose of which is "to assist Parties not included in Annex I in achieving sustainable development and in contributing to the ultimate objective of the Convention, and to assist Parties included in Annex I in achieving compliance with their quantified emission limitation and reduction commitments under Article 3." It will be recalled that, notwithstanding strong support from some Annex I Parties for a New Zealand proposal to make wealthier developing countries also subject to specific commitments,[57] the Protocol introduces no new commitments for developing states.[58] What Article 12 accomplishes is to provide a mechanism whereby JI between Annex I and non-Annex I Parties may take place, with Annex I Parties implementing quantifiable emission reductions under Article 3 of the Protocol while non-

Annex I Parties implement the obligations set forth in the Convention.[59] Private and/or public entities may participate in projects which are subject to certification and verification in order for emission reductions to be "claimed".[60] The mechanism is to be supervised by an executive board.[61] The executive board and "operating entities" under Article 6 could perform a compliance function in respect of the CDM, in which case the issue of whether multiple compliance mechanisms will evolve under the Protocol, perhaps linked with specific flexibility mechanisms, will need to be addressed by the COP/MOP. As under Article 6, the establishment of auditing and verification criteria will also give rise to the need to establish non-compliance parameters.

As with JI between Annex I Parties, concerns that Article 3 commitments would be met wholly through the CDM are addressed in Article 12 (3) (b), which explicitly provides that certified emission reductions from such project activities may contribute to compliance with part of their Article 3 commitments (as determined by the COP).[62] A key concern for all three of the Kyoto mechanisms is to establish an appropriate level of reliance on these mechanisms, jointly and severally, in addition to domestic implementation. The setting of a precise level would constitute a yardstick against which compliance with the supplementarity requirement could be measured. Finally, as with JI, emission reductions deriving from CDM project activities must demonstrate that such reductions are additional to any that would occur in the absence of the certified project activity [Article 12 (5) (c)], thus providing a further benchmark for the application of an NCP.

Emissions trading

Article 3 of the Protocol envisages an emissions-trading system that will establish a market amongst Annex I Parties in emission credits. Thus, for example, if an Annex B Party[63] discovered that it risked exceeding its quota, it would have the option of acquiring some or all of the unused quota of another Annex B Party, thus increasing its total allowable emissions under the Protocol. However, it is left to the COP to define "the relevant principles, modalities, rules and guidelines, in particular for verification, reporting and accountability for emissions trading."[64] Nor is any time-scale for operationalizing emissions trading stated in the Protocol, though it is certainly expected to be operational during the first commitment period (2008–2012). Any trading is expressed to be supplemental to domestic actions to meet reduction commitments;[65] limiting the operation of the trading to developed states further meets the concern expressed by developing states that such states would meet their quotas without implementing necessary domestic measures to reduce emissions, simply through purchasing quota.

Conclusions

As outlined above, a great deal has been left for determination by the first meeting of the COP serving as MOP 1,[66] including the NCPs and mechanisms referred to in Article 18. Moreover, as has already been observed, no binding consequences arising out of non-compliance may be imposed under the Protocol without further amendment of that instrument in accordance with the procedures set forth in Article 20 thereof. It is a tall order to establish the NCP at the first MOP, particularly given that so much of the detail of the Kyoto mechanisms remains to be fleshed out.[67] In practice, it is SBSTA and the SBI that have been charged with the preparatory work to allow the COP/MOP to discharge its functions,[68] including an Article 18 NCP. Further guidance from the Parties on the modalities and schedule for operationalizing the flexibility mechanisms will come from COP 4.[69]

There are a number of factors which should be considered in establishing an NCP under the Kyoto Protocol. First is the list of general guiding principles – that any NCP agreed should be simple, facilitative, cooperative, non-judicial, non confrontational, timely, and transparent. In fact, these are many of the characteristics of the Article 13 MCP and are broadly consistent with the essential characteristics of an NCP identified by the Working Group charged with establishing the Montreal Protocol NCP.[70] As for the functions of an

NCP, these could include (a) data collection (e.g. national reports), (b) review of data, (c) investigation (e.g. further information requested, site visit), (d) recommendation(s) (to indicate the end of the review process, with full or partial compliance indicated), and (e) further measures (facilitative or sanctions).[71] A new body (or bodies) would have to be created, along the lines of the Committee under the Article 13 MCP or the Committee on Implementation under the Montreal Protocol. Membership issues (e.g. size, duration of tenure, geographic distribution, and personal or government representation)[72] could prove contentious, as has been the case for the composition of the Article 13 MCP Committee. For example, should the body reflect the traditional UN approach of equitable geographic distribution, or should other principles govern (such as weighting in favour of Parties undertaking specific timetables and commitments under the Protocol)? Who should take actual decisions, particularly in respect of binding consequences of non-compliance? Should this be the COP (the procedure followed by the Montreal Protocol and under the Second Sulphur Protocol)? One benefit of such division of function between an NCP body and the COP is that this encourages the NCP to be less confrontational and will facilitate cooperation between the NCP body and the "defaulting" state.

In terms of the measures taken by a NCP body in the event of non-compliance, studies of the most fully operational NCP – the Montreal Protocol NCP – have shown that a combination of facilitation and sanction (assistance and coercion) is the most effective in ensuring compliance with treaty obligations.[73] Facilitative measures might include interpretation of ambiguous provisions and financial assistance to meet obligations arising under the Protocol. However, since the obligations undertaken are by Annex I Parties, lack of financial and technical resources is unlikely to be a convincing explanation for non-compliance.

A typical coercive mechanism is to reduce or withhold the benefits of treaty participation, including access to Global Environment Facility (GEF) funding[74] or to the proposed Multilateral Carbon Fund, if established, but a sanction of little relevance to non-complying Annex I Parties. This is part of the application of a sanction of suspending rights and privileges enjoyed under the Protocol, which could range from limiting permitted reliance on ERUs under JI and the CDM to reducing or denying access to an international emissions-trading system. There are few examples of multilateral trade sanctions being applied for non-compliance,[75] a rare exception being the NCP agreed by the International Commission for the Conservation of Atlantic Tuna (ICCAT) in 1996.[76] The compatibility of any measures adopted with other treaty obligations, including General Agreement on Tariffs and Trade (GATT)/World Trade Organization (WTO) obligations, will require further, careful analysis. Some fisheries arrangements provide for a reduction in total allowable catch for a subsequent fishing period, where the total allowable catch for the existing management period has been exceeded. An analogous approach under the Protocol would be increasing reduction commitments in a second commitment period; however, without the establishment of such a period, such a mechanism would be inoperative. Since the MOP is to institute consideration of Annex B at least 7 years before 2012 – i.e. in 2005 – this might be the stage at which to link consideration of future commitments with analysis of "significant progress"; however, any change in Annex B requires the amendment procedures of the Protocol to be complied with and the written consent of the Party concerned.[77]

Article 18 specifically mandates the development of an indicative list of consequences of non-compliance with the provisions of the Protocol, "taking into account the cause, type, degree and frequency of non-compliance." It has been suggested that an NCP could be simplified and shortened through the prior classification of non-compliance consequences – automatic or discretionary – depending on the type, degree, and frequency of non-compliance. This is closer to a coercive, sanction-based regime and is probably most suited to breach of quantifiable, non-derogable, and fixed obligations. As already indicated, however, if binding consequences are stipulated, amendment of the Protocol is required.

In addition to considering the prior classification of non-compliance responses, there is the additional possibility of a listing of presumptively non-complying acts and/or omissions. Indeed, since Article 18 links the development of an indicative list of consequences with, *inter alia*, the type of non-compliance, it is difficult to see how some classification of non-complying acts may be avoided if Article 18 is to be implemented fully. There are two, potentially compatible, approaches to setting non-compliance triggers. The first, a "bottom-up" approach, might arise from monitoring and reporting requirement: for example, Article 3 (3) requires States to submit data regarding GHG sources and sinks, which are reviewed by expert review teams pursuant to Articles 7 and 8; such analysis of national reports under Articles 7 and 8 could be linked with the Article 18 NCP in a "bottom-up" approach to NCP. A "top-down" approach is the prior classification of certain acts and omissions as prima facie instances of non-compliance. This might include various temporal triggers for assessing compliance with the provisions of the Protocol, viz. 2005 [has demonstrable progress in implementing commitments been exhibited as required under Article 3 (2)?], 2007 [has a national system for reductions been implemented as mandated by Article 5 (1)?], and 2008–2012 [have emission reductions been met within the commitment period as stipulated by Article 3 (1)?].

An additional NCP design issue is to determine the entities entitled to invoke the NCP. There are at least five possibilities:

1. one Party against another Party (or groups of Parties)
2. a Party in respect of its own conduct
3. the Secretariat
4. other Convention bodies, including the COP
5. states and/or non-state entities (NGOs for example) outside the Convention regime (or limited to those entities with observer status).

This goes beyond any existing NCP, the original Montreal Protocol trigger utilized only (1), but has evolved to incorporate (2) and (3). The proposed Article 13 MCP procedure would permit (1), (2), and (4) (the COP). However, there would no doubt be considerable objection to widening participation in the NCP, particularly if binding consequences of non-compliance are agreed.[78]

There are thus a large number of design issues to be addressed in implementing Article 18 of the Protocol, many of which are linked to the details of the flexibility mechanisms yet to be established. A key concern in the forthcoming negotiations, as the flexibility mechanisms are fleshed out, will be to ensure that the substantive commitments under the Protocol do not lead to irresistible pressures to weaken the non-compliance mechanism under Article 18. Without such a mechanism, there is no realistic alternative for ensuring the effective implementation of the Protocol.

Notes

1. This chapter is part of ongoing research by the author, in conjunction with Professor Malgosia Fitzmaurice of the University of London, into the relationship between non-compliance procedures, the law of treaties, and state responsibility. I am indebted to Professor Fitzmaurice for many of the insights contained herein.
2. For cogent analysis of the many legal issues which arise in regulating the boundary between compliance and responsibility, see M. Koskenniemi, "Breach of a Treaty or Non-Compliance? Reflections on Enforcement of the Montreal Protocol," *Yearbook of International Environmental Law* 123–162, 1992.
3. In particular, joint implementation, the clean development mechanism, and tradeable emission permits – the so-called flexibility mechanisms.
4. It is not intended to sketch in any detail here the existing procedures, a task in any event which has already been comprehensively performed in the literature on non-compliance. In addition to the sources cited below, see generally P. Szell, "The Development of Multilateral Mechanisms for Monitoring Compliance" in W. Lang (ed.), *Sustainable Development and International Law*. London: Kluwer Law International, 1995, 336 pp, and J. Cameron, J. Werksman, and P. Roderick, *Improving Compliance with International Environmental Law*, 1996, 341 pp.
5. Or, perhaps more accurately, dispute avoidance.
6. G. Handl, "Controlling Implementation of Compliance with International Environmental Commitments: the Rocky Road from Rio." *Colorado Journal of Environmental Law & Policy* 5: 305, 329, 1994. However, as discussed further below, non-compliance responses may be facilitative or coercive. In the latter case, incrimination for non-compliance may be one mechanism to achieve a return to compliance, analogous to "name and shame" techniques under certain international human rights instruments.
7. Article 6, 1987 Montreal Protocol to the 1985 Ozone Layer Convention.
8. Article 9, 1979 Convention on Long-Range Transboundary Air Pollution Treaty (LRTAP).

9. Article 19, 1989 Basel Convention on the Control of Transboundary Movements of Hazardous Wastes and their Disposal.
10. 1987 US/USSR Treaty on the Elimination of Intermediate Range and Shorter Range Missiles.
11. Article 13 FCCC.
12. Article 17 (1) Convention on the Elimination of Discrimination Against Women.
13. See, for example, "Consideration of the Establishment of a Multilateral Consultative Process for the Resolution of Questions Regarding Implementation", a Note prepared by the Interim Secretariat (to the FCCC), 26 July 1994, Paras 11–14.
14. See, generally, J. Heister, E. Mohr, F. Stahler, P. Tobias Stoll, and R. Wolfrum, "Strategies to Enforce Compliance with an International CO_2 Treaty" (1997) *International Environmental Affairs* 9(1): 22–24 ("Reasons for Noncompliance").
15. Mitchell identifies three principal sources of non-compliance: preference, incapacity and inadvertence. See R.B. Mitchell, "Compliance Theory: an Overview" in J. Cameron, J. Werksman, and P. Roderick, *Improving Compliance with International Environmental Law* (1996), Chapter 1, at pp. 11–13. Earthscan: London.
16. See Fitzmaurice and Redgwell, *Non-Compliance Procedures* (forthcoming).
17. For recent analysis, see D.G. Victor, "The Operation and Effectiveness of the Montreal Protocol's Non-Compliance Procedure" in D.G. Victor, K. Raustiala, and E.B. Skolnikoff, *The Implementation and Effectiveness of International Environmental Commitments* (1998), Chapter 4. Boston, Mass.: MIT Press.
18. As Szell observes, it was the first such agreement to "fill the gap" between reporting and dispute settlement with a "meaningful procedure": Szell, above, note 4, at p. 99.
19. Article 8 requires the first MOP to consider and approve procedures and institutional mechanisms for determining non-compliance with the provisions of the Protocol, and for treatment of Parties found to be in non-compliance. The procedures established pursuant to Article 8 of the 1987 Montreal Protocol are without prejudice to the operation of Article 11 of the Ozone Convention (dispute settlement provisions): UNEP/OxL.Pro.3/L.4 (Decision III/2). MOP3 requested the Ad Hoc Working Group of Legal Experts to compile indicative lists under Article 8 of the possible situations of non-compliance with the Protocol and of "advisory and conciliatory measures to encourage full compliance"; See Decision III/2(a)(ii), Montreal Protocol MOP3, UNEP/OxL.Pro.3.L.4. In the event, only an indicative list of measures is found as Annex V to Report of MOP4: UNEP/OxL.Pro4/5/15, 23 November 1992. It sets an escalating response from assistance through to a caution to suspension of rights and privileges under the Protocol.
20. The IC reviews specific cases of non-compliance, debates general issues of implementation and compliance, makes recommendations to other Convention bodies, and issues a publicly available report after each meeting. Issues of non-compliance may be referred to the IC by Parties concerned with their own, or other Parties', compliance or by the Secretariat.

21. Article 7 of the Protocol sets forth detailed data-reporting requirements. As Werksman observes, the early work of the Montreal Protocol Implementation Committee focused on concerns raised by the Ozone Secretariat regarding compliance with such requirements: see above, note 4, at p. 97. One interesting phenomenon has been the Committee's willingness to overlook non-compliance evidenced in data in an effort to ensure participation in and eventual compliance with the Protocol: B. Kingsbury, "The Concept of Compliance as a Function of Competing Conceptions of International Law" (1998) *Michigan Journal of International Law* 19(2): 345. This emphasis on cooperation over conflict, and a certain flexibility in permitting adherence to treaty obligations over time, suggests a certain progressive character to the obligations.

22. "Without regular, detailed, and objective reporting of performance, any meaningful supervision of a state's observance of its commitments [is] impossible": Szell, above, note 4, at p. 98; see also K. Sachariew, "Promoting Compliance with International Environmental Legal Standards: Reflections on Monitoring and Reporting Mechanisms" (1991) *Yearbook of International Environmental Law* 2: 33.

23. 24 ILM 484 (1985). See further J. Carlos di Primio, "Data Quality and Compliance Control in the European Air Pollution Regime" in D. Victor *et al.* (eds), above, note 17.

24. 1984 Protocol on Long-Term Financing of the Cooperative Programme for Monitoring and Evaluation of the Long-Range Transmission of Air Pollutants in Europe (EMEP), 24 ILM 484 (1985).

25. Protocol on the Reduction of Sulphur Emissions or their Transboundary Fluxes by at least 30%, 27 ILM 707 (1988).

26. See also Article 3 (3) of the 1991 Protocol concerning the Control of Emissions of Volatile Organic Compounds or their Transboundary Fluxes, 31 ILM 568 (1992).

27. The 1994 Sulphur Protocol entered into force on 5 August 1998; the 1991 VOC Protocol entered into force on 29 September 1997. In 1997 an Implementation Committee was established for review of compliance by Parties with protocols to LRTAP by Decision 1997/2 of the Executive Body of the Convention. That decision urges the Parties to the VOC and Sulphur Protocols to consider its use for review of compliance in accordance with Article 3 (3) (VOC) and Article 7 (Sulphur) of the Protocols.

28. 32 ILM 1069 (1993). See Article 23, which empowers the Commission established pursuant to Article 10 to assess the compliance of Contracting Parties and to call for steps to bring a non-complying Contracting Party back into compliance. These provisions have not yet been implemented, since this Convention entered into force only on 25 March 1998, with the first meeting of the OSPAR Commission held in July 1998.

29. At COP3 (September, 1995), the Parties to the Basel Convention requested the Consultative Sub-Group of Legal and Technical Experts to examine all the issues relating to the establishment of a mechanism for monitoring implementation and compliance with the Convention (Decision III/11). At COP 4 (February 1998), the Parties endorsed the Sub-group's proposal to continue its step-by-step approach to examination of these issues (Decision IV/21). In

addition, the Sub-group was requested to consider whether the dispute-settlement mechanism of Article 20 of the Basel Convention "continues to meet the needs of the Parties to the Convention."

30. In this sense, a continuum may be perceived from communication of information and review thereof through to non-compliance and culminating in dispute settlement. This is what Szell refers to as "filling the gap" with an effective mechanism. See above, note 4; see also the note on implementation (Article 13 FCCC) prepared by the interim secretariat, above, note 13, at Paragraph 18 (continuum from communication of information and review – Article 12 – to the multilateral consultative process – Article 13 – through to dispute settlement – Article 14). However, Szell also points out the risk of an inverse relationship between the stringency of NCP and the toughness of the commitments which Parties are willing to undertake (*ibid.*, at p. 107), a point echoed by Victor, see above, note 17, at p. 139.

31. Even where concrete obligations have been established, compliance with which has been ensured, the effectiveness of the treaty regime is not thereby ensured. Compliance is not synonymous with effectiveness, since the latter depends in part upon the strength of the obligations and their clarity. Low standards, and/or ambiguous ones, reduce effectiveness even where "compliance" has been ensured. On effectiveness, see generally D.G. Victor, K. Raustiala, and E.B. Skolnikoff (eds.), *The Implementation and Effectiveness of International Environmental Commitments* (1998).

32. For excellent analysis of the FCCC, see J. Werksman, "Designing a Compliance System for the UN Framework Convention on Climate Change," in J. Cameron, J. Werksman, and P. Roderick, *Improving Compliance with International Environmental Law* (1996), Chapter 4.

33. Article 14 (1) FCCC.

34. Articles 14 (5) and (6). Article 14 thus represents a comprise between a mandatory or voluntary procedure and its binding or non-binding effect: see further D. Bodansky, "The United Nations Framework Convention on Climate Change: A Commentary" (1993) *The Yale Journal of International Law* 18(2): 451. It is very similar in language to the dispute-settlement clauses found in other recent international environmental agreements such as the Ozone Convention (Article 11), the Basel Convention (Article 20) and the Biodiversity Convention (Article 27).

35. See Bodansky, *ibid.*, at p. 548.

36. As stipulated in Article 13 itself, which provides that "[t]he Conference of the Parties shall at its first session, consider the establishment of a multilateral consultative process, available to Parties on their request, for the resolution of questions regarding the implementation of the Convention "

37. Decision 14/CP.3 of COP 3 (FCCC/CP/1997/7/Add.1) invited the Group to complete its work before the fourth session of the Conference of the Parties in Argentina in 1998.

38. The Provisional Agenda for COP4 suggests that the President of the Conference may initiate informal consultations with a view to resolving the outstanding issue of the composition of the proposed Multilateral Consultative Commitee (MCC). Parties are asked to be prepared to nominate relevant experts

for the MCC in order that the Conference may designate members for the first period of office should such informal consultations reach a successful outcome. See Note by the Executive Secretary, Provisional Agenda and Annotations, FCC/CP/1998/1, 28 August 1998, Paras. 51–52.

39. FCCC/AG13/1998/2, 9 July 1998.

40. Paragraph 3 sets out how issues will be taken up, whilst Paragraph 8, still containing square brackets in relation to size and equitable geographic distribution of membership, addresses the Constitution of the Committee. Its mandate is set forth in Paragraphs 6 and 7.

41. Paragraph 7 further provides that the Committee shall not duplicate the activities of other Convention bodies.

42. Paragraph 4 emphasizes that the MCP is separate from, and without prejudice to, the provisions of Article 14 FCCC on dispute settlement. This reflects the view of most delegations in negotiating the text that the two mechanisms should be complementary, not competing: Bodansky, above, note 34, at p. 548.

43. Paragraph 12 further mandates that the conclusions and any recommendations of the Committee must be sent to the Party or Parties concerned for consideration, and that an opportunity to comment thereon must be provided. Written comments by the Party or Parties concerned are then to be forwarded to the Conference of the Parties, along with the Committee's conclusions and any recommendations.

44. Protocol, Article 18. Koskienniemi has raised the interesting and complex issue of the effect of non-compliance procedures upon traditional rules of state responsibility in terms of the wrongdoing State's traditional defences to responsibility: see above, note 2.

45. Thus, at best, such provision plays a largely symbolic role as a deterrent: see Note by the interim secretariat, above, note 13, at para. 13.

46. For general analysis of the Protocol, see P. Davies, "Global Warming and the Kyoto Protocol." *International and Comparative Law Quarterly* 47(2), April 1998, 446–461.

47. Protocol, Article 16. In this connection it should be noted that Paragraph 14 of the draft terms of reference of the MCP clearly envisages the evolution of those terms over time in the light of experience, decisions of the COP, and of any amendment to the Convention. The terms of reference further provide that they may be amended by the COP (Para. 14).

48. Article 16 of the Protocol provides that "[a]ny multilateral consultative process that may be applied to the Protocol shall operate without prejudice to the procedures and mechanisms established in accordance with Article 18." Article 18 of the Protocol refers to non-compliance.

49. Article 20 sets forth the formal requirements for amendment to the Protocol at an ordinary session of the COP. Amendments may be proposed by any Party, require 6 months notice and, if not adopted by consensus, require a three-quarters majority of Parties present and voting. There is the further requirement for acceptance by three-quarters of the Parties to the Protocol for the amendment to become binding, and then only on those Parties having accepted it. Thus whilst it is not possible to opt out of general non-compliance procedures once a Party to the Protocol and such procedures have been agreed by the

COP (unless of course any such procedures otherwise provide for opt-out), it is possible to remain outside any binding consequences of non-compliance through non-acceptance of such in a treaty amendment.

50. It is not intended to suggest that the FCCC is anomalous in this respect, since many treaties take a rigorous approach to amendment.

51. Article 11 of the Montreal Protocol empowers the meeting of the Parties, *inter alia*, "to consider and approve the procedures and institutional mechanisms specified in Article 8 [Non-compliance]."

52. A lengthy list is appended as Annex II to the SBSTA Report of its Eighth Session in Bonn; however, the list is not negotiated. It is based on submissions by the G77 and China, suggestions of other Parties, by Canada and others (including Australia, Iceland, Japan, New Zealand, Norway, the Russian Federation, Ukraine, and the USA) and by the UK on behalf of the EC and its member states.

53. See the Report of the Subsidiary Body for Implementation on its Eighth Session, Bonn, 2–12 June 1998, FCCC/SBI/1998/6, 6 August 1998 and the Report of the Subsidiary Body for Scientific and Technological Advice on its Eighth Session, Bonn, 2–12 June 1998, FCCC/SBSTA/1998/6, 12 August 1998. The meetings of SBSTA and the SBI on the Kyoto Mechanisms were held jointly, as reflected in the draft Conclusions by the Chairmen of both bodies on the suggested elements for a work programme on Mechanisms of the Kyoto Mechanisms, FCCC/SB/1998/CRP.2, 12 June 1998.

54. Article 6 of the Protocol provides that:

1. For the purpose of meeting its commitments under Article 3, any Party included in Annex I may transfer to, or acquire from, any other such Party emission reduction units resulting from projects aimed at reducing anthropogenic emissions by sources or enhancing anthropogenic removals by sinks of greenhouse gases in any sector of the economy, provided that:
   (a) Any such project has the approval of the Parties involved;
   (b) Any such project provides a reduction in emissions by sources, or an enhancement of removals by sinks, that is additional to any that would otherwise occur;
   (c) It does not acquire any emission reduction units if it is not in compliance with its obligations under Articles 5 and 7;
   (d) The acquisition of emission reduction units shall be supplemental to domestic actions for the purposes of meeting commitments under Article 3;
2. The Conference of the Parties serving as the meeting of the Parties to this Protocol may, at its first session or as soon as practicable thereafter, further elaborate guidelines for the implementation of this Article, including for verification and reporting.
3. A Party included in Annex I may authorize legal entities to participate, under its responsibility, in actions leading to the generation, transfer or acquisition under this Article of emission reduction units.

4. If a question of implementation by a Party included in Annex I of the requirements referred to in this paragraph is identified in accordance with the relevant provisions of Article 8, transfers and acquisitions of emission reduction units may continue to be made after the question has been identified, provided that any such units may not be used by a Party to meet its commitments under Article 3 until any issue of compliance is resolved.

55. Protocol, Article 6 (4).

56. A similar provision applies to the "EC bubble," namely, that in the event of the failure by Member States acting jointly within the EC to meet their total combined level of emission reduction levels, then individual Member States will remain responsible for the level of emissions notified in accordance with Article 4 (2): see Article 4 (6).

57. Including Australia, Canada, Japan, and the USA. See further P. Davies, above, note 46.

58. Article 10 of the Protocol reaffirms existing commitments under the Convention on the part of both Annex I and non-Annex I Parties. At the request of Argentina, the issue of "voluntary commitments by non-Annex I Parties" has been placed on the provisional agenda for COP 4 in Buenos Aires and is expected to be the object of informal consultations: Provisional Agenda and Annotations, A Note by the Executive Secretary, FCCC/CP/1998/1, 28 August 1998, item 6, Para. 105.

59. As Davies explains, "The CDM has a dual purpose in that it enables developing countries to operate projects which result in emissions reductions and thus to contribute to the objective of the convention, and also allows Annex I countries who finance such projects through the CDM to use emission reductions attributable to such projects to reduce their own emission totals." Above, note 46, at p. 457. This dual purpose is set forth in Article 12 (3).

60. Protocol, Article 12 (5). Only projects in which Parties participate voluntarily, which produce quantifiable long-term benefits related to the mitigation of climate change and result in emission reductions over and above what would occur without such a certified project, will qualify for certification under Article 12 (5).

61. Protocol Article 12 (4).

62. While emission reductions from jointly implemented projects in the period 2000–2008 may be used by Annex I Parties in meeting their own emissions-reduction target under the Protocol, projects from the pilot phase (which is due to conclude no later than the end of 1999) will not be eligible: see further Davies, above, note 46.

63. The Protocol provides that it is Parties listed in Annex B thereto which may participate in emissions trading for the purposes of meeting their Article 3 commitments (Article 17).

64. Protocol Article 17.

65. *Ibid.*

66. Entry-into-force requirements are set forth in Article 24 of the Protocol.

67. Note, however, that the first MOP will take place only after the Protocol enters into force, the provisions relating to which are contained in Article 24.

Fifty-five Parties to the Convention must become Parties to the Protocol, including Annex I Parties accounting for 55 per cent of total CO_2 emissions for 1990, in order for the Protocol to enter into force 90 days from the fifty-fifth ratification, acceptance, approval, or accession, satisfying such condition. A relatively high threshold is required to ensure the effectiveness of the Protocol and of steps taken in complying with the specific targets and timetables embodied therein.

68. See Decision 1/CP.3, para. 6, *ibid.*, and the Note by the Chairmen of SBSTA and SBI on matters related thereto, FCCC/CP.1998/3, 10 September 1998. Annex I thereof proposes that procedures and mechanisms relating to non-compliance under Article 18 will be allocated to the SBI. It will be recalled that Article 15 of the Protocol establishes the SBI and SBSTA as such bodies for the Protocol, with the provisions of Articles 9 and 10 FCCC applying, *mutatis mutandis*, to the Protocol.

69. Matters relating to the Kyoto Protocol, in particular the flexibility mechanisms (JI, CDM, and emissions trading) are on the agenda for COP 4 where the task of operationalizing the flexibility mechanisms will continue: Provisional Agenda and Annotations, *ibid.*, item 5, at Paras 96–98.

70. Namely, to avoid complexity, to be non-confrontational, transparent, and with decision-making by the COP, not a subsidiary body: Szell, above, note 4, at p. 99.

71. W. Lang, "Compliance Control in International Environmental Law: Institutional Necessities" (1996) *Heidelberg Journal of International Law* 56(3): 685–688.

72. Membership issues are highly important since these influence the legitimacy and effectiveness enjoyed by a committee and any recommendations made by it.

73. See, for example, Victor, above, note 17, at p. 139.

74. On the experience of the Russian Federation under the Montreal Protocol, see J. Werksman, "Compliance and Transition: Russia's Non-Compliance Tests the Ozone Regime." *Heidelberg Journal of International Law* (1996) 56(3): 750 (who raises, *inter alia*, the interesting question whether restricting Russia's trade in CFCs amounts to "multilateral enforcement of retorsion against a defaulting state").

75. As Werksman discusses, *ibid.*, the limited restriction on Russian trade in CFCs agreed at the seventh Meeting of the Parties falls within this category, though the compatibility of such restriction with the GATT/WTO did not arise with the Russian Federation not yet a member. In this instance, the Russian Federation was limited to trade with other members of the CIS, and to restricting further export to Article 5.1 (developing) and other countries. For the text of the decision, see (1996) 26/2/3 *Environmental Policy and Law* 120–121.

76. See C. Carr, "Recent Developments in Compliance and Enforcement for International Fisheries" (1997) 24:4 *Ecology Law Quarterly* 847, at pp. 857–860. The NCP for Contracting Parties has three steps: (1) explanation for non-compliance and indication of steps to remedy/prevent further non-compliance; (2) where annual quota is exceeded, a reduction of the next year's total annual catch to match overfishing (quantifiable non-compliance with proportionate

response); and (3) where quota is exceeded for two consecutive management periods, the ICCAT Commission may further reduce quota and, as "an absolute last resort," recommend trade measures against the defaulting State. A similar mechanism was established in respect of non-contracting Parties in 1994, including the possibility of prohibiting imports of bluefin tuna products from the defaulting, but non-contracting, State. This made ICCAT "the first international fisheries organization to authorize the use of multilateral trade measures against non-contracting parties that compromise its conservation and management objectives": *ibid.*, at p. 857. Such a recommendation was made in 1996 in connection with Atlantic bluefin tuna and its products from Belize, Honduras, and Panama: *ibid.*, at p. 858. Concerns about compatibility with GATT/WTO obligations were evidently raised: *ibid.*, at p. 858 (note 55).

77. It may be necessary to consider in the design of the NCP whether coercive measures ought to be considered according to their impact on the specific non-complying state to avoid the inequitable application of such measures as between states.

78. A role for NGOs and for individuals has also been discussed under the Montreal Protocol, it was rejected as unnecessary (at least in the early stages of the development of the process), in part due to concerns regarding the non-confrontational character of the process and in part due to a perception that the concerns of such entities could be channelled through other bodies with standing in the NCP.

4

WTO Rules and Climate Change: The Need for Policy Coherence

GARY P. SAMPSON

Introduction

An important challenge facing the World Trade Organization (WTO) is dealing satisfactorily with the increasingly complex interface between trade policy and considerations relating to the environment. Current or future measures taken as part of national programmes to address greenhouse-gas (GHG) emissions and the associated climate-change concerns provide good examples of the complexity of this interface.

The goal of the UN Framework Convention on Climate Change (UNFCCC) is to establish institutional and economic mechanisms, backed by legal obligations, to enable the negotiated reductions in global emissions of GHGs to be achieved. The Convention came into force on 21 March 1994; in its Article 3.5, the Convention addresses its relations with the trade regime. This Article states:

> The Parties should cooperate to promote a supportive and open international economic system that would lead to sustainable economic growth and development in all Parties, particularly developing country Parties, thus enabling them better to address the problems of climate change. Measures taken to combat

climate change, including unilateral ones, should not constitute a means of arbitrary or unjustifiable discrimination or a disguised restriction on international trade.

The Convention does not provide for any specific trade-related environmental measures. The nature and scope of any Protocol or another legal instrument, and the subsequent implementation of the measures enacted, will determine whether any potential trade-related developments or trade issues would arise.

The Kyoto Protocol to the United Nations Convention on Climate Change was adopted on a consensus basis by 160 developed and developing countries at the third session of the Conference of the Parties in December 1997.[1] The Protocol is to promote the "progressive phasing out of market imperfections, fiscal incentives, tax and duty exemptions and subsidies in all greenhouse gas emitting sectors that run contrary to the objective of the Convention and application of market instruments" (Article 1 (a) (v)). This is very much in line with the WTO objective of the progressive removal of trade restrictions and distortions. Further, the Protocol states that the Parties shall strive to implement policies and measures "in such a way to minimize adverse effects ... on international trade." (Article 2:3).

The results of Kyoto were significant and a number of key principles were agreed, including the use of market-based mechanisms to achieve the negotiated reductions in GHG emissions within specified time periods.[2] The next step in the process is to define the detailed means to achieve the targets; a variety of measures are candidates, many of which are already in force in Parties to the Convention. Energy, carbon and other taxes; mandatory and voluntary standards; subsidies for environmentally friendly production processes; labelling and certification schemes; and the sale and transfer of emission permits within or between groups of countries all provide examples.

In addition, novel mechanisms for the fulfilment of commitments are provided for in the Kyoto Protocol. Annex 1 Parties are allowed to act within "bubbles" or regional groupings to achieve jointly their emission-reduction commitments. Countries adopting this procedure will have met their reduction commitments if their total aggregate emissions do not exceed the total of their combined amounts as set out in Annex B.[3] In the event of failure to achieve the aggregate target, each of the countries concerned will be held responsible for its individual commitment as specified in the Annex.

The specific measures employed to reduce emissions will certainly have a bearing on world trade. They will affect the costs of production of traded goods and therefore the competitive position of producers in the world market. Offsetting measures will be called for by those whose competitive position is adversely affected by cheaper imports not subject to the same measures in the country of origin. Measures such as these may well raise complex questions with respect to WTO consistency and the conditions under which border taxes, for example, can be adjusted to accommodate a loss of international competitiveness. Similarly, enforcement mechanisms that could legitimize discrimination between products in international trade because of the manner in which they were produced in other countries touches on one of the fundamental principles of the WTO.[4] Further, preferential trading of goods and services between countries – within "bubbles" – is permitted within the WTO only if certain strict conditions are met.

Not surprisingly, the possibility of an eventual conflict between the rights and obligations of the WTO and what emerges from the future negotiations to address climate change concerns has been flagged by a number of authors.[5] While the potential for conflict may exist, it should be kept in perspective. First, while the outcome of future negotiations on mechanisms to reduce emissions is a moving target, the WTO Agreements are established and well known. Decisions will be taken by governments with a full awareness of the implications with respect to their WTO commitments. As with any multilateral environmental agreement (MEA), acceptance of a legal instrument relating to the reduction of emissions would mean that an individual government has agreed to be subjected to the obligations of that instrument. If trade measures not authorized by the WTO are provided for, then the WTO Member would have agreed to forgo its WTO rights. The fact that the legal rights and obligations are not consistent with the WTO is a problem only if WTO-inconsistent measures are applied to WTO Members not Parties to the Agreement. In this respect, Sir Leon Brittan,[6] Vice-President of the European Commission, recently expressed a balanced degree of concern:

> Most of the governments that signed up to the Uruguay Round also accepted the outcome of Kyoto. There is a clear need for policy coherence here, and we owe it to ourselves to ensure that we do not make our task more difficult by taking on obligations that are incompatible.

The purpose of this chapter is to review the WTO provisions that could be relevant with respect to measures taken to address climate-change concerns. The outline is as follows. There is first an overview of how the WTO Members view MEAs in general. This is based largely on the discussion in the Committee on Trade and Environment (CTE) in the WTO. Where relevant, the Climate Change Convention and the Kyoto Protocol are referred to. Second, some relevant WTO principles are singled out and discussed in the light of the objectives to reduce GHG emissions – in particular, the constraints they could place on measures to reduce emissions. Third, a number of specific measures that could be employed to achieve the desired reductions are discussed with a view to establishing their "coherence" with WTO rules. The objective is not so much to be comprehensive as to concentrate on some of the more important principles and measures that are relevant for the rules of the two regimes. The chapter closes with conclusions.

WTO, MEAs, and climate change

In the CTE there has been considerable discussion on the current and potential relationship between MEAs and the WTO.[7] As the WTO and MEAs represent two different bodies of international law, it is clear that the relationship between them should be fully understood and coherent. In this context, much of the discussion is relevant for a full appreciation of the relationship between the WTO Agreements, the Climate Change Convention, the Kyoto Protocol and any subsequent legally binding instruments to address climate change.

What has clearly emerged is the acceptance by Members that the WTO has no special expertise regarding how to deal with environmental problems such as the heating of the upper atmosphere. Nor is it well placed to make judgements on the most appropriate means to achieve objectives or targets such as GHG-emission reduction. A consensus has emerged that MEAs are the best way of coordinating policy action to tackle global and transboundary environmental problems cooperatively. Members of the WTO are, however, concerned with trade measures applied pursuant to MEAs which can affect WTO Members' rights and obligations. Of the many MEAs currently in effect, while only about 20 contain trade provisions, some – such as the Climate Change Convention and the Kyoto Protocol – are potentially important in commercial and political terms.

There are considerable differences between the trade provisions of the various MEAs – in particular, regarding the kinds of trade measures that MEA Parties are authorized or required to apply and the conditions pursuant to which the measures are taken. Some – such as the Convention on the International Trade in Endangered Species of Wild Fauna and Flora (CITES), the Montreal Protocol, and the Basel Convention – provide for discrimination in world trade if specific conditions are not met.[8] A case for the existence (and even strengthening) of MEAs can be made on the grounds that no General Agreement on Tariffs and Trade (GATT) or WTO trade dispute has arisen so far over the use of trade measures applied pursuant to an MEA.[9] Nevertheless, doubts have been expressed by some WTO Members about the WTO consistency of certain trade measures applied pursuant to some MEAs – in particular, discriminatory trade restrictions and sanctions applied by MEA Parties against non-parties that involve extrajurisdictional action.

It has been suggested that the WTO should formally recognize the possibility for inconsistent WTO measures to be applied under certain specified Agreements. The discussion in the CTE reveals that different views exist on this matter. One school of thought is that, when account is taken of the limited number of MEAs that contain trade provisions and of the fact that no trade dispute has arisen over the use of those provisions, no real problem exists.[10] The reasoning continues that, with some limited resort to the WTO dispute-settlement procedures, existing WTO rules could be considered to provide sufficient scope to allow trade measures to be applied pursuant to MEAs, and that it is neither necessary nor desirable to exceed that scope. According to this view, the proper course of action to resolve any underlying conflict is for WTO Members to avoid using trade measures in MEAs that are inconsistent with their WTO obligations.

Another view is that, because of the increasing commercial and political importance of some MEAs that clearly deal with transborder problems (e.g. the effects of GHG emission), it is perhaps important to adopt a preventive attitude and provide greater certainty as concern grows about the collective impact of individual countries on the global commons. As a result, various proposals have been advanced in the CTE with a view to establishing a framework for the relationship between MEAs and the WTO. Although these proposals differ in nature, scope, and level of ambition, they are all based on the view that the WTO should be supportive of action at the multilateral level for the protection of the environment.

The proponents of this approach develop the view that, subject to specific conditions being met, certain trade measures taken pursuant to MEAs should benefit from special treatment under the WTO provisions; this approach has been described as creating an "environmental window" in the WTO. In terms of the test of the "necessity" of discriminatory measures to fulfil an environment objective (see below), the interpretation of necessity could be influenced by the existence of a broad-based MEA. In the case of the Kyoto Protocol, it will enter into force following the ratifications from 55 countries accounting for at least 55 per cent of carbon emissions in 1990. The issue then emerges as to whether it is appropriate to provide for differentiated treatment for trade measures applied pursuant to the environment agreement, depending on whether they apply between

Parties or against non-Parties and whether the measures are specifically mandated in the environment agreement itself.[11]

In this respect, there is not a great deal of specificity in the Kyoto Protocol regarding the measures that can be applied to meet the objectives. Articles 2 and 3 describe the measures for the implementation of the reduction commitments. The Protocol specifies that Parties are bound to adopt policies or measures in a manner to promote sustainable development. Examples are policies or measures to enhance energy efficiency, protect and enhance sinks and reservoirs, promote research and development, increase the use of new and renewable forms of energy and environmentally sound technologies, phase out fiscal incentives and exemptions in GHG-emitting sectors, and promote the application of market instruments. Such actions are to be taken in accordance with national circumstances.

On the basis of experience of the discussion of MEA dispute-settlement procedures in the CTE, it seems reasonable that an eventual dispute between WTO Members who are Parties to the Protocol in the application of these measures should in the first instance be pursued under the dispute-settlement procedures of the Convention. It has also been suggested in the CTE that MEA Parties might stipulate ex ante that they intend any trade disputes among them, arising out of implementation of the obligations of the MEA, to be settled under the MEA's provisions. It could be argued that this approach can help to ensure the convergence of the objectives of MEAs and the WTO while safeguarding their respective spheres of competence, thus overcoming problems arising from overlapping jurisdictions. It has been suggested that there may be value in strengthening MEA dispute-settlement mechanisms, but this matter lies outside WTO competence.[12]

If, however, the Convention, Protocol, or any follow-up Agreement does not provide for the trade measures under dispute, then what is permissible under the WTO is relevant. It is reasoned below that the relationship between the measures that are candidates for implementation to reduce carbon emissions and WTO obligations is a complex one. For example, any measure taken under the General

Exceptions provision of the WTO must be either necessary to protect human, animal, or plant life or health (Article XX (b)), or related to the conservation of exhaustible natural resources, and made effective in conjunction with restrictions on domestic production or consumption (Article XX (g)). Interpretation of what is necessary and the geographical location of the resources being protected, for example, raises difficult questions.

In creating an environmental window and giving a special importance to any specific MEA in the context of WTO rules, account would have to be taken of the fact that countries may not wish to join the Agreement for a variety of reasons. If a country had chosen not to join an agreement relating to emission reduction, who would judge the merit of that decision and the reasons why a country would take that decision? The country in question may find the scientific evidence unpersuasive, it may not be able to afford to join, or it may not have access to the necessary technology on favourable terms. It may not agree with a given environmental objective or with the means to achieve the objective, or it may consider there are more pressing national policy problems that deserve higher priority.[13,14]

It has been proposed in the CTE that, with respect to measures applied among Parties but not specifically mandated in any legal instrument to deal with emission reduction, and those applied against non-Parties which are specifically mandated in the legal instrument, these could be tested through WTO dispute settlement against procedural and substantive criteria which would be set out in an "Understanding" to be established by WTO members. The Understanding would not apply to trade measures taken against non-Parties to the instrument that were not specifically mandated by it, nor would it apply to unilateral measures; these would continue to be subject to existing WTO provisions.

As with the Climate Change Convention, most of the MEAs that are the focus of the CTE's work contain mechanisms for resolving disputes. As with the "Dispute Settlement Understanding" of the WTO, MEAs emphasize the avoidance of disputes. They include provisions to increase transparency through the collection and exchange of information, coordination of technical and scientific research, and collective monitoring of implementing measures, as well as consultation provisions. These range from non-binding, consensus-building mechanisms to binding, judicial procedures of arbitration and – in certain cases – resort to the International Court of Justice.

In the event of a dispute between two WTO Members, one a non-party to a legal instrument to address the climate change over trade measures applied pursuant to the instrument, the WTO would provide the only available dispute-settlement mechanism since the non-party would have no rights under, nor access to, the climate change dispute-settlement mechanism. The point has been noted in the CTE that, in such circumstances, it would be important for the WTO dispute-settlement body to avoid becoming involved in purely environmental conflicts; however, a WTO dispute-settlement panel could seek relevant environmental expertise and technical advice.

WTO rules and climate change

The WTO does not inhibit governments from protecting (as they wish) against damage to the environment resulting from the production and consumption of *products* produced within national boundaries. Final products, for example, can be taxed and other charges levied for any purpose thought to be appropriate by national governments. If carbon dioxide emissions and energy use are considered to be excessive by a government, the products can, for example, be taxed in a form and to the extent necessary. Similarly, there are no problems from a WTO perspective with governments levying taxes according to the manner in which a product is produced within their territory. There can, for example, be domestic taxes on production methods that are directed to reducing energy consumption or carbon emissions in the process of production.

It is important for measures taken for climate-change purposes, however, that the WTO flexibility extends only to regulation of *products* produced domestically, imported *products* and domestic *production processes*. It does not extend to flexibility in the extraterritorial application of measures relating to production processes in exporting countries. The *manner* in which a foreign product is produced is not a basis on which WTO rights and obligations are established. An imported product cannot be discriminated against only on the grounds that the production process was energy intensive, for example. The underlying thesis is that, should any country wish to influence the manner in which products are produced in other countries – however appropriate this may be thought to be by the importing country – this should not be translated into discriminatory trade measures. The relevance of this for a legal instrument that has as its objective the reduction of GHG emissions is clear. If a product imported into a country has been produced by a process that emits more GHG than is thought acceptable according to norms established in the importing country, it cannot be treated in a different manner to that for a like product" (i.e. a product with the same physical characteristics) produced domestically, solely because of the production process employed.

Thus, for measures to be WTO consistent, products that have the same physical form are to be considered to be "like" products by the importing country, irrespective of whether they have been produced abroad in an environmentally friendly manner or not. There is, however, flexibility in the WTO rules to deal with these situations. The possibility of imposing WTO-inconsistent measures is provided for. If a product were to be treated differently at the border because of the way in which it was manufactured – emitting too much carbon dioxide – an "exception" could be sought from WTO obligations. Additional flexibility exists, as there are specific circumstances under which WTO members can invoke measures that normally would constitute a breach of WTO obligations. The circumstances under which measures can be employed are spelled out in the General Exceptions Article XX provision. Exceptions to WTO obligations can be sought, provided that the measure is *necessary* to protect human, animal, or plant life or health (Article XX (b)). Exceptions are also provided for measures related to the conservation of exhaustible natural resources (Article XX (g)). This general exception provision is clearly designed to permit governments to maintain or implement laws that they feel are necessary to preserve the lives of people, flora, fauna, and exhaustible natural resources.

On the basis of past experience in the GATT/WTO, it would appear, however, that the measures taken to protect the fauna and flora should be taken with respect to the fauna and flora inside the boundaries of the country taking the action. As noted above, in the case of GHG emissions, owing to the transboundary nature of the problem, the production process is in the exporting country and the externality is experienced outside the borders of the country where that product is produced. Furthermore, if the trade action is taken pursuant to that accepted within the context of a legal instrument addressing the reduction of GHG emissions, where Parties consider it necessary to take such action to implement the objective of the instrument, then added support would be given to the necessity test of Article XX (b) (i.e. for action taken *vis-à-vis* a non-Party to the MEA). With respect to the notion of exhaustible natural resources, since precedents have arisen in GATT as to whether clean air is a natural resource, presumably the question could be addressed as to whether cool air is also a natural resource that could be exhausted.

According to Article XX, however, any measure that breaches WTO obligations for this purpose should not be used as a means of arbitrary or unjustifiable discrimination between countries, or as a disguised restriction on international trade. Further, that the measures must be *necessary* to protect the environment means that other less trade-restrictive options are not available. In the case of measures to restrict trade in products that have been associated with excessive carbon dioxide production, it could mean, for example, that an attempt has already been made to deal with the problem through an Agreement to address climate change.

An additional and important consideration is that on the basis of decisions relating to disputes brought to the WTO (and GATT) in the past, any exception applies only to the lives and resources which are in the territory of the country taking the action. While this limits the intrusion of some countries into the practices of others, it leaves open a number of questions relating to transboundary considerations such as the effects of global GHG emissions.

Another area of importance to the WTO is the role of voluntary standards, mandatory regulations, and conformity-assessment procedures when used for environmental purposes. Flexibility is also provided for here. The WTO Technical Barriers to Trade (TBT) Agreement establishes obligations to ensure that voluntary standards, mandatory regulations, and conformity-assessment procedures do not have as their objective the restriction of trade. However, the Agreement provides considerable flexibility to accommodate environmental concerns: while it encourages the adoption of international standards and technical regulations (which may well relate to reducing carbon emissions in the production of products) to encourage the harmonization of regulations and therefore to facilitate trade, it specifically recognizes that priorities with respect to the environment differ between countries. The Agreement formally acknowledges that this can be fully reflected in domestic regulations, and therefore permits the adoption of different standards and regulations by any WTO Member. This could relate the amount of energy used in the production of a good, or the level of carbon dioxide emission within its borders. The principal obligation (apart from such factors as transparency) is that standards and technical regulations should not be implemented in such a way that they restrict trade to a greater extent than that necessary to achieve the policy objective. This is the concept of proportionality.

A further point of relevance is that a WTO Member may wish to subsidize a production process to facilitate the adoption of technology producing less carbon, or could be competing in the world market with another country that is doing so. The WTO Subsidies Agreement has as its main purpose the prohibition of governments providing direct assistance to their own industries to improve their competitive position. The Agreement, however, identifies certain non-actionable subsidies. Included in the list of non-actionable subsidies is assistance to promote the adaptation of existing facilities to new environmental requirements imposed by law and/or regulations which result in greater constraints and financial burdens on firms. These subsidies are, however, carefully circumscribed to avoid them constituting trade barriers to improve competitiveness.

A final additional flexibility for WTO Members to derogate from their WTO obligations for environmental purposes is to invoke a waiver under Article IX of the GATT. In exceptional circumstances, a waiver to a WTO obligation can be granted, subject to approval at a minimum by three-quarters of the WTO membership. A waived obligation is time limited: it must be renewed periodically, and a trade measure applied pursuant to a waiver could still be challenged in WTO dispute settlement on the grounds of non-violation, nullification, and impairment of WTO rights.

National measures to reduce emissions

The undertaking of commitments to reduce carbon emissions means that measures will be adopted to implement these reductions at the national level, some of which may be specifically provided for. Article 2 of the Kyoto Protocol, for example, states that:

> Each Party included in Annex 1, in achieving its quantified emission limitation and reduction commitments under Article 3, in order to promote sustainable development shall implement and/or further elaborate policies and measures in accordance with its national circumstances, such as: Enhancement of energy efficiency in relevant sectors ... protection and enhancement of sinks ... promotion of sustainable forms of agriculture ..., etc.

While measures such as this certainly have the potential to influence international competitiveness, as noted above, the qualification is that these measures should be implemented in such a way as to "minimize adverse effects on trade" (Article 2:3).

Recent studies have specifically addressed the situation where national measures, such as energy-efficiency standards or carbon and energy taxes, which are not applied to imports, provide foreign competitors with an economic advantage. It has been argued that it is likely that, as countries develop their national response strategies, trade measures will play an increasingly important role.[15] Carbon and energy taxes have been introduced to date in five European countries[16] and all include some form of compensatory measures, ranging from total exemptions for certain sectors, reduced rates for most energy-intensive processes, ceilings for total tax payments, to subsidies for energy audits, etc.[17] According to Richard Baron (1997), exemptions and other such features were introduced to accommodate competitiveness of concerns of energy-intensive industries which argued that they would greatly suffer from similar operating in countries without such taxation.[18]

What is clear from WTO rules is that, with respect to border tax adjustments, indirect taxes levied on products because of the energy consumed or the carbon dioxide emitted should not be used to provide a competitive advantage for domestic products. Thus, border taxes should not be in excess of taxes on like products manufactured and sold domestically. This is clear. However, the problem of discriminatory taxes applied to products with the same physical characteristics (i.e. like products) according to the production processes employed (e.g. because of the energy consumed or carbon dioxide emitted) raises serious questions in the WTO. One of the major unresolved questions before the WTO CTE remains how to address the question of indirect taxes, such as taxes on energy inputs applied on process and production methods.

A further consideration is the use of labelling and certification to convey information to consumers on product energy-efficiency levels. Already, this is used in a number of countries, including Australia, the United States, and Sweden. However, what remains unanswered in the WTO is the use of eco-labelling and certification schemes such as product and performance standards – which are traditional areas of GATT/WTO jurisprudence – and also labels that convey how much energy was used in making the product.

Novel measures and schemes will probably be introduced to implement emissions reductions: in particular, there is likely to be an international "emissions trading" regime allowing industrialized countries to buy and sell emissions credits amongst themselves. They will also be able to acquire "emission-reduction units" (ERUs) by financing certain kinds of projects in other countries. In addition, a "clean development mechanism" (CDM) will enable industrialized countries to finance emissions-reduction projects in developing countries and to receive credit for doing so. The operational guidelines for these various schemes must still be further elaborated.[19] As far as tradeable emission permits are concerned, this is a new area of international policy. Questions to be addressed include whether tradeable emission schemes fall under the WTO General Agreement on Trade in Services, and whether joint implementation schemes would be considered an environmental subsidy under the WTO Agreement on Subsidies and Countervailing Measures and therefore exempt from WTO disciplines on subsidies.

Conclusions

Should future commitments to achieve reductions in GHG emissions provide for measures that under WTO law would be considered illegal, this does not present a problem in itself as long as Parties to the Agreement voluntarily agree to forgo their WTO rights. From a WTO perspective, the relevance of any legal instrument to deal with climate change relates to the possibility of setting differentiated WTO disciplines for trade measures applied pursuant to the Agreement, based on whether it specifically mandates the measures and whether they are applied among Parties or against non-Parties. It is clear, however, that of the measures likely to be employed to meet either national or international emission targets, the potential exists for a number of important aspects of the key provisions of the WTO to be investigated with the need for their clarification becoming increasingly important.

Notes

1. For a comprehensive overview, see Brendan F.D. Barrett and W. Bradnee Chambers, *Primer on Scientific Knowledge and Politics in the Evolving Global Climate Regime CPO 3 and the Kyoto Protocol*, United Nations University, Institute of Advanced Studies, Tokyo, June 1998.
2. The developed countries commit themselves to reducing their collective emissions of six key greenhouse gases by at least 5 per cent. This group target will be achieved through cuts of 8 per cent by Switzerland, most Central and East European states, and the European Union (the EU will meet its target by distributing different rates to its members states); 7 per cent by the US; and 6 per cent by Canada, Hungary, Japan, and Poland. Russia, New Zealand, and

Ukraine are to stabilize their emissions, while Norway may increase emissions by up to 1 per cent, Australia by up to 8 per cent, and Iceland by 10 per cent. The six gases are to be combined in a "basket," with reductions in individual gases translated into "CO_2 equivalents" that are then added up to produce a single figure.

3. The European Union will, for example, be bound by a specific commitment to a reduction of 8 per cent.

4. See WTO (1997), *Taxes and Charges for Environmental Purposes: Border Tax Adjustment*, WT7CTE7W/47, Geneva, 2 May, 1997.

5. See Donald M. Goldberg, "The Framework Convention on Climate Change", in *The Use of Trade Measures in Select Multilateral Environmental Agreements,* R. Housman *et al.* (eds.), pp. 42–65. Geneva: UNEP and CIEL, 1995. See also, UNCTAD (1996), *Legal Issues Presented by a Pilot International Greenhouse Gas Trading System*, by Richard B. Stewart, Jonathan B. Wiener, and Philippe Sands. Geneva: UNCTAD.

6. See Leon Brittan (1998), in *Policing the Global Economy: Why, How and for Whom*, Saddrudin Aga Khan (ed.), pp. 36–42. London: Cameron and May, 1998.

7. WTO members recognized some time ago the complexity of the relationship between trade policy and environment policy. As a result of discussions, which coincided with the latter stages of the Uruguay Round, the WTO General Council established a Committee on Trade and Environment (CTE) in January 1995. The CTE mandate and terms of reference are contained in the Marrakesh Ministerial Decision on Trade and Environment of 15 April 1994. They are far-reaching and indicate an early concern on the part of the WTO Members with the compatibility of WTO rules with MEAs. This Decision also mandated the CTE to report to the first biennial meeting of the Ministerial Conference when the work and terms of reference of the CTE were reviewed in the light of recommendations of the CTE. This report was heavily negotiated, forwarded to Ministers, and adopted in Singapore. The CTE has now structured its work around the ten items listed in the Decision on Trade and Environment. Indeed, the Secretariat of the Climate Change Convention has been invited to the CTE and has described the principal features of the Convention, particularly the trade-related features, to WTO Members. The CTE is kept fully informed of developments in the Climate Change Convention.

8. For a discussion of a variety of MEAs and WTO rules see Robert Housman *et al.* eds., *The Use of Trade Measures in Select Environmental Agreements*, No. 10 in Environment and Trade Series Geneva: UNEP, 1995.

9. See WTO (1996), *Report of the Committee on Trade and Environment*, November, WT/CTE7W740, Section II, Item I.

10. The following views have emerged from discussions in the CTE, see WTO (1996), *op. cit.*

11. See WTO (1996), *op.cit.*

12. The 1982 Convention on the Law of the Sea, and in particular the 1994 Agreement Relating to the Implementation of Part XI of the Convention (Section: 6 Production Policy), attributes competence to the WTO in settling disputes involving trade-related measures, notably production subsidies and trade-restricting measures.

13. Another approach is to examine whether recourse to arbitration, as provided for in the WTO Disputes Settlement Understanding Article 25, can be an appropriate means of resolving trade and environment disputes. See WTO, *op. cit.*

14. This consideration is formally recognized in Principle 7 of the Rio Declaration, which states that there is a "common but differentiated responsibility" of States in resolving environmental problems of a global nature.

15. See Donald M. Goldberg, *op. cit.*

16. Denmark, Finland, the Netherlands, Norway, Sweden.

17. See Richard Baron *et al.* (1996), *Economic/Fiscal Instruments: Taxation*, Working Paper 4, Policies and Measures for Common Action, Annex I Expert Group on UNIFCCC, OECD/IEA, Paris, Section 3.2.2.3.

18. See Richard Baron (1998), *Policies and Measures for Possible Common Action*, Working Paper 14, OECD/IEA, October p. 47.

19. See UNCTAD (1996), *op. cit.*

5

International Trade Law and the Kyoto Protocol: Potential Incompatibilities

W. Bradnee Chambers

Introduction

Early environmental treaties make little mention of potential incompatibilities with international trade rules. Even environmental treaties as recent as the Basel Convention on the control of transboundary movements of hazardous wastes and their disposal (BASEL, 1989), and the Montreal Protocol (1987) of the Vienna Convention for the Protection of the Ozone Layer (1985), on substances that deplete the ozone layer – both of which contain provisions that restrict trade and could therefore be inconsistent with existing international trade rules – make no mention of the relationship to international trade. However, the growing realization that trade and environment are inextricably linked has forced policy makers to address potential problems of overlap and conflict between the burgeoning regimes of nascent law in these two areas.

Agenda 21, the global agenda for action on sustainable development, which came into being at the Earth Summit in Rio de Janeiro in 1992, openly recognized that "universal, multilateral, and bilateral treaty-making" on the environment "should not constitute a means of arbitrary or unjustifiable discrimination or a disguised restriction on international trade, and that unilateral actions to deal with environmental challenges outside the jurisdiction of the importing country should be avoided."[1] These sentiments were echoed in two multilateral environmental agreements (MEAs) that emerged from the Rio Conference – the Biodiversity Convention and the Climate Change Convention.[2]

A call for provisions balancing trade and the environment also emerged on the trade side following the Earth Summit at Rio. The conclusion of the Uruguay Round of the General Agreement on Tariffs and Trade (GATT, 1994) saw the birth of the World Trade Organization (WTO). The preamble of the WTO agreement explicitly recognizes that trade must take into consideration the goals of environmental protection and sustainable development. At the same time, a new Committee on Trade and the Environment (CTE) was created with the mandate of assessing the role of the WTO in environmental matters. The North American Free Trade Agreement (NAFTA) negotiations also delved heavily into the trade and environment debate, which resulted in the clear recognition by NAFTA of the necessity for compliance with certain trade-related MEAs.[3] The NAFTA negotiations also led to the creation of an important environmental side-agreement to NAFTA, the North American Agreement on Environmental Cooperation (NAAEC).

This emergence of international discourse at the interface of new bodies of international law indicates that there is a growing recognition in the international community of the need for an integrated approach to environment and trade policy-making. With this background, the prospect for an integrated international law of environment and trade looks quite hopeful. However, in spite of the respective acknowledgements and concessions described above, which have been made within the main charters of these areas of law, increasing numbers of academics and practitioners alike have called attention to incompatibilities that could arise between MEAs and international trade agreements. None of these bodies of law have very long track records, but some of the cases that have occurred suggest that policy makers have not yet adequately addressed the trade/environment relationship. Furthermore, to a large extent, environmental agreements continue to be negotiated in relative isolation from other international agreements, including those on trade.[4]

The Global Climate Change Convention and its most recent incarnation, the Kyoto Protocol to regulate and control the use of greenhouse gases (GHGs), have tremendous economic and commercial significance, in that they have the potential of impacting domestic economies and affecting international trade more than any other MEA to date. Thus it is incumbent upon the Parties of the convention, before adopting specific rules, to consider the incompatibilities with international trade that could arise and, on this basis, to draft a coherent and balanced agreement that is compatible with (and complementary to) existing international legal regimes. It is in an effort to further this end that this chapter points to possible incompatibilities between the Kyoto Protocol and the WTO and, to a lesser extent, the European Union (EU) and NAFTA.

The Kyoto Protocol and potential measures affecting trade

The Kyoto Protocol negotiated in December of 1997 lays the foundation for its Parties to achieve average reductions in emissions of the main GHGs of 5.2 per cent by the year 2012. The responsibility for attaining this quantitative commitment, as prescribed under Annex B of the Protocol, is borne by the most-developed countries. In reaching their emission targets, Annex B Parties are given the flexibility to use different implementation methodologies. The first method is through adopting specific domestic policies and measures (PAMS) set out in the Framework Convention on Climate Change (FCCC) and in Article 2 of the Kyoto Protocol. The second method of implementation is through what are known as "flexible mechanisms" or the "Kyoto mechanisms." These mechanisms allow Parties to achieve their targets in the following ways: (a) by emissions trading with other Annex I Parties (Article 17); (b) by regional arrangements known as cooperative "bubbles" (Article 4); (c) by implementation of projects aimed at reducing anthropogenic gases by reducing sources and enhancing or creating sinks (Article 6); or (d) by using a mechanism referred to in the Protocol as the "clean development mechanism" (CDM), which involves exchanging the implementation of clean technologies on the one hand for emission credits on the other (Article 12).

Of these two methods of implementation, the first technique (policies and measures) is not considered to be trade related. It is clear, however, that PAMs may affect trade directly when they lead to domestic legislation that imposes regulation in the form of border taxes or technical restrictions on imported products, or indirectly when they lead to selective subsidies of particular products or processes. The second method of implementation has been referred to by some analysts as trade-related environmental measures (TREMs). These are measures within agreements for protecting the environment, which use trade instruments to achieve their objectives. The implications of these two implementation techniques for trade rules are considered below but, before their possible incompatibilities with the WTO are determined, the WTO rules are examined and their relation to MEAs is considered.

Like products and MEAs (NT, MFN, and Article XX Exceptions)

The relationship of WTO rules to those of the MEAs is still not completely clear. Article I is a fundamental principle of the WTO and grants most-favoured-nation (MFN) status to reciprocal countries "with respect to custom duties and charges of any kind" on imports or exports of all like products from contracting parties. Although undefined in Article I, MFN status refers to the granting of the same treatment to domestic products as to foreign "like products."[5] Analogously, in the area of internal taxation and regulation, Article III of the WTO provides the basic requirement to treat "like products" in the same way. This is referred to as the National Treatment (NT) principle.

The key to understanding why many commentators put MEAs at potential odds with the WTO is the relationship of the MFN and

NT principles to definition in the WTO agreement of "like products." "Like products" has come up in various contexts under the WTO but the most well-known application within a trade and environment setting occurred in the two panels of the Tuna Dolphin case.[6] In evaluating Article III, the first Panel concluded that the application of "laws, regulations or requirements affecting the sale, offering for sale, purchase, transportation, distribution or use of products" must be no less favourable in its treatment of imported products than in its treatment of "like" domestic products. The term "like products" was deemed to refer to the state of the product when it arrives at the border, not (as was maintained in the case of yellowfin tuna imported from Mexico) the method by which it was harvested or produced.[7] In reaching this conclusion, the Panel referred to a 1970 Working Party Report on Border Tax Adjustments, which addressed, *inter alia*, the issue of "like products." The report stated that the criterion for determining the "alikeness" of products should be decided upon on a case-by-case basis, and should take account of "the product's end-uses in a given market, consumers' tastes and habits, which range from country to country, the product's properties, nature and quality."[8] The report did not specify either production methods or processes as a criterion. The second Tuna Dolphin[9] panel, brought up by the EU as an intermediary importer, went further in its opinion on the "like product" and "process and production method" (PPM) issue, stating that Article III "calls for the treatment accorded to domestic and imported like products, not for the comparison of the policies or practices of the territory of where the product originated from."[10]

In other words, under a strict interpretation of the WTO clauses designed to prevent unfair constraints on commerce, whether the production process of a final product entails a GHG-emitting fossil-fuel-intensive method such as the burning of coal, or something as clean as wind or solar energy, is irrelevant to a WTO decision. The inability in the WTO to discriminate between products on the basis of how they were produced runs contrary to the objectives of environmentalism and most environmental agreements. The WTO does, however, provide exceptions under Article XX that could potentially confront such problems of incompatibility between MEAs and the WTO. The two sub-Paragraphs that relate to the environment under Article XX are (b) and (g), and state the following:

> Subject to the requirements that such measures are not applied in a manner which constitutes a means of arbitrary or unjustifiable discrimination between countries where the same conditions prevail, or a disguised restriction on international trade, nothing in this Agreement shall be construed to prevent the adoption or enforcement by any contracting party of measures:
> (b) necessary to protect human, animal or plant life or health;
> (g) relating to the conservation of exhaustible natural resources if such measures are made effective in conjunction with restrictions on production or consumption . . . .

Sub-Paragraphs (b) and (g) fall under a general list of possible "carve-outs" ranging from the importation and exportation of gold and silver[11] to products of prison labour.[12] Despite the expanse of different exceptions under Article XX, most abide by somewhat common rules for determining their permissibility. Recently, however, the Shrimp Turtle Appellate Body ruling gave a rather different application of these rules for Article XX (g); sub-Paragraphs (b) and (g) are, therefore, dealt with separately below.

XX (b)

Sub-Paragraph (b) requires that a number of criteria be met before an exception to the WTO rules is granted. The first criterion is that the measure enacted by the domestic authority on the import must be "primarily aimed" at achieving one of the specified objectives deemed by the WTO Agreement as a legitimate exception. In other words, if the measure is really created either to protect human, animal, or plant life, then it should be clearly and apparently aimed at achieving this result, and not be readily construed as aimed at "laying disguised barriers to trade or imports." To illustrate this point, EU law actually gives a good example: during the 1981 Christmas season, Britain imposed a ban on imported meat and poultry, claiming that it was necessary under an EU provision (Article 36),[13] which is similar to WTO's Article XX, to protect British turkeys from being afflicted by a type of poultry disease.[14] The ban coincided with a period of intense frustration on the part of British farmers with their European poultry competitors. Conveniently, one of the effects of the ban was to give the British farmers a corner on the British turkey market during a season of elevated sales. The European Commission brought the case before the European Court of Justice and the Court ruled against the British government, finding that the measure had been aimed at protecting local markets rather than being motivated by a valid concern for the protection of poultry flocks. Another example, which demonstrates this test in a WTO and in an environmental context, is the above 1991 Tuna Dolphin case. The case found that US tuna regulation was unfairly requiring Mexican tuna fisherman to meet "maximum incidental dolphin taking rates." The regulation was unfair because the rates were established only after the season had ended, which meant that, even if the Mexican fisherman had wanted to meet the regulation, it was impossible because they did not know the rates in advance. Consequently, the Panel, on the basis of this evidence, found that the US measure was not primarily aimed at the protection of dolphins but, rather, was a disguised barrier to trade.[15]

A second criterion that must be met in XX (b) is that an exception cannot be invoked to protect humans, animals, or plants outside its national jurisdiction. Returning to the landmark Tuna Dolphin case, the Panel noted "that a country can effectively control the production or consumption of an exhaustible natural resource only to the extent the production or consumption is under its jurisdiction." This criterion suggests that Parties cannot invoke Article XX to protect the global commons, which could restrict the use of measures or policies pursuant to certain MEAs. In determining whether the exception under consideration was a necessary one, however, the report of the same panel also used arguments to the effect that the US action was unjustified because it had not exhausted other efforts under international law to protect dolphins: "The United States had not demonstrated to the panel ... that it had exhausted all options reasonably available ... in particular through the negotiation of international cooperative agreements ...". Although not substantiated thus far in other WTO panels, this ruling implies that internationally adopted standards such as those pursuant to MEAs could be grounds for justifying an exception.[16]

Thus, the Panel leaves the jurisdictional question unsettled. It is, perhaps, reasonable to interpret these results as indicating that a unilateral action that has an extraterritorial effect has more weight as a legitimate exception to international trade law if it is carried out pursuant to recognized enabling provisions or endowed by an MEA than if it is carried out without any explicit reference to, or authorization under, an MEA. Such an interpretation would be in keeping with the way certain other exceptions contained in Article XX have been treated. For instance, GATT is explicit when it comes to balancing other areas of international law such as the United Nations Charter. Article XXI (c) provides that the GATT should not restrict any Member from "taking action in pursuance of its obligations under the United Nations Charter for the maintenance of international peace and security." Trade sanctions under Security Council Resolutions, which are authorized under Article 39 and 41 of the UN Charter, have become commonplace responses to the challenge of peacefully solving international disputes.[17] The United Nations Charter is, of course, a universally accepted document having a substantially constitutive nature. Legally speaking, this could suggest that international agreements that mirror similar degrees of universality, such as the Climate Change Convention with over 180 signatories, should be treated with the same validity and authority as other agreements considered as legitimate exceptions under Article XX (b).

The last criterion required by XX (b) is the most controversial in the trade and environment debate. This criterion is known as the minimal derogation test, or is sometimes referred to as the "necessary test." This test was examined extensively under the Section 337 case but in relation to sub-Paragraph (d), which protects patents, trademarks and copyrights and the prevention of deceptive practices. The case established that "a contracting Party cannot justify a measure inconsistent with other GATT provisions as 'necessary' in terms of Article XX (d) if an alternative measure which could be reasonably be expected to be employed and which is not inconsistent with other GATT provisions is available."[18] It further stated that, if an alternative measure is not available, the measure selected must be the least inconsistent (that is, of the available measures) with the GATT. The environmental context of the "necessary test" was upheld for sub-Paragraph (b) in the Thai Cigarettes case[19] and thereafter in the two Tuna Dolphin decisions.[20] In effect, what this test constituted was a stringent threshold that an action or measure must first pass before its legitimacy as an exception can even be considered. In practice, what this has meant is that the WTO essentially gives predominance to the trade rules rather than to environmental measures.

The one-sidedness in favour of trade in XX (b) has led some countries to propose different options to balance the substantive rights of WTO members with that of the right to protect the environment. In the context of the CTE, two main scenarios have been considered: first, an *ex post* approach that would grant a waiver to MEAs on a case-by-case basis under Article IX of the WTO; secondly, an *ex ante* approach that would define under what conditions an environmental measure pursuant to an MEA would be allowed. The latter approach is sometimes referred to as an "environmental window" and would involve an amendment to be negotiated by the WTO Parties.

Neither of these approaches would be required, however, if the interpretation of Article XX (b) gave a more balanced proportionality test between the environmental measure and the inconsistency with the GATT rules. The article requires a "rule of reason" that judges the measure "necessary" in order to protect human, animal, or plant life or health while being proportional to the rules and principles under the WTO. Such a rule is essentially a test of reasonableness: could an alternative measure have achieved the same level of protection to human, animal, or plant life? If so, would the measure have been feasible to implement; would it be cost effective; could it be monitored; would it be consistent with national legislative practices, etc. If such reasonableness is taken into account, a level of equity will be reached between the environment and trade that is not currently reflected in the overly strict "necessary" test of XX (b). Unfortunately, to date, panels seem to have created considerable precedent in favour of trade objectives over environmental ones.

XX (g)

The WTO Appellate Body Shrimp Turtle Decision of 12 October 1998, however, does suggest that the WTO interpretation of some of the key issues relating to at least Article XX (g) exceptions is beginning to change. Article XX (g) has become a much more likely foundation for a defence of discriminatory domestic policies aimed at environmental protection. The 1998 Shrimp Turtle appellate body decision clarified past WTO interpretations of the (g) provision and put in place a series of tests that appear to strike a more appropriate balance between the trade and environment regimes.

The first test requires a determination as to whether the resource at issue is exhaustible. The Shrimp Turtle ruling dealt with this question at some length because the Principals to the dispute argued that a "reasonable interpretation of the term exhaustible is that it refers to finite resources such as minerals rather than biological or renewable resources."[21] The Appellate body did not agree with this argument and ruled that, as a species of plant or animal can become endangered, it is exhaustible. This allows Article XX (g) to be used in a much wider range of circumstances than those with which it had previously been associated; this wider range potentially could involve climate change. The WTO has not yet been called upon to make a ruling on this issue, although past precedents suggest that such an argument could succeed.

A comparable question was raised in the Reformulated Gasoline Panel, involving a dispute between the United States and Venezuela over compositional and performance specifications for reformulated gasoline entering the United States.[22] The Panel noted that clean air could be considered to be an exhaustible natural resource as it has value, is natural, and can be depleted. Taking this ruling into account, the global climate, with similar attributes to clean air, could also be considered as falling within the definition of Article XX (g).

The second criterion in XX (g) is the examination of the relationship between the measure enacted to protect the natural resource and its resulting effect — in other words, whether the objective of the measure is aimed at or, as the sub-Paragraph states, "relates to" the protection of an exhaustible resource. To establish the intent of the measure, the Body stated that a substantial relationship must exist between the measure's effect and the objective of protecting an exhaustible resource. The Body referred to the method it set in US – Gasoline, that a "close and genuine relationship of ends and means" must exist in order to establish the "substantial relationship." In the case of Shrimp Turtle, Section 609, the domestic legislation in question was believed to meet this "substantial relationship" requirement because the target of the domestic legislation was fishing technology that endangered sea turtles and exempted artisan practices and aquaculture shrimping. The measure also differentiated between waters certified either as having no threat to turtles or as already having implemented protection schemes. The Body felt that Section 609 was not a "blanket measure" and was therefore "related to" the objective of protecting endangered sea turtles. A second requirement set by US – Reformulated Gasoline was an examination of whether the measure was applied equally on restricting domestic production and consumption. In the Shrimp Turtle Appellate case, the fact that the United States imposed the same turtle excluder regulations on the domestic shrimp industry was considered adequate to meet this requirement. It was considered to be evidence that the US action stemmed from a genuine environmental concern and was not a disguised trade barrier.

The last test in sub-Paragraph (g) is the "chapeau test", which is, perhaps, the most difficult to interpret and apply. The chapeau (or cap) sets out certain basic provisions that the measure must meet. It states that discrimination must not be present and that it must not be unjustifiable or arbitrary in circumstances where the same conditions exist between the exporters and importers. In applying the chapeau, the Appellate Body recognized that a balance must be struck between the right to invoke the exception and the rights of Members to the main provisions contained in the WTO. Demarcating the line where these rights are balanced is the key to applying the chapeau and, to a large extent, the Body stated that this line would depend on the facts of the case. It also stated that, on the basis of the negotiating history of Article XX, the chapeau was clearly put in place to conditionalize or limit the use of the exceptions in Article XX; however, as mentioned earlier, it must be interpreted in the modern context – which includes interpreting the chapeau in keeping with that of the Preamble of the WTO Agreement, which includes the goal of sustainable utilization of world resources.

In the Shrimp Turtle case it was the non-transparency and inflexibility of the US regulation and the fact that basic standards of fairness and due process in the certification procedures were not present that led the Appellate Body to the conclusion that Section 609 was both unjustifiable and arbitrary discrimination.[23]

The Shrimp Turtle ruling can be viewed as a success in many ways, but it did leave open the question of whether unilateralism could be justified by an Article XX exception. Until the Shrimp Turtle case, it had been assumed by the majority of observers that exceptions could be justified only on the basis of some form of multilateralism such as a multilateral agreement, widely practised and documented standards, or accepted principles of international law. Clearly, this was what was hinted at in the Dolphin Tuna case. Shrimp Turtle, however, ran contrary to this widely held belief. The Body stated that:

> What we *have* decided in this appeal is simply this: although the measure of the United States in dispute in this appeal serves an environmental objective that is recognized as legitimate under paragraph (g) of Article XX of the GATT 1994, this measure has been applied by the United States in a manner which constitutes arbitrary and unjustifiable discrimination between Members of the WTO, contrary to the requirements of the chapeau of Article XX. For all of the specific reasons outlined in this Report, this measure does not qualify for the ex-

emption that Article XX of the GATT 1994 affords to measures which serve certain recognized, legitimate environmental purposes but which, at the same time, are not applied in a manner that constitutes a means of arbitrary or unjustifiable discrimination between countries where the same conditions prevail or a disguised restriction on international trade. As we emphasized in *United States – Gasoline*, WTO Members are free to adopt their own policies aimed at protecting the environment as long as, in so doing, they fulfill their obligations and respect the rights of other Members under the *WTO Agreement*.

This leaves open the question of the scope of Article XX (g) and whether discrimination can be justified for exhaustible resources outside national jurisdictions. In the future, this will undoubtedly beckon attempts by governments to justify unilateralism and protectionism.

The Kyoto Protocol and potential incompatibilities with the WTO

Non-specific trade-related environmental measures

Conflicting policies and measures (PAMs)

Article 2 of the Kyoto Protocol sets forth a menu of PAMs that each Party should adopt to achieve its quantified emission-limitation and -reduction commitments under Article 3 (QELROs), and to promote sustainable development. These include policy options such as, *inter alia*, the enhancement of energy efficiency in relevant sectors of national economies, the promotion of sustainable forms of agriculture and forest management, the development of new and renewable forms of energy, and the creation of other measures to reduce GHG emissions. Article 2 (b) also reiterates the importance of the policies and measures found in Article 4 of the Convention.

To fulfil these commitments domestically, Parties are expected to translate the PAMs into laws, policies, and binding regulatory regimes that will curb their use of GHGs and enable them to meet their respective targets by the year 2012, the end of the first commitment period. The possibilities for domestic legal instruments that could be employed are, theoretically, endless but some plausible examples are taxes on fossil-fuel-intensive sectors, technical regulations such as pollution controls, and subsidies on products or sectors that are deemed to be comparatively environmentally sustainable or to have minimal negative impact on climate. The economic impact of PAMs could be far-reaching, as the Climate Change Convention pledges to reduce the use of fossil fuel, the most common source of energy for virtually all sectors of society. Such domestic, PAM-guided regimes are likely to affect the competitiveness of national industries. One important area of concern arises in connection with the application of PAM-motivated constraints to imported products. For example, when the competitiveness of domestic industry is diminished by domestic environmental regulation and similar domestic regulatory measures are placed on imported products to restore the competitiveness of domestic products, by levelling the playing field, the potential for conflicts with WTO rules that regulate the flow of international trade could arise.[24]

For this reason, the PAM issue is one that needs to have better consideration within the climate-change framework. In particular, more attention needs to be given to Article 4.2 sub-Paragraph (e) (i) of the Climate Change Convention, which calls on parties to coordinate their national policies so that conflicts over different implementation techniques do not arise. Although the national communications do normally contain the general polices taken to reduce emissions, perhaps, in an effort to increase transparency, a separate notification and registry system could represent one concrete option.

Differentiated responsibility between developed and developing countries

The reduction of domestic competitiveness could become even more acute upon consideration of the fact that the responsibilities under the FCCC and Kyoto Protocol are different for developed[25] and developing countries, respectively,[26] and also for the economies in transition (EIT) of the former Soviet Union. Developed countries are obligated to achieve substantial reductions of their emissions by the year 2012, whereas developing countries do not have the same responsibilities. Similarly, EIT countries have been granted greater flexibility to implement the Climate Change Convention and Kyoto Protocol.

At the same time, many of the countries that are Parties to the Kyoto Protocol also belong to the WTO agreement and have responsibilities pertaining to the equal or fair treatment of domestic and foreign products. Would a developed country be justified if, in pursuing its international obligations under the Kyoto Protocol, it imposed domestic legislation on a developing country that does not share the same international obligations?

Non-Parties

Very similar to the differentiated-responsibility problem is a circumstance where conflict emerges in the WTO regime, between two Parties, but one Party is not a member of the Kyoto Protocol. For instance, Party A pursues a domestic measure that is pursuant to the Kyoto Protocol but is discriminatory to Party B, a non-signatory to the Protocol. Since both Parties are WTO members, does Party A have the right to impose a measure that is justified according to an international regulation that Party B does not recognize? In terms of the Climate Change Convention this is not such a serious problem, as there are over 180 members with significant overlap with the WTO membership and the Convention is non-binding. The Kyoto Protocol, on the other hand, had been ratified only by 32 members when this book went to press, and will and could leave out significant countries such as the United States, if the climate in the US Senate is not favourable.

The issue of non-Parties has been one of the greatest concern to the WTO CTE which, in its 1996 report to the Singapore Ministerial Meeting, issued caution to MEAs when drafting trade related provisions that might affect non signatories. The Report states that disputing Parties to an MEA and which are also WTO Members have the right to bring that dispute to the WTO, but should first try to resolve it through the MEAs dispute-settlement mechanisms. The report, however, is decidedly vague on disputes pursuant to an MEA arising between Parties and non-Parties but which concerns countries that are both WTO members. As is discussed later, clearly under international law the only available means of solving the dispute would be recourse to the forums where both Parties are signatories.

Trade-related environmental measures: Flexible mechanisms

Trade-related environmental measures (TREMs) have generated the most concern amongst trade experts and environmentalists in terms of potential conflict with WTO rules. From the environmental perspective, concern stems from the possible interference that WTO provisions or conditions might impose on the TREM. This is despite the acknowledgement, by WTO officials, that it is the architects of MEAs who are probably in the best position to oversee the use of TREMs. From a trade perspective, TREMs are viewed with caution as their full impact is yet to be tested and their potential to interfere with trade remains a possibility. That no TREM-related case has, so far, been brought before the WTO has only added to debate, speculation, and anxiety.

In reviewing TREMs, the WTO CTE has often used for discussion an example of discrimination pursuant to an MEA, against a MEA non-signatory, concerning Parties that are both signatories to the WTO. As mentioned above, that is just such a case that might put the WTO in the unwanted position of being the only forum available to the non-Party to resolve the dispute.[27]

There seems to be a marginally lower level of concern for trade discrimination on goods that are traded outside their environmental regime but are also regulated by an MEA. Examples of such goods are hazardous wastes, endangered species, and ozone-depleting substances (ODS). These are controlled by the Basel Convention, the Convention on the International Trade in Endangered Species of Wild Fauna and Flora (CITES), and the Montreal Protocol, respectively. All of these agreements call for discrimination and the regulation of trade in goods that, prior to the MEA regime regulations, were openly traded with commercial value on international markets. In the case of the Montreal Protocol, a desire not to interfere (inadvertently) with WTO rules led to the creation of a subgroup under the Ad Hoc Working Group of Legal and Technical Experts during Protocol negotiations. The subgroup considered the compatibility of the regulation of ODS of the Protocol with the GATT. The group concluded that the two were compatible as the Protocol provisions would most likely be justifiable under GATT Article XX.[28] At the time, the WTO CTE did not exist and the issue of compatibility in this issue area was not the focus of as much concern as it is today.[29]

The new twist compared with other MEAs is that Article 17 of the Kyoto Protocol effectively introduces a completely new product to be traded – Parts of Assigned Amounts (PAA). Prior to the Protocol, emissions had never been traded on international markets and this has raised fundamental questions about whether PAA should even come under the jurisdiction of the WTO, given that they are inherently limited to the Kyoto Protocol.

In the absence of express rules limiting PAA-related issues to the UNFCCC, difficulties may arise because there is no legal barrier preventing a country from bringing the case before the WTO dispute settlement. The broad rules of the Dispute Settlement Understanding (DSU) apply to disputes pursuant to every imaginable good or service traded on the international market. Of course, arguments could arise of how to identify a PAA: is it a good or a service? Some might argue that, as it has a physical aspect, it should be considered to be a good. It may, for example, be a by-product of the manufacturing process, such as hazardous waste or used oil. No clear definition of a *good* has been provided within the GATT and, therefore, there is no solid basis from which to make an assessment. Alternatively, an argument could also be made that the emission is not the object of the trade. The object of the trade is, rather, the PAA permit – the *right to emit*. Under the General Agreement on Trade in Services (GATS), permits or credits would be considered a negotiable instrument and therefore a financial service. Whether a service or a good is important only to the point of establishing which WTO agreement applies – the GATS or GATT. To all intents and purposes, however, the GATS and the GATT work on similar principles. The question, then, is which parts (if any) of the Protocol enabling and regulating this trade would be likely to come into conflict with these principles.

As it stands, the "relevant principles, rules, modalities, rules and guidelines"[30] of Article 17 are still undefined. However, several possibilities are on the negotiating table. Among these are calls for the tight regulation of the emissions-trading system by means of a monitoring and verification process. For instance, if the selling party were in compliance with its emission requirements, the trade would be unrestricted; however, if monitoring showed a potential for non-compliance or a serious compliance problem, then the trade would be banned or the seller would be sanctioned for trading while out of compliance.[31] Such a compliance system would, of course, have implications for WTO rules on "like-products" and PPM.

Another restriction in the emissions-trading system that could have implications to the WTO are the provisions restricting the trading of emissions to Annex B Parties only. This is, of course, a blatant barrier to trade, particularly from the perspective of developing countries (non-Annex B Parties), which have large inventories of emissions credits[32] and might wish to trade on the emissions market, but could do so only by becoming Annex B members.[33]

A third area of conflict is the nature of the potential sanctions under consideration for the Protocol's compliance system. Article 18 of the Kyoto Protocol calls its Parties to create an indicative list of sanctions for non-compliance. Although unlikely to succeed, there have been some unwise calls that the list should include trade sanctions on fossil-fuel-intensive products.[34] This, of course, would again violate the basic WTO discipline of non-discrimination.

In Chapter 7, Jacob Werksman raises the fundamental question of whether WTO rules would be even a consideration in the Kyoto Protocol's emission-trading schemes. His contention is that emissions trading is essentially not a trading system but rather a system of mutually recognized allowances between Parties to emit GHG. The implication is that emissions trading is neither a good nor a service. He admits, however, that certain design choices in the Protocol that affect the allocation and regulation of emission allowances could also have implications for the competitiveness of goods or services governed by WTO disciplines.

The debate of whether emission trading falls under the WTO or not, or whether it is a good or a service, is one that has no easy answer. It is also, perhaps, one that can be avoided if the Protocol (as is suggested by Gary Sampson in Chapter 4) develops a solid trading system, not unlike the WTO's system, which envisions the potential problems and requirements of regulating an international market. This includes creating a dispute-settlement and -enforcement mechanism that can solve inconsistencies among the parties quickly and efficiently. If such a regulatory regime were created, there would be more likelihood that disputes would be resolved within the framework of the Protocol and therefore less incentive to the recourse of going to the WTO. Furthermore, Parties could avoid completely the possibility of cases arising in the WTO if they explicitly set out in the Protocol that WTO rules are not applicable to emissions trading or its related provisions.

Perhaps the simplest way to solve the whole debate, however, is for the Kyoto Protocol to define "emissions" explicitly as outside the definitional scope of either a service or a good for the purposes of the international trade rules and to recognize that disputes arising in relation to emissions trading must be solved within the Kyoto Protocol.

Other trade agreements: European Union and NAFTA

European Union (EU)

Under EU law there are few potential incompatibilities with the Kyoto Protocol. The EU has developed a relatively strong legal framework, which carefully defines the relationship of Member States and the EU *vis-à-vis* international agreements. On environmental matters the EU has non-exclusive powers to enter into international agreements on the environment – which means that (depending on the competence) the Community and the Member States can participate together as a whole or separately. The competence depends on whether the Community has adopted internal rules on the environmental matter at hand. If it has, the Community alone has the competence to participate. In practice, if no internal rules exist or if they are of a "minimal requirement" (meaning that they are only loosely construed), then the Member States and the Community decide together, through the Council, how they will negotiate and sign the international agreement.[35] In the case of the Climate Change Convention, the Member States gave the competence of the negotiations to the Community.[36]

Once an international agreement has been concluded, it can become binding on Member States in several ways. First, international agreements can be given "direct effect" under European Community law. This means that the agreement can confer rights and obligations that are directly applicable to individuals within a Member State's national legal system. The determination of whether an international agreement can actually confer direct effect is done on a case-by-case basis; generally, however, the European Court has been reluctant to grant its application easily. Direct effect largely depends on the nature of the agreement. For instance, if the Community explicitly gives its Parties the task of implementing the international agreement through national legislation, or if its language is imprecise or hortatory, it is unlikely to have any direct effect. If, however, the agreement has direct obligations and comes closer to conferring rights on individuals, then it may have direct effect. Of course, the question of direct effect becomes a moot point if the Community implements the provision of the agreement as a Community regulation under Article 189 of the EU Treaty, which in most cases, gives automatic direct effect.

A third way in which an international agreement such as the Kyoto Protocol could be implemented in EU law is as a directive. Directives are binding, but not explicit. They give the overall effect of what must be achieved, while the "form and the method" of the legislation is left up to the Member State to legislate. In some cases a directive can have direct effect, if the language is "unconditional and sufficiently precise," as laid down in *Van Duyn* v. *Home Office*.[37] Increasingly, EU law is becoming more binding on states to ensure that directives are implemented in national legislation. In *Francovich* v. *Italy*, the European Court ruled that a Member State could be held liable for damages suffered by individuals as a result of the Member State's failure to implement a directive.[38]

Because of the manner in which international agreements are negotiated and then implemented, it is unlikely that inconsistencies between EU and Member State law will occur in connection with the Kyoto Protocol. Problems could arise, however, if a Member State decided to implement the Protocol in a manner inconsistent with that used by other EU members. As previously mentioned, one of the dynamic features of the Protocol is that it allows Parties various choices of means of implementation. Consider, for instance, the hypothetical case of a Member State that chooses to introduce a measure according to the Protocol but which differs from the method that the other EU Member States have agreed, as a group, to adopt.[39] Even if such measures are applied equally both to the domestic product in question and the corresponding EU-imported product, it is prohibited.[40] Article 30 of the EC treaty states that "Quantitative restrictions on imports and all measures having equivalent effect shall ... be prohibited between Member States." Article 36 does give some powers to derogate from Article 30, but the European Court (ECJ) has limited these powers to a large extent. In what is considered by many analysts to be an example of creative judicial decision-making, the ECJ in *Cassis de Dijon*[41] stated that domestic measures inconsistent with Article 30 "may be recognized as being necessary in order to satisfy mandatory requirements relating in particular to the effectiveness of judicial supervision, the protection of public health, the fairness of commercial transactions and the defense of the consumer." Environmental protection was not included in the list; however, since the 1988 Danish Bottle case[42] it, too, has been considered a mandatory requirement.

In a case where discrimination could arise between Member States that have decidedly different methods of implementing the Kyoto

Protocol, there is no easy answer. Any responsible ruling would have to look at the application of Article 30's proportionality principle, which calls for an evaluation of the degree to which the measure is required, on the one hand, as weighed against the extent of trade restriction the measure would entail, on the other. The judgement would also have to be preceded by a determination of whether an alternative means existed to accomplish the same objective. Arguably, in determining the alternative means, it would require the Member State to employ the method of implementation adopted by the Community as a whole when the latter acceded to the international agreement. Therefore, it is reasonable to conclude that, since the EU has positive legislation that has a harmonizing effect (as contained in Articles 30 and 36) on its Member State's environmental laws, and since the EU in practice tends to work cooperatively in negotiating and implementing international agreements, the Kyoto Protocol would cause few incompatibilities or problems under EU law.

North American Free Trade Agreement (NAFTA)

NAFTA is a relatively progressive trade agreement in terms of the environment. Its architects have had the foresight to draft its provisions to address many of the potential problems that could arise between it and MEAs. Perhaps the most innovative provision is Article 104, which expressly sets out the relationship of NAFTA rules with certain MEAs containing trade-related measures. The Article states that, in the case of an inconsistency between specific trade rules of the NAFTA and certain international environmental agreements that are identified in NAFTA Annex 104.1, the obligations of the international environmental agreements will have legal prevalence. At present, four agreements are contained in the Annex 104.1: (a) the Convention on International Trade in Endangered Species of Wild Fauna and Flora; (b) the Montreal Protocol on Substances that Deplete the Ozone Layer (c) the Basel Convention on the Control of Transboundary Movements of Hazardous Wastes and their Disposal and (d) the Canada–United States and Mexico–United States agreements concerning the transboundary movement of hazardous waste.

In effect, Article 104 gives supremacy to the obligations contained in the MEAs. The only qualification is that the Party, when it has a choice of equally effective means of achieving a given obligation, should choose a measure that is the least inconsistent with the NAFTA rules. The Article further elaborates that the Parties may agree in writing to amend the Article by adding more treaties to the list contained in the Annex. Since the Kyoto Protocol contains several trade-related provisions it, too, should be added to the Annex's list. To do so would render moot any debate over incompatibilities between the NAFTA and the suggested market mechanisms of the Protocol, such as emissions trading. The fact that the Kyoto Protocol has not been added to the Annex, however, leaves the question of exception pursuant to it up to the provisions contained in Articles 904 (2) and 907 (2), and the definition of legitimate objectives in Article 915.

According to Article 904 (2) a NAFTA Party is permitted to set a level of protection, including environmental protection, that it deems appropriate as long as the objective is legitimate. Article 915 defines a legitimate objective as:

(a) safety
(b) protection of human, animal or plant life or health, the en
vironment or consumers, including matters related to quality and identifiability of goods and services; and
(c) sustainable development;
considering, among other things, where appropriate, fundamental climatic or other geographical factors, technological or
infrastructural factors, or scientific justification but does not
include the protection of domestic production;

An innovative provision built into NAFTA, which is absent under the WTO, is that legitimate objectives are judged according to other factors such as climate, geography, scientific justification, and risk assessment.[43] Interestingly, this provision, which is found in Articles 915 and 907, could provide an alternative argument for defending domestic measures enacted to protect the global commons pursuant to an MEA. For example, if the Party can argue that the environment of the global commons is linked to the domestic environment, then the measure could be acceptable on the grounds of Article 915.2. For example, on the issue of climate change, a Party to NAFTA and to the Kyoto Protocol that has considerable low-lying territory might justify a high domestic standard on fossil-fuel emissions by citing the Intergovernmental Panel on Climate Change (IPPC) finding that GHGs are having a discernible impact on climate, together with its further finding that the effects of this impact will be greater in areas more susceptible to climate change, such as low-lying regions. Then, in consideration of its extensive low-lying territory, it could make an argument on the basis of the scientific evidence on the higher sensitivity or susceptibility to climate change of low-lying areas, that a particularly stringent standard is required to protect its lowlands.

One of the greatest challenges to NAFTA from the Kyoto Protocol will be the "common but differentiated responsibility principle." Both Canada and the United States are Annex 1 Parties and have made commitments to targets of 6 and 7 per cent targets, respectively; however, Mexico remains a non-Annex 1 Party and is therefore not subject to a quantitative reduction target. However, all three countries belong to NAFTA, a binding trade agreement. This situation will undoubtedly lead to trade advantages, distortions, and perceived inequities within NAFTA.

Treaty compatibility: Successive treaties and Article 30 of the Vienna Convention

The issue of treaty compatibility is dealt with under the 1969 Vienna Convention of the Law of Treaties (VCLT) and, to a limited extent, the work of this convention has bearing on the relationship between the Kyoto Protocol and international trade rules. The Vienna Convention is of a general nature and cannot provide a panacea for the kind of problems that might arise at the juncture of these two competing areas of international law, environment, and trade. In spite of its limitations, however, it seems appropriate to suggest that the present and future participants in the further development and evolution of the Kyoto Protocol take heed of the precautions which have been outlined at the Vienna Convention and read carefully between its lines, as well as studying those provisions that are more specifically germane to environmental protection and trade.

Article 30 is the only specific provision of the Vienna Convention which directly refers to treaty compatibility. However, the Article stipulates rules only for treaties which have the same common subject matter, which raises the question of whether the principles therein can actually be applied to treaties which have clearly different purposes, such those concerning trade and environment respectively. If this fundamental question is put aside for a moment and an assumption is made that environment and trade measures are considered to fall into the same subject category (since they are inseparable from one another), then the guidelines set out by Article 30 are directly pertinent. These guidelines are summarized below.

First, if a treaty establishes a subordinate relationship to another treaty within its text, then the other treaty will take precedence. Second, if all the Parties to an earlier treaty sign a new treaty, the common provisions of the two treaties will have precedence over the other provisions but, according to *lex posterior derogat priori*, the uncommon provisions will remain in force. Third, for new treaties that do not include all the original parties, the rule is also commonsensical: the Parties that have signed the new treaty are bound by it over the former treaty, whereas the Parties that did not sign it remain bound by the original treaty. Thus, the provisions of Article 30 of the Vienna Convention could be considered as a basis for establishing rules or principles of compatibility or balance between an environmental treaty like the Kyoto Protocol and trade law such as that embodied in the WTO Agreement.

However, the Parties to the Vienna Convention still have much to consider in light of the difficult questions emerging from the conflicts that are now occurring at the interfaces of competing bodies of international law. Such conflicts are inevitable, and are likely to continue to occur even after a more integrated system of international law comes into being. At the moment, however, the settlement of certain important issues with regard to these conflicts is particularly urgent at the interface of trade and environment law.

One of the intents of Article 30 is to clarify the rights and responsibilities that accrue to nations that sign successive treaties with related subject matter, so that Parties with multiple memberships in international agreements will be capable of interpreting the interactive effect and implications of these agreements on the basis of a full knowledge of the issues involved in their overlaps, gaps, conflicts, contradictions, and so on.

Unfortunately, in practice, this is far from the reality. National and international agendas for multilateral political negotiations have become overwhelmed with the number and the range of international treaties, agreements, and unsettled disputes. Often, because of the ad hoc manner in which environmental issues arise on political agendas, there is no integration between international environmental treaty negotiations. This, of course, leads to treaties in which the normative assumptions, principles, or provisions incidentally overlap those of other treaties, in either complementary or conflicting fashion. The conflicts between treaties and agreements may be small or large, simple or complex. In the case of environment and trade, they are both complicated and large.

Article 30 seems only rudimentary in light of the practical demands for a more comprehensive and sophisticated framework for the construction and interpretation of international law.

Moreover, if the remarks of I.M. Sinclair, one of the original negotiators, are accepted as definitive, namely that "in determining which treaty is earlier and which the later, the relevant date is from the adoption of the text and not that of its entry into force,"[44] then, although many treaties on trade, such as the Technical Barriers to Trade (TBT) Agreement (GATT, 1994) or the revised WTO text after the 1994 Uruguay Trade Round would have precedence over the 1992 FCCC, nevertheless the 1997 Kyoto Protocol would prevail over any of the recent WTO amendments.

Another important consideration here is the interpretation of the words in Article 30 "relating to the same subject matter." It has been argued that the maxim *generalia specialibus non derogant* (general things do not derogate from special things) should be used as a guideline for treaty compatibility. This maxim dictates that, in determining the relationship between two treaties that are not directly related, the specific clause should prevail over the general clause. For environmental treaties, which are often general in nature, this could have disadvantageous repercussions.

This brief analysis of the Vienna Convention leads to the conclusion, which is generally agreed on by other authors, that its rules on treaty compatibility are residuary. Clearly, in an ideal world, the best way to avoid incidental conflicts between treaties would be always adequately to consider inter-treaty relationships in advance of striking and signing new agreements. This, of course, has little relevance to the real-world situation. Nevertheless, it is equally clear that if and when potential incompatibilities, such as those set out in this chapter, are predicted or anticipated, it would behove all concerned to exercise a mutual effort in the direction of taking appropriate preventative measures. The objective of establishing the relative strength of respective treaties and their provisions *vis-à-vis* one another is clearly part of this task, albeit a daunting one.

Conclusions

In conclusion, it is apparent from the general analysis of the Kyoto Protocol and its relationship with international trade law that certain incompatibilities exist and could develop into difficult and complicated situations in practice. This is particularly true with regard to the possible policies and measures that Parties might pursue to reach their quantitative emissions targets. Potential problems exist at the interface between the emissions-trading provisions of the Kyoto Protocol and the trade-protective measures of the WTO. If the details as to how the respective parameters of the two bodies of law are supposed to interact are not clearly settled and distinguished, the Protocol will founder under overwhelming pressure from the international trade law side, in part created by the great energy and momentum with which the latter is being formed.

However, the incompatibilities described in this paper and the serious problems to which they are likely to give rise will be largely avoided if the widening community of participants in the ongoing process of refining the Kyoto Protocol are able to draft specific rules and principles that establish clear guidelines as to which treaty should prevail in a given circumstance and why. One of the most important areas in which such specific rules and principles are needed is that of potential conflicts among the member Parties to the Kyoto Protocol, while they are attempting to fulfil their respective obligations under the Protocol. Some of these potential conflicts have been described in the form of hypothetical examples in this chapter as a means of generating concrete proposals for such rules and principles.

In addition to the specification of such rules and principles, it is also imperative that the Parties to the Kyoto Protocol devise and come to an agreement that brings into existence a strong mechanism which enables both the enforcement and the sustainability of the Protocol, and establishes in adequate detail the organizational, financial, and tangible means whereby compliance will be maintained, disputes among nations will be resolved, and conflicts among agreements settled.

Specifically, the Parties to the Protocol should consider adopting the following recommendations:

1. Create an ad hoc working group of legal and technical experts under the UNFCCC to examine the potential incompatibilities between the FCCC/Protocol and the WTO.

2. Re-energize the PAMs debate in the negotiations, concentrating on developing, concretizing, and coordinating the various policy options so that they are more integrated and consistent with international trade rules. In essence, give effect to the measures suggested in Article 4.2 (e) sub-Paragraph (i) of the Climate Change Convention.

3. Define "emissions" for the purpose of international trade rules so that it does not fall into the same category as either products or services under the WTO rules on "like" products or services.

4. Create a strong overall dispute-settlement and flexible-mechanism dispute-settlement system so that MEA conflicts are solved within the FCCC.

5. Explicitly recognize in the Kyoto Protocol that disputes arising from the provisions of the FCCC should be resolved within the FCCC.

6. Give effect to the principle "minimize the effects (of environmental protection measures) on international trade" as contained in Article 3.5 of the Convention and Article 2(3) of the Protocol.

7. By the same token, give effect to a reciprocal principle – "minimize the effects of international trade on the environment" – in international trade-law agreements.

In short, these specific suggestions first call for reflection on the potential problem of compatibility. However, following such considerations must be policy responses that weave what are now only abstract principles, soft law, or merely ideas into specific, binding, treaty provisions that will help concretize the climate-change regime into a strong and effective agreement that is compatible with international trade law.

Notes

1. Agenda 21; 39.1 (d); A/COF.151/26 (vol. 111) 14 August 1992.
2. The Biodiversity Convention makes only indirect reference (Article 22), but the Climate Change Convention has several references to its relationship with trade agreements (Article 3.5, 4.2 e).
3. Article 104.
4. A rough indication of this can be made by scrutinizing the participants list to UNFCCC, COP 3, COP 4, or COP 5.
5. MFN status has been defined by the International Law Commission as "accorded by the granting State to the beneficiary state, or to persons or things in a determined relationship with that state, not less favorable than treatment extended by the granting state to a Third state or to persons things in the same relationship with that third State." 1978 Yearbook of the ILC, vol. II pt. 2; ILM 1518 (1978), Article 5.

6. Tuna Dolphin Panel 1, 1992 BISD 29S/9. The application of "like products" has come up in various other contexts: see Report of the panel regarding Spanish tariffs coffee on raw coffee, BISD 28S/102 (1982); Australian Subsidies on Ammonium Sulphate Panel, BISD II/188 (1952), par. 9; Japanese Alcohol Panel, BISD 34S/83 (1988), par. 5.5 (b).

7. The WTO has referred to the way in which a product is produced as the "process and production method" (PPM).

8. Report of the Working party on Border Tax Adjustments, BISD 18S/97 (1972) pr. 18.

9. Tuna Dolphin Panel 2, 1993 39S/155.

10. Ibid.

11. GATT Article XX (c).

12. GATT Article XX (e).

13. Article 36 states that provisions of the EU Treaty shall: "not preclude prohibitions or restrictions on imports, exports or goods in transit justified on the grounds of public morality, public policy, or public security; the protection of health and life and humans, animals or plants ... Such prohibitions or restrictions shall not, however, be a disguised restriction on trade.

14. Case 40/82 [1982] ECR 2793; see, for a general description of Article 36, S. Weatherill and P. Beaumont, *EC Law*, Penguin Books, 1993 pp. 393–426.

15. See 1991, Tuna Dolphin Panel 1, note 4 above.

16. This aspect of the Panel's ruling in the Tuna Dolphin case is further considered below in the section on the standards and the "necessary test" issue. For additional discussion of this point see James Cameron and Zen Makuch, "Implementation of the United Nations Framework Convention on Climate Change: International Trade Law Implications" in Cameron, Demaret and Geradin, *Trade and Environment: The Search for Balance*, vol. 1, Cameron and Mae 1994, p. 31.

17. See Edmond Govern, *International Trade Regulation*, Globefield Press 1995, which points out that sanctions have been placed *inter alia* on Rhodesia in 1966 (Res. 232), South Africa in 1977 (Res. 418), Iraq in 1990, (Res. 661), Libya in 1992 (Res. 748), Serbia and Montenegro in 1993 (Res. 757) and Haiti in 1993 (Res. 841), all of which would be considered exceptions under Article XXI (c).

18. Section 337 case, 7 November 1990, BISD 36S/345.

19. Thai Cigarettes case, 7 November 1990, BISD 37S/200.

20. Dolphin Tuna case.

21. Appellate Body report, Shrimp Turtle case, WT/DS58/AB/R, 12 October 1998, p. 47, par. 127.

22. Appellate Body report, Reformulated Gasoline case, WT/DS2/AB/R, 20 May 1996.

23. Jacob Werksman, "United States Import Prohibitions of Certain Shrimp and Shrimp Products." Case Note, *Review of European Community and International Environmental Law (RECIEL)*, 8 (1): 78–83, 1999.

24. It must be noted that an uncoordinated PAM arising in a WTO dispute and justified using Article XX would have to pass the chapeau requirements, one of which is that measures cannot be taken that would discriminate between countries where the same conditions prevail. The effect of this statement is that

a country cannot discriminate against another country in an attempt to force that country to comply with its own regulatory programme or policy goals.

25. Under the Climate Change Convention these countries are referred to as Annex I countries.

26. Under the Climate Change Convention these countries are referred to as non-Annex I countries.

27. Although CTE and Ministerial debates have expressed the same concern, the concern was first identified by the Report by Ambassador Ukawa (Japan), Chairman of the Group on Environmental Measures and International Trade, to the forty-ninth Session of the Contracting Parties, L/7402.

28. Duncan Brack, *International Trade and the Montreal Protocol*. London: Royal Institute of International Affairs, 1996, p. 67.

29. Ibid, p. 68.

30. Article 17, Kyoto Protocol FCCC/CP/1997/l.7/Add.1.

31. See Donald M. Goldberg, Stephen Porter, Nuno LaCasta and Eli Hillman, "Responsibility for Non-compliance under the Kyoto Protocol's Mechanism for Cooperative Implementation," Center of International Environmental Law (CIEL) and EURONATURA, 1998; Environmental Defense Fund, "Cooperative Mechanisms under the Kyoto Protocol: The Path Forward," June 1998, UNCTAD, "Greenhouse Gas Emissions Trading: Defining the Principles, Modalities, Rules and Guidelines for Verification Reporting and Accountability – Draft Version," June 1998.

32. If developing countries prescribed to Annex B they would undoubtedly be entitled to the highest number of emission credits because of their level of development.

33. Annex B Parties have several substantive responsibilities such as reporting obligations and emission targets.

34. EDF.

35. For a detailed analysis of EU and its external relations see MacLeod, Hendry and Hyett, *The External Relations of the European Communities*, Oxford 1996.

36. The Member States cited as the basis for giving authority to the Community on the negotiation of the FCCC as Article 130s(1) and Article 228(3).

37. *Van Duyn v Home Office*, Case 41/74 [19/4] ECR.

38. *Francovich and Others v Italy* Case C-6, C-9/90.

39. The EU has agreed to implement the Kyoto Protocol according to differentiated targets under Article 4, which aggregately equal 8 per cent. To achieve their respective targets they will employ policy instruments such as (1) positive and negative economic incentives; (2) changes in subsidies – phasing out subsidies on fossil-fuel-intensive energies, while encouraging subsidies on renewables; (3) negotiated agreements between public authorities and specific industrialized sectors; these would offer in principle, maximum flexibility for industry to act in a cost-effective way; (4) technical options – new technologies, increased R&D; (5) socio-economic research – lifestyles, barriers to new technologies.

40. Article 30 was strictly interpreted in *Procureur de Roi v Dassonville* Case by the European Court stating the phrase "measures having equivalent effect" encompassing all trade rules enacted by Member States which are capable of

hindering, directly and indirectly, actually and potentially, intra-Community Trade" 8/74 [1974] ECR.

41. *Rewe-Zentrale* v *Bundesmonopolverwaltung fur Branntwein* Case 120/78 [1979] ECR.

42. *Commission* v *Denmark* Case 302/86 [1988] ECR.

43. Article 907 states that "A Party may, in pursuing its legitimate objectives, conduct an assessment of risk." This risk assessment of course must "avoid arbitrary or unjustifiable distinctions between similar goods and services."

44. See I.M. Sinclair, *The Vienna Convention on the Law of Treaties*, Manchester University Press, 1973; p 68.

6

Greenhouse-Gas Emissions Trading and the World Trading System[1]

ZHONG XIANG ZHANG

Introduction

On 11 December 1997 in Kyoto, Japan, 160 countries reached a historical agreement on limiting greenhouse-gas (GHG) emissions. In comparison with the United Nations Framework Convention on Climate Change (UNFCCC) at the Earth Summit in June 1992, which committed Annex I countries[2] only to "aim" to stabilize emissions of carbon dioxide (CO_2) and other GHGs at their 1990 levels by 2000, the so-called Kyoto Protocol sets legally binding emissions targets and timetables for these countries. Together, Annex I countries must reduce their emissions of six GHGs by at least 5 per cent below 1990 levels over the commitment period 2008–2012, with the European Union (EU), United States, and Japan required to reduce their emissions of such gases by 8, 7, and 6 per cent, respectively (UNFCCC 1997). Although proposals had been made for differentiation of allowed emissions on the basis of indicators such as population, gross domestic product (GDP), or carbon intensity of the economy, the differentiated targets agreed upon at Kyoto were purely political. The Protocol will become effective once it is ratified by at least 55 Parties whose CO_2 emissions represent at least 55 per cent of the total from Annex I Parties in the year 1990.[3] Pushed by the United States, the Kyoto Protocol also accepts the concept of emissions trading in principle, under which one Annex I country will be allowed to purchase the rights to emit GHGs from other Annex I countries that are able to cut GHG emissions below their assigned amounts (i.e. their targets); however, the Kyoto Protocol leaves the design of the market and its rule entirely to subsequent conferences. Structured effectively, the market-based emissions-trading approach, pioneered in the US SO_2 Allowance Trading System (McLean 1997), can provide an economic incentive to cut GHG emissions while also allowing flexibility for taking cost-effective actions. It is generally acknowledged that the inclusion of emissions trading in the Protocol is in line with the underlying principles in Article 3.3 of the UNFCCC, which states "policies and measures to deal with climate change should be cost-effective so as to ensure global benefits at the lowest possible cost," and reflects an important decision to address climate-change issues through flexible market mechanisms.

As the successor to the General Agreement on Tariffs and Trade (GATT), the World Trade Organization (WTO) was created in 1994 upon the completion of the Uruguay Round of multilateral trade negotiations (WTO 1995). Its Committee on Trade and Environment (CTE) has been established to coordinate the policies in the field of trade and environment. The Committee's work programme includes a review of "the relationship between the provisions of the multilateral trading system and trade measures for environmental purposes, including those pursuant to multilateral environmental agreements" (WTO 1995: 470). Although emissions trading has been identified for future discussion in the Committee, it has not thus far been examined. It remains unknown whether WTO provisions would cover an emissions-trading scheme, in part because no interpretation exists on whether a legal definition of emissions trading would be interpreted as either trade in a good or trade in a service (Vaughan 1997). No doubt, the inclusion of emissions trading in the Kyoto Protocol will catalyse the international consciousness for the potential of emissions trading. Clearly, this will provide a stimulus to addressing the market-based instrument in the Committee.

This chapter examines the relationship between GHG-emissions trading and the world trading system.[4] The next main section explains why emissions trading is considered to be the most promising way to control GHG emissions, and the three subsequent main sections discuss, respectively, the basic requirements for setting up a successful emissions-trading scheme, some trade-related aspects of emissions trading, and joint implementation (JI) with developing countries. The chapter ends with some conclusions.

Why emissions trading?

GHGs are uniformly mixed pollutants, i.e. one ton of a GHG emitted anywhere on earth has the same effect as one ton emitted somewhere else on earth. Translated into the language of abatement strategies, this means that it does not matter where reductions in GHG emissions take place; what matters is whether we are able to reduce the emissions effectively on a global scale. Given the fact that the costs of abating GHG emissions differ significantly among countries (see, for example, IPCC 1996) and that, unlike sulphur dioxide (SO_2) emissions, there are no local "hot spots" for GHG emissions,[5] GHG-emissions trading seems to enjoy an even better prospect for trading than SO_2. This large potential of efficiency gains, backed up with the widely regarded successful O_2 Allowance Trading System in the United States,[6] conveys the message that emissions trading is a very attractive abatement option. How, then, does emissions trading compare with carbon taxes, another economic instrument that is widely believed to be able to achieve the same emissions target at lower costs than the conventional command-and-control regulations?

In economic theory, the two instruments can achieve identical results given both perfectly competitive markets and certainty (Weitzman 1974; Pezzey 1992). In practice, however, there could be major differences between these two instruments.

Probably the most valid arguments in favour of tradeable permits rather than taxes so far are as follows.

First, tradeable GHG-emissions permits, unlike carbon taxes, are a form of rationing and the great advantage is that, in this way, one can be sure of achieving the target agreed.[7] This feature seems to be appealing more than ever because Annex I parties to the Kyoto Protocol are obligated to comply with their legally binding emissions targets. This also makes the "ecological transparency" argument against emissions trading no longer valid.[8] By contrast, the actual achievements in reductions of CO_2 emissions by a proposed carbon tax remain uncertain because of imperfect knowledge of the price elasticities of demand and supply for fossil fuels, especially for the large price increases caused by carbon taxes for major emissions cutbacks (Cline 1992). This implies that setting the initial tax will be a hit-and-miss affair, and could thus induce hostile reactions from countries, industries, and consumers although it is not clear how serious an objection this is (Pearce 1991). Moreover, in the context of global warming, the delays in adjusting the insufficient carbon tax to the desired level will imply more CO_2 emissions emitted into the atmosphere than would otherwise have occurred, thus leading to additional committed warming.

Another complication of the carbon tax is the initial difference in energy prices. As a consequence of existing distortions by price regulations, taxation, national monopolies, barriers to trade, and so on, there are initially great differences in energy prices, both between fuels and across countries (Hoeller and Coppel 1992). If CO_2 emissions are then to be reduced by similar amounts in two countries, ceteris paribus, lower taxes are required for the country with low prices before the tax imposition than for the country with the higher pre-tax prices. Thus, an eventual cost-efficient regime of international carbon tax would presumably need to remove existing distortions in international energy markets — otherwise, countries with the lower pre-tax prices would enjoy free-rider benefits.

Third, and most importantly, emissions trading offers a built-in feature of resource transfers by emission sources to developing countries. Such transfers are crucial to getting developing countries engaged in controlling GHG emissions (Wiener 1997). Of course, it is not impossible to include transfers in an international scheme of carbon taxes, but the trouble with it is that we need an international agency to collect carbon taxes. Given the fact that the United Nations still have difficulty in collecting their membership fees and that no other institution is of higher international jurisdiction than the United Nations, this will leave some doubt about its capacity to collect international carbon taxes. Even if such an agency manages to obtain the proceeds and uses them as transfers, there are still serious doubts as to whether it can efficiently manage such transfers.

Fourth, emissions trading is more attractive to firms than are carbon taxes, because the latter scheme extracts revenues from firms without offering any compensation, not to mention the political difficulties of introducing such taxes in countries such as the United States. So, even if a firm has to buy permits now to cover all of its emissions, it still can acquire the value of those additional permits by selling them in the future if its actual emissions are lower than the allowed limit. This in turn creates an incentive for firms to comply with their "caps".

Basic requirements for setting up emissions trading

Even if international emissions trading is considered to be the most promising way to control GHG emissions (IPCC 1996, UNCTAD 1995), then what are the basic requirements for setting up a successful scheme?

First, there should be legally binding national emissions targets and timetables for reducing GHG emissions for countries that would wish to participate in an international emissions-trading scheme. Those countries should be committed to the binding obligations.

Second, there should exist a reliable national registration of individual emissions sources that will participate in an emissions-trading scheme. Without such an inventory of sources and their present emission levels, it would be impossible to design schemes for permit allocation by way of grandfathering permits (see ch. 7, p. 172). Moreover, since countries (not sources) sign the Kyoto Protocol and it is the responsibility of the governments to ensure that their countries are in compliance with the national emissions limits, inter-source trading would have to be accounted for at the national level. This also underlines the need for such an inventory.

Third, there should be in place some system of monitoring and reporting emissions. This is to ensure (among other purposes) that, if banking of permits were allowed, emissions permits to be sold by any sources would at least represent part of their real emissions reductions from the allowed emissions levels. This, combined with the above requirement for good emissions inventories, would provide certainty about the validity of permits traded, thus increasing confidence and incentives for inter-source trading.

Fourth, there should be effective enforcement aimed to detect those in non-compliance and to apply sanctions. Although enforcement is necessary for effective application of other instruments as well (e.g. charges and regulations), this requirement is of particular importance to emissions trading because, under an emissions-trading scheme, firms that operate in a country without adequate enforcement can emit without handing over their permits. Consequently, they can sell their permits to firms in other countries, thus leading to exceeded emissions in the sellers' country. By contrast, when charges or regulations are used, firms that defraud cannot sell permits to sources in other countries. Clearly, if enforcement were not adequate, it would be easy for a firm to sell permits or to refrain from buying permits without taking adequate measures to reduce its emissions. Consequently, an emissions-trading scheme would lead to higher overall pollution levels compared with instruments such as charges or regulations. Besides, enforcement at the international level often proves to be more difficult and less likely to be effective than at the national level because of the absence of an institution with the international jurisdiction to enforce policy. This further underlines the importance of national legal mechanisms for enforcement.

Annex I countries would so far qualify for engaging in emissions trading according to the first condition, but not all Annex I countries would do so if the other three conditions need to be fulfilled. Strictly speaking, this suggests that an emissions-trading scheme might initially start with only a handful of Annex I countries, although it does not preclude its subsequent expansion to include other qualified countries according to the rules of procedure agreed before trading begins. Such an expansion would bring more emission sources into an international emissions-trading scheme; it would reduce the leakage effects that occur when reduced GHG emissions in countries with caps are counteracted by increased emissions elsewhere in other countries without caps; it would lower the costs of abating emissions; and it would increase the scope for efficiency gains.

According to Article 17 (formerly numbered Article 16 *bis*) of the Kyoto Protocol, the Parties with targets included in Annex B, which lists 38 countries and the European Community, may participate in emissions trading for the purpose of fulfilling their commitments under Article 3 of this Protocol (UNFCCC 1997).[9] While the Article has a loose stance on the qualifying requirement as we propose, it indicates that emissions trading is limited to Annex B countries. Even with the scope of participation, given great differences in environmental monitoring and enforcement infrastructures among Annex B countries, however, it will probably take years to agree on the commonly accepted rules and guidelines "for verification, reporting and accountability for emissions trading" pursuant to the Kyoto Protocol. Even if they could have been worked out after lengthy negotiations, the scope of participation is very narrow, even in comparison with the WTO Members, who represent only part of the world community.[10] Because non-Annex I countries have not committed themselves to any targets, pressure has been placed on Annex I countries to take trade measures to protect their domestic industries against competition from those countries that do not adopt GHG-emissions limits. If so, this will have far-reaching implications for the international trading system. This brings us to the next issue.

Some trade-related aspects of emissions trading

The issue of compatibility of using trade measures against foreign environmental practices with the GATT was not given much attention until the findings of two GATT disputes panels on trade measures unilaterally taken by the United States in the US–Mexico Tuna Dolphin disputes were made public (Hudec, 1996). Both panel reports (GATT 1991, 1994), which are commonly referred to as Tuna Dolphin I and Tuna Dolphin II, found the US restrictions on tuna imports from Mexico, which did not meet the US standards on dolphin-safe fishing practices, in violation of GATT. The panel in Tuna Dolphin I ruled that all trade restrictions directed against environmental harms have to be territorial. Moreover, such restrictions cannot be justified under Article III if they relate to the process of production rather than to the product itself. The panel explained that, if governments could regulate imports according to the production process by which they were made, the rules of the GATT's Article III would allow governments to require imports to conform to any type of social regulation currently imposed on the production process of domestic producers. It would allow governments to condition market access on compliance with domestic laws governing working conditions. The panel in Tuna Dolphin II concluded that Article XX does not preclude governments from pursuing environmental concerns outside their national territory, but such extra-jurisdictional application of domestic laws would be permitted only if aimed primarily at having a conservation or protection effect. The second panel ruled that the US restrictions were in violation of GATT because they aimed to force other countries to change their own policies in order to comply with the US standards.

The preceding discussion promotes the concern about the compatibility of an international emissions-trading scheme with the GATT/ WTO. In what follows, I examine whether such an emissions-trading scheme has the potential to bring parties into conflict with the WTO provisions in dealing with the allocation of permits, non-compliance with emissions targets, emissions-trading system enlargement, and trade measures against non-Members of an emissions-trading club.

Allocation of permits

The Kyoto Protocol has set the caps on aggregate GHG emissions for Annex I countries. If trading among private parties is authorized, the next issue is how these governments allocate the assigned amounts within their countries. The allocation process itself represents the establishment and distribution of private property rights over emissions, and itself lies outside the mandate of the WTO (Vaughan 1997).

The allocation of permits depends on the structure of national emissions-trading systems. Such systems could be modelled as either *"upstream,"* or *"downstream,"* or *"hybrid"* systems. An upstream trading system would target fossil-fuel producers and importers as regulated entities, so would reduce the number of allowance holders to oil refineries and importers, natural gas pipelines, natural gas processing plants, coal mines, and coal-processing plants (Hargrave 1998). For example, if such a system were to be implemented in the United States, the total number of allowance holders would be restricted to about 1,900. Even with such a relatively small number of regulated sources, market power would not be an issue. In the above upstream system for the United States, the largest firm has only a 5.6 per cent market allowance share. Firms, with each having less than 1 per cent share, would hold the lion's share of allowances (Cramton and Kerr 1998). Implemented effectively, an upstream system would capture virtually all fossil-fuel use and carbon emissions in a national economy. Firms would raise fuel prices to offset the additional cost. In an upstream system the number of firms that have to be monitored for compliance is relatively small and thus is easier to administer. Moreover, existing institutions for levying excises on fossil fuels, which exist in most industrialized countries, can be used to enforce the scheme (Zhang and Nentjes 1998). However, one of the drawbacks of an upstream system is that it provides no incentive for energy end-users to develop disposal technologies, the aspect that is deemed critical in seeking long-term solutions to solving climate-change problems.

In contrast, a downstream trading system would be applied at the point of emissions. As such, a large number of diverse energy users are included. This would offer greater competition and stimulate more robust trading, thus leading to increased innovation. However, such a system would be more difficult to administer, especially concerning emissions from the transportation sector and other small sources. On the other hand, it would avoid the possibility that some energy users would not respond to the price signal, which might occur in an upstream system because of market imperfections such as high transaction costs, high discount rates, and imperfect information, although the extent of their responsiveness depends on the degree of competition and on whether price increases are actually passed on to the consumers. To keep a downstream trading system at a manageable level, regulated sources could be limited to utilities and large industrial sources. Governments could then address un-capped sources through other regulatory means such as carbon taxes. In doing so, however, the governments need to establish additional programmes. This would be an administrative burden and, in some countries, there would be great political difficulties involved in introducing carbon taxes. Moreover, the actual achievements in reductions of CO_2 emissions by a proposed carbon tax remain uncertain (as previously mentioned) because of imperfect knowledge of the price elasticities of demand and supply for fossil fuels. This would put the governments at risk of non-compliance with the emissions commitments.

Alternatively, national trading systems could be modelled as hybrid systems (Zhang and Nentjes 1998). A hybrid system is similar to a downstream trading system in the sense that regulated sources at the levels of energy users are also limited to utilities and large industrial sources. On the other hand, like an upstream trading system, a hybrid system would require fuel distributors to hold allowances for small fuel users and to pass on their permit costs in a mark-up on the fuel price. As such, small fuel users are exempted from the necessity (and transaction costs) of holding allowances. Yet the rise in fuel price will motivate them to reduce fuel consumption or to switch from fuels with a high carbon content, such as coal, to fuels with a low carbon content, such as natural gas.

No matter how national trading systems are modelled, importers and domestic producers of fossil fuels should be treated equally in obtaining emissions allowances under the "like product" provisions in the WTO. Moreover, regardless of whether individual countries choose to empower private trading, the ultimate responsibility for fulfilling the Kyoto commitments would remain with the national government as a Party to the Protocol.

Given the great concern about international competitiveness, however, the allocation of permits does have the potential to bring Parties into conflict with the WTO provisions. Some fear, for example, that governments could allocate the permits in such a manner that domestic firms would be favoured over foreign rivals; this would violate the WTO principle of non-discrimination. The allocation of permits could also be designed in such a manner that certain sectors would have an advantage over others and further enhance their existing imperfect market competition. This makes the unequal treatment explicit, which can be much more easily hidden from the general public if the conventional command-and-control regulations are used. This, in turn, would have a price-distortion effect similar to that of a subsidy, and would be in conflict with the WTO rules that prohibit the use of export subsidies for such a purpose. All this clearly indicates that the manner in which countries allocate their assigned amounts should be compatible with these WTO principles and should not constitute a means of arbitrary or unjustifiable discrimination or a disguised restriction on international trade.

However, it should be pointed out that although grandfathering is thought of as giving implicit subsidies to some sectors, grandfathering is less trade-distorted than the exemptions from carbon taxes. To understand their difference, it is important to bear in mind that grandfathering itself also implies an opportunity cost for firms receiving permits: what matters here is not how you get your permits, but what you can sell them for – that is what determines opportunity cost (Zhang and Nentjes 1998). Thus, relative prices of products will not be distorted to any great extent and switching of demands towards products of those firms whose permits are awarded gratis (the so-called substitution effect) will not be induced by grandfathering. In this way, grandfathering differs from the exemptions from carbon taxes. In the latter case, substitution effects exist. For example, the Commission of the European Communities (CEC) proposal for a mixed carbon and energy tax provides for exemptions for the six energy-intensive industries (i.e. iron and steel, non-ferrous metals, chemicals, cement, glass, and pulp and paper) from coverage of the CEC tax on grounds of competitiveness. This not only reduces the effectiveness of the CEC tax in achieving its objective of reducing CO_2 emissions but also causes those industries that are exempt from paying the CEC tax to improve their competitive position in relation to those industries that are not. There will therefore be some switching of demand towards the products of these energy-intensive industries, which is precisely the reaction that such a tax should avoid (Zhang 1997a).

With the great concern that a government that grandfathers permits to a domestic firm could give it a competitive advantage over a similar firm in another country where permits are not awarded gratis, in the opinion of some there is a need for the harmonization of allocation of permits. However, I think that individual governments should be left free to devise their own ways of allocating permits on the following grounds.[11] First, I think this is not necessarily the case, because even if a firm obtains emissions permits by auction, its government still can, if necessary, protect its international competitiveness by means of recycling the revenues raised through auctioned permits to lower other pre-existing distortionary taxes, such as taxes on labour and capital.

Second, although auctioning at least part of the assigned amounts to subnational legal entities alleviates to some extent the concern about international competitiveness, any attempts to produce an agreement on a common rate are likely to run into concerns about national sovereignty and thus would encounter significant political difficulties. Take the above CEC proposal for a carbon—energy tax as an example. National sovereignty considerations to some extent explain why the CEC proposal for a carbon–energy tax failed to gain the unanimous support of its member states, partly because some member states opposed an increase in the fiscal competence of the Community and thus opposed the introduction at a European level of a new tax on grounds of fiscal sovereignty (Bill 1997).

Third, given great differences in national circumstances, setting a uniform rule of allocation will restrict the rights of individual governments to select the option that is best suited to their own national circumstances. Indeed, the failure of the above CEC carbon–energy tax is to some extent because some member states are loath to restrict themselves to the common CEC-specified policy-and-measure design to stabilize CO_2 emission and how to do it. It is conceivable that some countries whose economies are heavily distorted would decide to auction permits, and that the revenues generated through auctioned permits could then be used to reduce pre-existing distortionary taxes, thus generating overall efficiency gains. Parry *et al.* (1997), for example, show that the costs of reducing US carbon emissions by 10 per cent are four times more under a grandfathered carbon permits case than under an auctioned case. This disadvantage reflects the inability to make use of the revenue-recycling effect in the former case.

Fourth, and importantly, leaving individual governments the freedom to devise their own ways of allocating assigned amounts to sub-national entities would ensure that any individual government maintains its right to determine the domestic policies and measures that would be taken to meet its Kyoto obligations. For example, a government that wants to use taxes or regulations for domestic emissions control could retain the sole right to trade. Alternatively, a government could allocate its assigned amounts to private entities to trade.

Emissions-trading system enlargement

The Kyoto Protocol allows Russia to emit the same volume of GHGs as (the then) Russia did in 1990. Given the fact that CO_2 emissions in Russia declined over the past years after the collapse of the Soviet

Union in 1991 and are expected to continue to decline, that means that Russia should be left as the biggest seller of emissions permits among Annex I countries once emissions trading takes place. The United States has reached a conceptual agreement with Australia, Canada, Japan, New Zealand, Russia, and Ukraine to pursue an umbrella group to trade emissions permits (USDOS 1998). It is believed that the United States is counting on emissions trading with Russia to achieve half of its 7 per cent reduction target set in the Kyoto Protocol.[12] Although the United States insists on bringing non-Annex I countries into an emissions-trading scheme, which has widely been seen as creating a source of such permits for the United States to buy and therefore achieve its own agreed reductions through offshore compliance,[13] it might seem that the United States does not want the EU to breathe Russian "hot air"[14] because the addition of the EU to the group would raise the prices of the Russian emissions permits that the American firms would have to pay.[15] On the other hand, Russia would not welcome the addition of non-Annex I countries, such as China and India, to the group because these new entrants would raise the supply of overall permits on the market and depress the prices of those permits held by Russia. This is also one of the reasons for the developing countries' opposition to emissions trading because they feel that it leaves them out of the system at this stage, although for some legitimate reasons these countries do not want to join in an emissions-trading club at this moment. Although these are just political speculations, they underline the importance of establishing clear rules of procedure about admitting new entrants before emissions trading begins.[16]

There are two avenues to establish such rules of procedure. One is based on voting to admit new entrants. So far, any decisions made by the Conference of the Parties to the UNFCCC have been generally adopted by consensus. If admitting new entrants requires consensus by all current Annex B countries eligible for emissions trading, this confers on Russia a de facto power of veto. Thus, if the avenue to admit new entrants rests on voting, a three-quarters majority vote of the current Annex B countries present and voting at the meeting could be adopted to prevent exploitation of market power.

The second avenue rests on automatic phase-in once one prospective country meets predetermined criteria. In my view, the second avenue is superior to the first. Such criteria should include under what conditions, how, and when a new entrant could be incorporated into the emissions-trading scheme. Once such criteria are set, they should remain stable in the short run although this by no means precludes any adjustments that might be required in the future.

Similar reasons hold for expansion to include GHGs other than CO_2 and the uptake of GHG by sinks,[17] because a comprehensive coverage of both gases and options will induce more cost-effective abatement options. On the other hand, a workable emissions-trading scheme requires that emissions of whatever pollutant is to be included have to be measured with reasonable accuracy. This requirement implicitly precludes including all gases in the initial trading scheme. However, limiting trading to a subset of gases is not likely to be effective unless the Protocol is further amended to partition the assigned amounts into two categories – tradeable and non-tradeable gases – with separate goals being assigned for each (UNCTAD 1998). Without a separation of categories, there appears to be a lack of any legal basis for rejection of the legitimate claim from those countries that use the flexibility inherent in the equivalence process to substitute freely among the gases, because Article 5.3 of the Protocol has authorized that the global-warming potentials are used to translate non-CO_2 GHGs into carbon-equivalent units in determining each Annex I party's compliance with its assigned amounts.

No matter what kind of rules are established, they would, no doubt, have profound implications for the world trading system.

Non-compliance with the agreed emissions targets

The Kyoto Protocol itself does not contain stipulations on what actions, if any, should be taken in the event that a country were found to be in non-compliance. Without clear criteria to judge compliance, it is difficult to believe that many of the Annex I countries will be willing to ratify the Protocol. The United States had proposed penalizing a country that failed to meet its target by imposing ever-larger reduction obligations over a subsequent period (the so-called borrowing with a penalty); however, negotiators at Kyoto blocked the only compliance mechanism on the table because they fear that it would not bring any additional pressure to bear on a country that simply continues to disregard its commitments. It is then natural to consider the use of trade measures – usually in the form of a trade restriction – to enforce a country to comply with its commitment. In this case, caution should be taken because all WTO retaliation is limited to a "compensatory" amount – that is, an amount equivalent to the value of the trade obligations being nullified or impaired by the other Party. Its main significance is that it rejects a more aggressive approach towards sanctions – the approach under which a legal sanction must be large enough to produce the desired change of behaviour (Hudec 1996).

Trade measures against non-members of an emissions-trading club

Because non-Annex I countries have not committed themselves to any targets, Annex I countries have been pressed by their powerful lobbying groups to take trade measures to protect their domestic industries against competition from non-Annex I countries. What kind of trade measures could potentially be applied against non-members of an emissions-trading club in order to counter the trade effects of honouring their Kyoto commitments? One possibility might be that Annex I countries comply with their Kyoto commitments, but use border adjustment taxes based on embodied carbon content of goods imported from non-Annex I countries to keep non-Annex I countries' emissions at their baseline levels.[18] Another possibility is that Annex I countries abide by their Kyoto commitments, but set imports of energy-intensive goods from non-Annex I countries at their baseline levels or set exports of energy-intensive goods from non-Annex I countries at their baseline levels. The third possibility is that Annex I countries abide by their Kyoto commitments but provide subsidies up to the levels at which their exports of energy-intensive goods remain at their baseline levels. Although these trade measures appear to include only the component designed to reduce GHG-emissions leakage, they are, in principle, in conflict with the GATT/WTO principles of most-favoured nation and non-discrimination. Such taxes could fall foul of the "like product" provisions in the GATT's Article I and Article III, which are designed to prevent a country from discriminating against imports on the basis of their territorial origin (WTO 1995). There are formidable technical difficulties involved in identifying (and it may even be completely impossible) the appropriate carbon contents embodied in virtually all traded products unless non-Annex I exporting countries are willing to cooperate in certifying how the products are produced. In the absence of any information regarding the carbon content of the products from non-Annex I countries, importing Annex I countries may prescribe the tax rates based on their domestically predominant method of production for the imported products.[19] Such a practice will violate the GATT rules that do not allow trade measures to be taken on a basis of the differences in process and production methods (PPM), and appears to deprive non-Annex I countries of enjoying the very basis of comparative advantage in their production. Moreover, such tariffs would be likely to violate commitments made by the WTO contracting countries not to raise import taxes above "bound tariff" levels, i.e. maximum tariffs for goods listed in an annex to the GATT (WTO 1995). The WTO rules also prohibit the use of export subsidies to give certain sectors an advantage over others.

Are there any potential avenues within the WTO rules to accommodate Annex I countries on this score, should they decide to pursue the above offsetting trade measures? One avenue would be that Annex I countries could claim general exceptions under the GATT's Article XX, which states that:

> Subject to the requirement that such measures are not applied in a manner which would constitute a means of arbitrary or unjustifiable discrimination between countries where the same conditions prevail, or a disguised restriction on international trade, nothing in this Agreement shall be constructed to pre-

vent the adoption or enforcement by any contracting party of measures:

... (b) necessary to protect human, animal or plant life or health;

... (g) relating to the conservation of exhaustible natural resources if such measures are made effective in conjunction with restrictions on domestic production or consumption; ... (WTO 1995: 519).

Article XX itself sets out the exceptions that authorize governments to employ otherwise GATT-illegal measures when such measures are necessary to deal with certain enumerated social policy problems. Since Annex I countries participating in emissions trading are obligated to limit their GHG emissions, whereas non-Annex I countries are not bound by such commitments, the same conditions do not exist for Annex I countries and non-Annex I countries. Therefore, Annex I countries could argue that the discrimination in the trade restrictions is neither arbitrary nor unjustifiable, thus meeting the requirement in the preamble to Article XX.[20] Under Article 2.2 of the Agreement on Technical Barriers to Trade, technical regulations shall not be more trade restrictive than necessary to fulfil a "legitimate objective," which is defined as including the protection of human health or safety, animal or plant life or health, or the environment (WTO 1995); the offsetting trade measures could be based on a legitimate environmental objective and not merely on formal membership of an international agreement (Brack 1996). Thus, if any non-Annex I countries voluntarily assume binding emissions targets (a prerequisite for engaging in emissions trading, through amendment to the Annex B of the Kyoto Protocol),[21] they should be exempted from such trade restrictions. This is of particular importance to newly industrializing countries because they are the countries that are most likely to make such voluntary commitments among non-Annex I countries. This is not without precedent: for example, the Montreal Protocol[22] has included the provision that exempts non-Parties from trade measures if they are determined by the Parties to be in compliance with the phase-out schedules. Indeed, the United States has proposed at Kyoto to allow non-Annex I countries to adopt GHG controls voluntarily so that non-Annex I countries can also be brought into an emissions-trading club. However, the group of 77 and China[23] blocked the US proposal. The underlying reasons for their objections are given below. First, on ethical grounds, non-Annex I countries think that Annex I countries have caused the climate-change problem and should thus clean it up themselves before asking non-Annex I countries to take action. Second, non-Annex I countries insist that the US demand for developing countries' commitments goes against an earlier UN agreement (known as the Berlin Mandate) adopted at the first Conference of the Parties to the UNFCCC in Berlin in April 1995, which specifically indicated that "a protocol or another legal instrument" adopted at the third Conference of the Parties in Kyoto should "not introduce any new commitments" for non-Annex I countries. Third, there is the widespread fear that the opportunity to trade emissions permits might eventually lure others in the group, especially the Latin American nations, to be drawn into making commitments of their own. Then rich Annex I countries might use emissions trading as a means of buying their way out of responsibility for climate problems and at the same time postponing the radical changes in their own consumption patterns and passing the responsibility on to the poor, while GHG emissions limits grow subsequently more restrictive for the developing countries.

In addition, Annex I countries might argue that to support the operation of an emissions-trading scheme that is designed to protect health and conserve depletable fossil fuels, some kind of offsetting trade measures would be required and qualify for the exceptions under Article XX (b) and Article XX (g) because international emissions leakage would otherwise frustrate its intent (Babiker et al. 1997). Furthermore, although such measures would not be the least trade distorting, they are much less trade restrictive than the tariff suggested by Hoel (1996), which also includes the optimal trade tariff term.

Another avenue rests on Article 1.1 of the Agreement on Subsidies and Countervailing Measures, under which a subsidy is defined as including "government revenue that is otherwise due is foregone or not collected" (WTO 1995). Although a narrow interpretation of this clause would limit claims to cases in which taxes are levied but not collected, its broad interpretation would expose the absence of environmental taxes to charges of unfair subsidization (Esty 1994). Annex I countries could argue, therefore, that the absence of emissions targets for non-Annex I countries would be equivalent to giving an implicit unfair export subsidy biased towards their energy-intensive sectors (the so-called ecological dumping), because the costs of environmental degradation are not part of the prices of those exported products.

Although Annex I countries could justify their offsetting trade measures according to Article XX and the definition of lax environmental regulation as a countervailable subsidy, non-Annex I countries of the WTO would, no doubt, resist such interpretations. As environmental issue was simply not a public issue in 1947 when GATT was signed, exploring the environmental exceptions to the general free-trade requirements in GATT depends as much on interpretation as on the actual clauses (Charnovitz 1991). Given the fact that a three-quarters vote of the entire membership is required for the membership to adopt legal interpretation of any WTO agreement (WTO 1995), the above interpretations might stand little chance of being accepted by non-Annex I countries that form the majority of the WTO Members.

In addition, lessons from the Montreal Protocol may be instructive. The Protocol prohibits trade with non-Parties in ozone-depleting substances (ODS) themselves, products containing ODS, and possibly products made using (but not containing) ODS. The trade restrictions were used together with financial assistance (i.e. Multilateral Fund in this case) and technology transfer as a means to coerce or force countries to become Parties. Although the Protocol has succeeded in securing universal participation by means of the "carrot and stick" approach as the signatories to it make up more than 95 per cent of current world consumption and production of ODS, the fact remains that restrictions are discriminatory. Although the restrictions have not been contested by the WTO Members, the WTO Secretariat has voiced its opposition to such uses of trade restrictions, and its CTE has opted not to welcome their replication in an emissions-trading scheme (Barrett 1994; Vaughan 1997), because such measures appear to violate the GATT/WTO principles of most-favoured nation, national treatment, and non-discrimination. In the Montreal Protocol, these discriminatory restrictions are not that important (given the scope of its membership, which is wider than that of the WTO itself), since most of the potential for trade conflict arises with non-Parties to the Protocol. However, if such restrictions were used in climate problems, the economic implications could be substantial because an emissions-trading club is only a small subset of the WTO Members – at least at its initial stage. Moreover, there may be some legitimate reasons[24] why many non-Annex I countries, if not all, might want to remain outside an emissions-trading club unless side payments are offered to these countries so that they are not made worse off as Members than they would be as non-Members. Thus, it seems unfair to discriminate against them on merely this basis. Is there, then, any way out? This leads to another major subject.

Joint implementation with developing countries

Countries may differ with respect to assimilative capacities and to tastes and preferences for environmental quality. Thus, the harmonization of environmental policy would not be always necessary from an environmental point of view, and may lead to sub-optimal use of the environment from an economics point of view. On the other hand, from the industrialized countries' perspective, the lack of developing countries' involvement in combating climate change aggravates their short-term concerns about international competitiveness. Non-participation by developing countries increases emissions leakage that could arise in the short term, as emissions controls lower world fossil-fuel prices and, in the long term, as industries relocate to developing countries to avoid emissions controls at home. In addition, it raises the spectre of developing countries becoming "locked in" to more fossil fuel-intensive economy and eliminates the Annex I

countries' opportunity to obtain low-cost abatement options. Testi-
fying on 4 March 1998 before the House of Commerce Subcommittee on Energy and Power about the domestic economic implications
of the Kyoto Protocol, Dr Janet Yellen (Yellen 1998), Chair of the
White House's Council of Economic Advisers, stated that when
there is no emissions trading at all, the cost of complying with the
Kyoto target for the United States would run to US\$125 per ton of
carbon. With emissions trading only among Annex I countries, the
cost would drop to \$30–50/ton. With fully worldwide emissions
trading, the cost would further drop to \$14–23 per ton. This clearly
explains why the United States puts heavy emphasis on the involvement of developing countries. Indeed, recent Indonesian bush fires
choking South-East Asia served as a graphic reminder that developing countries have an important part to play in protecting the environment against global warming.

For some time to come, however, many developing countries
would not be qualified to participate in an international emissions-
trading scheme. This promotes the concern: how can we encourage
their participation in combating global climate change, given the
fact that there are a great deal of low-cost abatement options there?
One widely recognized option to bring the developing countries on
board is by means of JI.[25] Indeed, many countries in the Organization for Economic Co-operation and Development (OECD) are keen
to see JI as a key part of the Kyoto Protocol, even although it is not
without conceptual and operational problems – such as the form of
JI, criteria for JI, the establishment of baselines against which the
effects of JI projects can be measured, and the verification of emissions reductions of JI projects (Zhang 1997a, b). In brief, JI means
that the investor in one country invests in emissions-abatement
projects in another (host) country where the costs of abating GHG
emissions are lower than those involved when trying to achieve an
equivalent degree of abatement within the home country and is
credited, in whole or in part, for emissions abatements in its own
GHG accounts. By shifting the burden of carrying out abatement in
non-Annex I countries, JI thus offers the potential for lowering the
global costs of abating GHG emissions and succeeds in reducing

GHG-emissions leakage without discriminating against such countries (Barrett 1994). In the WTO jargon, JI offers a positive incentive for countries to participate in an international agreement:

> When cooperation is not voluntarily forthcoming, positive incentives are the best way to achieve sustained inter-governmental cooperation. Positive incentives can include offers of financial assistance and transfers of environmentally friendly technology directly related to the problem at hand, as well as more broadly based offers, for example, to increase foreign aid, to lessen debt problems and to make non-discriminatory reductions in trade barriers. (GATT 1992)

However, bringing the developing countries on board and integrating JI credit trading into an international GHG-emissions scheme promotes another concern about the credibility of the scheme. How can such an international scheme incorporate credits from JI projects and at the same time ensure that confidence in the scheme is not compromised? One option would restrict the amount of JI credits that could be bought by Annex I countries for compliance from non-Annex I countries. Another option, which is superior to the first option, would be to discount the credits awarded to JI projects. Such reduced crediting could provide an "environmental bonus" and, at the margin, allow for the uncertainty about reported emission reductions of JI projects. Moreover, I advocate a predetermined discount factor, a view shared by the Center for Clear Air Policy (CCAP 1997). In order to reflect the characteristics of a JI project and the differing quality of GHG monitoring and reporting infrastructures across countries, such a discount factor should differ according to both type of project and country and should be accordingly adjusted over time for those countries in order to reflect the improvement in their monitoring and reporting infrastructures. I think that a predetermined discounting approach is superior to a market-driven discounting approach, because the former would protect against the introduction of false credits into an emissions-trading scheme and provide non-Annex I countries with financial incentives to opt for binding commitments and develop their stringent monitoring and reporting infrastructures. In addition, only verified and certified JI credits would become part of the emissions-trading scheme. Once certified, these credits could be treated as equivalent in quality to all other permits.

It should be pointed out that the group of 77 and China have not proved very receptive to the concept of JI, for some legitimate reasons. It is also unclear if the US Congress will support such a mechanism, although for reasons very different to those used for the group of 77 and China. Given the fact that JI, by definition, will not shift the burden of paying for abating GHG emissions into non-Annex I countries, which could result in a large outflow of investment capital from the United States to non-Annex I countries, some influential congressmen in the United States have already begun to regard JI as foreign aid.[26]

Conclusions

The Kyoto Protocol, despite its apparent flaws in its current form, is the first international environmental agreement that sets legally binding GHG-emissions targets and timetables for Annex I countries. Its Article 17 authorizes emissions trading between Annex I countries. If properly designed, emissions trading can effectively reduce these countries' abatement costs while assisting them to achieve their Kyoto obligations.

This chapter has examined the compatibility of an international emissions-trading scheme with the GATT/WTO. It has been found that, in dealing with the allocation of permits, with non-compliance with emissions targets, and with emissions trading-system enlargement, emissions trading has the potential to bring Parties into conflict with the WTO provisions. WTO will also have to resolve the very difficult question of what to do about Annex I countries of the WTO, should they decide to pursue the offsetting trade measures against non-Annex I countries of the WTO, who for some legitimate reasons have decided to remain outside an emissions-trading club. In this regard, JI may offer the way out because it succeeds in reducing GHG-emissions leakage without discriminating against such countries. However, the prospect for JI depends on how JI is implemented and on whether mutual mistrust between Annex I and non-Annex I countries can be removed. In any case, breakthroughs in low-cost energy-efficient technologies and the ways to transfer such technologies play a key role in acceptably drawing developing countries into the battle against global climate change. The ozone experience has shown that, when low-cost substitution technologies start to become available and when their transfers to developing countries take place on fair and most favourable conditions, there is little difficulty in persuading developing countries to join. This underlines the importance for governments to enhance energy R&D and for the WTO Committee on Trade and Environment to explore the possibility of envisioning a more flexible patenting and intellectual property rights scheme that allows developing countries to acquire such technologies on preferential terms under the Agreement on Trade-Related Aspects of Intellectual Property Rights.

It should be pointed out that, although GHGs offer an even more attractive case for application of emissions trading than many local pollutants already well handled with emissions trading, the US SO_2 Allowance Trading System cannot merely be transplanted to the international terrain where legal and institutional ingredients differ substantially from those in the United States. It will probably take years, if not decades, to set up such an international scheme. This raises the political question about the credibility of achieving Kyoto commitments and, at the same time, promotes the necessity of investigating effective national policies that can influence the behaviour of firms and consumers and establish the credibility of long-term goals. As such, interim measures before the beginning of the first commitment period in 2008 warrant special attention. They include national emissions-trading schemes with looser controls than are required by the Kyoto Protocol, crediting early emissions reductions below internationally accepted national baselines prior to 2008 within the jurisdiction of the advanced OECD countries, tax incentives to promote energy-efficient technologies, signals of carbon taxes to be levied at a specific future date, and government's role as a larger buyer to create stronger demand for energy-efficient technologies. Indeed, interim measures are necessary because Article 3.2 of the Kyoto Protocol requires Annex I countries to "have made demonstrable progress" in achieving their commitments by 2005.

Notes

1. This material was presented at the International Workshop on Market-based Instruments and International Trade, organized by the European Union Research Network on Market-based Instruments for Sustainable Development, Amsterdam, 19–20 March 1998. The author would like to thank the Netherlands Organization for Scientific Research for financial support, and Catrinus Jepma, Andries Nentjes, and Tom Tietenberg as well as the participants in the above Workshop for useful discussions and comments on an earlier version of the article. The usual caveat applies. This chapter has appeared as a paper in *Journal of World Trade* 32(5): 219–239, 1998.
2. Annex I countries refer to the OECD countries and countries with economies in transition. These countries have committed themselves to legally binding GHG-emissions targets.
3. Although the 55 per cent ratification threshold is lower than 75 per cent of the total Annex I emissions in 1990 proposed in earlier negotiation drafts of this chapter, it seems to be high. This threshold confers on the US a de facto power of veto, since the US accounted for nearly 40 per cent of the total Annex I emissions in 1990. Besides the US insistence on the high threshold, the EU was partly responsible for this because it was unwilling to assume any obligations without the US signing on, just as its previous proposal for a carbon–energy tax was subject to whether the US took similar actions.
4. The design of a workable emissions-trading scheme is the very important issue because it is essential to the success of emissions trading. This has been the focus of the UNCTAD Greenhouse Gas Emissions Trading Project (UNCTAD, 1998), the Annex I Expert Group on the UNFCCC, Zhang (1998), and Zhang and Nentjes (1998).
5. The "hot spots" here refer to those localized areas of high pollution concentration. This has been a major concern in designing a sulphur-emissions-trading scheme because of the spatial nature of that pollution.
6. As a reflection of its success, the System has cut the compliance costs to less than US$100 per ton of SO_2 removed (from early estimates of the expected costs ranging from US$180 to US$981/ton during Phase I and from US$374 to US$981/ton during Phase II) (McLean 1997).
7. The Kyoto Protocol adopts the "commitment period" of 5 years that was originally proposed by the US as the "budget period." The multi-year compliance is designed to avert the danger that a single-year target may pose due to fluctuations in economic performance or certain extreme weather conditions, and to provide countries with additional flexibility in meeting their targets. While enjoying such advantages, the multi-year compliance might undermine

the actual scope of a country's achievement in meeting its Kyoto obligations if monitoring, reporting, and enforcement would not be adequate. This underlines the importance of setting up a very strict institutional framework to ensure stringent monitoring, frequent reporting, and vigorous enforcement. The same holds for banking and borrowing of permits, which are another two ways to increase intertemporal flexibility and lower the cost of abating GHG emissions.

8. What I mean by the "ecological transparency" argument is that if there were no Kyoto Protocol, some governments would not be keen to adopt emissions trading because the quantity-based instrument would provide the public and their political opponents with a very clear reference to judge their performance.

9. In addition to Article 17, on the insistence of the EU, the Kyoto Protocol incorporates the "bubble" concept into the final text (Article 4). The "bubble" approach is often termed as "trading without rules" because it sets few restrictions on trading between parties. This makes it a potentially attractive instrument. Given great differences in environmental monitoring and enforcement infrastructures among Annex I countries, if it turns out to be too difficult to agree on the commonly accepted rules and guidelines, the "bubble" approach at least opens the possibility of trading emissions permits within the voluntarily formed group. However, the approach presents some drawbacks. First, it requires setting of a cap on overall emissions for the group as a whole and working out of a specific cap for each member country within the group in an agreement, the terms of which must be notified to the UNFCCC Secretariat at the time of ratification of the Protocol. This has not proved easy for the EU to arrange before Kyoto. The EU still has difficulty in redistributing the joint commitments because the Kyoto Protocol incorporates a basket of six GHGs, rather than the EU's originally proposed three gases before Kyoto, and the uptake of GHGs "by sinks resulting from direct human-induced land-use change and forestry activities," at first "limited to afforestation, reforestation and deforestation since 1990" (Article 3.3). Second, it narrows the scope of efficiency gains in comparison with inter-source trading, because it restricts the location where firms or countries comply with their caps and because it is likely to have frightening transaction costs. Third, in the case of the current EU bubble, because the European Community (EC) itself as a party to the Protocol, in addition to its member states, has the legitimate responsibility for reporting on the performance of the EU as a whole and ensuring that its declared targets as a whole under the notified agreement are met, the potential advantages of offering double coverage of reporting obligations and double assurance for abatement obligations could be hindered by the need to have complete and early information from individual member states (OECD 1998). In the event that the EC as a whole would fail to meet its own targets and if a non-compliance procedure would be established, the EC, together with those individual member states that have not achieved their own targets set out in the agreement, would thus be faced with sanctions under Article 4.6. In this case, who bears the responsibility of the EC itself? As such, some clarification for the clear division of responsibility in the terms of that agreement would be needed in the case where a regional economic integration organization itself was a party to the Protocol. Fourth, because Article 4 is framed in general terms and because no mandate to

negotiate further rules has been given to the Conference of the Parties to the UNFCCC, it might create potential loopholes in meeting the Kyoto obligations.

10. Currently, the WTO has 132 members. More than 30 others are negotiating the accessions.

11. See Zhang and Nentjes (1998) for other reasons that are not given here.

12. "Emissions Trading Discussions to Exclude EU", *Japan Times*, 25 February 1998.

13. See pp. 139–142 for a further discussion.

14. When emissions trading was allowed, a country whose legally binding GHG-emissions limits set by the Kyoto Protocol exceeded its actual or anticipated emissions requirements would be able to trade these excess emissions, thus creating the "hot air" that would otherwise have not occurred. The "hot air" problem is particularly acute in Russia, whose emissions are not expected to rise to its 1990 level until 2008. The "hot air" forms a "reservoir" from which some advanced Western countries, if not all, can simply buy emissions permits to make up any shortfall, instead of taking any serious domestic action. This is one of the reasons why some countries have called for imposing a percentage limitation on the use of emissions trading. Indeed, such limitation was included in earlier negotiation drafts of the article about emissions trading, but on the insistence of the US does not appear in the final Protocol. The only leftover from this debate is the provision that "such trading shall be supplemental to domestic actions." If a country like the United States would count on emissions trading with Russia to achieve half of its reduction target set in the Kyoto Protocol, emissions trading would then not be regarded as a "supplemental" means according to the common sense. As such, some clarification for interpreting the terms is needed. Besides, it should be pointed out that although emission trading makes the "hot air" problem explicit, the problem is related to targets setting, not to emissions trading *per se*. Even if such a flaw has now been built into the Kyoto Protocol, however, we have to deal with it in designing an effective emissions-trading scheme in order to minimize its damage. Instead of imposing a percentage limitation on the use of emissions trading, I propose a transaction tax on trades involving "taxable" allowances, with the tax rate to be set by the Conference of the Parties. Such a tax rate could be imposed only on the buyer and could differ to reflect the direction of emissions-trading flows, with a uniform zero or low rate for transactions within the advanced OECD countries themselves but a uniform high rate for transactions between them and countries with economies in transition. Setting a uniform low and uniform high rate is to prevent countries from attracting more trade by setting an even lower transaction tax rate of their own. An alternative strategy would allow emissions reductions below internationally accepted national baselines for the pre-2008 period within the jurisdiction of the advanced OECD countries prior to the beginning of the first commitment period to be credited for later use. This would also reduce their demand for the "hot air" during the commitment period.

15. That the EU was not invited to participate in the meeting of the above umbrella group, on 5–6 March 1998, in Washington, DC, which aimed to

discuss the specific ways to implement emissions trading, has triggered the speculation.

16. The interpretation that the relevant rules and guidelines should be established first before emissions trading begins is in line with Article 17 of the Kyoto Protocol, which puts the text of establishing the rules prior to who are eligible for emissions trading. This clearly indicates that those claims that emissions trading can start immediately are in violation of Article 17.

17. Sinks here refer to those vehicles for absorbing anthropogenic GHG emissions. Oceans, soils, and forests all offer some potential to serve as sinks for net carbon sequestration. For practical reasons, however, the Kyoto Protocol authorizes the uptake of GHG only "by sinks resulting from direct human-induced land-use change and forestry activities," at first "limited to afforestation, reforestation and deforestation since 1990."

18. The baseline levels in this Section refer to those emissions, imports, or exports when either Annex I or non-Annex I countries have not adopted emissions targets. As discussed in Zhang (1997a, b), establishing such future national baselines is not a simple matter.

19. This practice is by no means without foundation. For example, the US Secretary of the Treasury has adopted the approach in the tax on imported toxic chemicals (Poterba and Rotemberg 1995).

20. Brack (1996) has used this argument to justify the discriminatory trade measures applied against non-Parties to the Montreal Protocol.

21. Annex B to the Kyoto Protocol and Annex I to the UNFCCC are now identical in nature, although they are slightly different numerically. This deliberate change from Annex I into Annex B potentially allows a developing country to engage in emissions trading if it voluntarily adopts an emissions target and is inscribed in Annex B.

22. The Montreal Protocol on Substances that Deplete the Ozone Layer was signed in 1987. The Protocol has since been amended and strengthened in a number of aspects (see, for example, Brack 1996).

23. As has been the case in the international climate-change negotiations, the developing countries express their consensus views as the group of 77 and China's positions. Divergent or dissenting views are then expressed separately, representing either individual countries or smaller groups, such as the Alliance of Small Island States (AOSIS).

24. Such as disagreement about scientific evidence, different perspective on the responsibility for climate problems, different priority to divert its limited resources, different risk-acceptance thresholds, and disagreement about the burden-sharing of abating GHG emissions.

25. This kind of joint implementation between one Annex I country with emissions targets and one non-Annex I country without emissions targets has now been termed the clean development mechanism (CDM) under the Kyoto Protocol (UNFCCC 1997). However, we still use the customary term JI instead of the CDM.

26. Rep. Bill Archer (R-Texas), Chair of the House Ways and Means Committee, for example, said that "It is another form of foreign aid." (*Congressional Quarterly*, 29 November 1997).

References

Babiker, M.H, K.E. Maskus, and T.F. Rutherford. "Carbon Taxes and the Global Trading System," Department of Economics, University of Colorado, PO Box 173364, Denver, CO, USA, 1997, (mimeo).

Barrett, S. "Climate Change Policy and International Trade." In: A. Amano *et al.* (eds.), *Climate Change: Policy Instruments and their Implications, Proceedings of the Tsukuba Workshop of IPCC Working Group III*, Tsukuba, Japan, 17–20 January, eds A. Amano *et al.* 1994, pp. 15–33.

Bill, S. "European Commission's Experience in Designing Environmental Taxation for Energy Products," Presented at the European Union Advanced Study Course on Goals and Instruments for the Achievement of Global Warming Mitigation in Europe, 20–26 July 1997, Berlin.

Brack, D. *International Trade and the Montreal Protocol*. London: Royal Institute of International Affairs and Earthscan, 1996.

CCAP "Integration of Joint Implementation into an Annex I Greenhouse Gas Trading System: Summary of Key Points." Washington, DC: Center for Clean Air Policy (CCAP), 1997.

Charnovitz, S. "Exploring the Environmental Exceptions in GATT Article XX." *Journal of World Trade*, 25(5): 37–55, 1991.

Cline, W.R. *The Economics of Global Warming*. Washington, DC: Institute of International Economics.

Cramton, P. and S. Kerr. "Tradeable Carbon Allowance Auctions: How and Why to Auction," University of Maryland at College Park, MD 20742, USA, 1998 (mimeo).

Esty, D. *Greening the GATT: Trade, Environment and the Future*, Washington, DC: Institute of International Economics, 1994.

GATT. "*United States – Restrictions on Imports of Tuna.*" Report of the Panel DS21/R, 3 September, Geneva: General Agreement on Tariffs and Trade (GATT), 1991.

GATT *International Trade 90 91*. Geneva: General Agreement on Tariffs and Trade (GATT), 1992.

GATT "United States – Restrictions on Imports of Tuna." Report of the Panel DS29/R, 16 June, Geneva: General Agreement on Tariffs and Trade (GATT), 1994.

Hargrave, T. "US Carbon Emissions Trading: Description of an Upstream Approach." Washington, DC: Center for Clear Air Policy, 1998.

Hoel, M. "Should a Carbon Tax Be Differentiated across Sectors?" *Journal of Public Economics*, 59(1): 17–32, 1996.

Hoeller, P. and J. Coppel. "Carbon Taxes and Current Energy Policies in OECD Countries." *OECD Economic Studies*, No. 19, 167–193, 1992.

Hudec, R.E. "GATT Legal Restraints on the Use of Trade Measures against Foreign Environmental Practices." In: *Fair Trade and Harmonization: Prerequisites for Free Trade?* ed. J. Bhagwati and R.E. Hudec. Volume 2: Legal Analysis. Cambridge, Mass: The MIT Press, pp. 95–174, 1996.

IPCC. "Climate Change 1995: Economic and Social Dimensions of Climate Change." Contribution of Working Group III to the Second Assessment Report of the Intergovernmental Panel on Climate Change (IPCC). Cambridge: Cambridge University Press, 1996.

McLean, B. "The Evolution of Marketable Permits: the US Experience with Sulphur Dioxide Allowance Trading." In: *Controlling Carbon and Sulphur: Joint Implementation and Trading Initiatives* ed. D. Anderson and M. Grubb. London: Royal Institute of International Affairs, pp. 83–104, 1997.

OECD. "Ensuring Compliance with a Global Climate Change Agreement." ENV/EPOC(98)5. Paris: Organization for Economic Co-operation and Development (OECD), 1998.

Parry, Ian W.H., R.C. Williams III, and L.H. Goulder. "When Can Carbon Abatement Policies Increase Welfare? The Fundamental

Role of Distorted Factor Markets." Washington, DC: Resources for the Future, 1997.

Pearce, D. "The Role of Carbon Taxes in Adjusting to Global Warming." *Economic Journal* 101, pp. 938–948, 1991.

Pezzey, J. "The Symmetry between Controlling Pollution by Price and Controlling it by Quantity." *Canadian Journal of Economics* 25(4): 983–991, 1992.

Poterba, J.M. and J.J. Rotemberg. "Environmental Taxes on Intermediate and Final Goods When Both Can Be Imported." *International Tax and Public Finance* 2: 221–228, 1995.

UNCTAD. "Controlling Carbon Dioxide Emissions: The Tradeable Permit System." UNCTAD/GID/11. Geneva: United Nations Conference on Trade and Development (UNCTAD), 1995.

UNCTAD. "Greenhouse Gas Emissions Trading: Defining the Principles, Modalities, Rules and Guidelines for Verification, Reporting and Accountability." Geneva: United Nations Conference on Trade and Development (UNCTAD), 1998.

USDOS. "The Kyoto Protocol on Climate Change." Washington, DC: United States Department of State (USDOS), 15 January 1998.

UNFCCC. "Kyoto Protocol to the United Nations Framework Convention on Climate Change (UNFCCC)." Bonn: FCCC/CP/1997/L.7/Add.1, 1997.

Vaughan, S. "Tradeable Emissions Permits and the WTO." Presented at the European Union Advanced Study Course on Goals and Instruments for the Achievement of Global Warming Mitigation in Europe, Berlin, 20–26 July 1997.

Weitzman, M.L. "Prices vs. Quantities." *Review of Economic Studies* 41: 477–491, 1974.

Wiener, J.B. "Designing Markets for International Greenhouse Gas Control." Washington, DC: Resources for the Future, 1997.

WTO. "The Results of the Uruguay Round of Multilateral Trade Negotiations: The Legal Texts." Geneva: World Trade Organization (WTO), 1995.

Yellen, J. Statement before the House Commerce Subcommittee on Energy and Power on the Economics of the Kyoto Protocol, 4 March, Washington, DC: University Government Printing Office, 1998.

Zhang, Z.X. *The Economics of Energy Policy in China: Implications for Global Climate Change*. New Horizons in Environmental Economics Series. Cheltenham, England: Edward Elgar, 1997a.

Zhang, Z.X. "Operationalization and Priority of Joint Implementation Projects." *Intereconomics (Review of International Trade and Development)* 32(6): 280–292, 1997b.

Zhang, Z.X. "Towards a Successful International Greenhouse Gas Emissions Trading." Presented at the Seminar Organized by the United Nations Conference on Trade and Development, A Side Event of the Eighth Sessions of the Subsidiary Bodies of the UNFCCC Bonn, 8 June 1998.

Zhang, Z.X. and A. Nentjes. "International Tradeable Carbon Permits as a Strong Form of Joint Implementation." In: *Pollution for Sale: Emissions Trading and Joint Implementation* eds J. Skea and S. Sorrell. Cheltenham, England: Edward Elgar, pp. 322–342, 1998.

7

Greenhouse-Gas Emissions Trading and the WTO[1]

Jacob Werksman

Overview

This chapter explores selected aspects of the potential relationship between an international emissions-trading system (ETS) that may be developed as a means of implementing the Kyoto Protocol to the United Nations Framework Convention on Climate Change (UNFCCC),[2] and the rules and procedures of the World Trade Organization (WTO).[3] The primary objective of this chapter is to provide an assessment of the scope of the WTO's jurisdiction over various aspects of the design of an ETS. It thus offers an approach to exploring this relationship, rather than an exhaustive analysis of what conflicts might arise and how they may be resolved.

Precise conclusions about this relationship are difficult to reach because the rules governing the operation of the Kyoto Protocol have not yet been agreed internationally, and states have not yet narrowed the options available to them in the design of an ETS. Furthermore, substantial portions of the WTO regime have been in force for less than five years and the precise contours of these obligations have yet to be clarified through state practice and jurisprudence. Finally, it must be acknowledged that, in seeking to implement the Kyoto Protocol through the use of international market mechanisms, the Parties are undertaking an unprecedented experiment in international cooperation and regulation.

Introduction

When in force, the Kyoto Protocol will require its industrialized Parties (known as "Annex I Parties") collectively to reduce their overall emissions of greenhouse gases (GHGs) by at least 5 per cent below 1990 levels in the commitment period 2008–2012. Each Annex I Party will be bound by a specific commitment set out in Annex B to the Protocol.

These commitments "cap" emissions to between 8 per cent below to 10 per cent above each Annex I Party's 1990 levels, with each Annex I Party limited to emitting its respective "assigned amount." Negotiators designing the Kyoto Protocol recognized that the costs of reducing GHG emissions would vary among Annex I Parties. Emissions could be reduced most cost-effectively if governments and regulated entities were allowed to acquire or invest in emission-reduction opportunities in whichever countries they are cheapest to achieve. Emissions trading, in effect, allows those Annex I Parties with parts of assigned amount (PAAs) that are excess to their requirements, to sell these to Annex I Parties that need additional PAAs to remain within their Annex B caps.

The essential objective of the WTO is to liberalize markets in the trade in goods and services. It does this through the imposition of both relative and absolute standards of treatment of goods and services in the international and domestic market place. The WTO's relative standards prohibit WTO Members from the discriminatory treatment of "like" goods, services, and service suppliers on the basis of country of origin. The WTO's "absolute" standards prohibit or discourage Members from putting in place certain types of measures that directly or indirectly interfere with the trade in products and services.

This chapter analyses international emissions trading under the Kyoto Protocol on two, parallel levels: at one level, sovereign exchanges of PAAs will take place between Parties; at a second level, exchanges of emissions allowances may take place between private entities. The analysis concludes that WTO rules do not cover the transactions in PAAs at the sovereign level. Thus, WTO rules would not constrain the choice of any Party to the Protocol as to which other Party to the Protocol it wishes to trade PAAs with. For example, if the Kyoto Protocol rules allow it, a Party may choose not to engage in the exchange of PAAs with countries that have joined the Kyoto Protocol but that are in non-compliance with their commitments.

This chapter assumes that international "emissions trading" involving private entities will probably involve the transfer of government-issued permits or "allowances." Such emissions-trading systems will require the development of rules on the following:

1. transfer and mutual recognition of allowances (what standards and conditions will govern the validity of allowances within the jurisdiction of each participating country)
2. incidence of regulation (which entities will be required to hold allowances) and
3. allocation of allowances (by what means allowances will be issued and distributed to regulated entities).

An analysis of the compatibility of these rules with WTO disciplines requires an assessment of whether the rules will affect the trade in products and services that fall within the WTO's coverage.

Emissions allowances could not themselves be described as either products or services under the WTO, and thus rules governing *the transfer and mutual recognition of allowances* are not covered by WTO disciplines. Rules on transfer and mutual recognition could be set either by each participating country unilaterally, by two or more countries, and/or by the Conference of the Parties (COP) to the UNFCCC. These internationally agreed rules (and not WTO disciplines) will determine the circumstances in which Parties acting unilaterally or as a group may restrict the transferability of emissions allowances between private entities operating within different countries.

However, design choices regarding the *incidence of regulation* and of *allocation of allowances* will probably affect the competitive relationship between products and services that are governed by WTO disciplines. A wide range of energy and energy-related products and services may be considered to be covered by the General Agreement on Tariffs and Trade (GATT)[4] and/or the General Agreement on Trade in Services (GATS), which guarantee non-discrimination and market access. Rules requiring and allocating emission allowances may act to constrain or promote the import or export of energy or energy-related products or services. For example, if allowances for fossil fuels are demanded "at the border," these could amount to quantitative restrictions on the import of products or services, which may be prohibited by the GATT and/or GATS. Allowances required for the distribution or sale of energy products or services within the domestic marketplace may raise GATT or GATS concerns, if they are allocated on a basis that is either directly or indirectly discriminatory against or between foreign products, services, or service suppliers.

Measures implementing an emissions-trading system that are found to violate WTO rules on non-discrimination or market access may still survive a WTO challenge if they qualify for a general exception under either the GATT or the GATS. Recent WTO jurisprudence interpreting GATT general exceptions suggests that these exceptions will continue to be construed narrowly. However, national, regional, or international emissions-trading systems that are designed in a manner that is neither "arbitrary nor unjustifiable" nor a "disguised restriction on trade," and that are designed in accordance with the rules set by the Convention or Protocol, will qualify for a WTO exception.

By way of conclusion, this analysis assesses the likelihood of a WTO challenge of an ETS arising at all. Although a number of multilateral environmental agreements (MEAs) have employed trade-related measures, none has ever been the direct cause of a WTO dispute. However, no MEA has had the potential to affect so many sectors of the economy, so many economic interests, and such high volumes of trade in products and services, as does the climate-change regime. If an ETS, and the Protocol as a whole, is to be considered a success, powerful vested economic interests that trade in fossil fuel and fossil-fuel-dependent products and services, will be dislocated. This will increase the likelihood of a trade dispute. Disputes between Parties to the Protocol should be resolved by the Protocol's own compliance and dispute-settlement procedures. Disputes between Parties to the Protocol and non-Parties that are WTO Members may be the most likely to end up in WTO dispute settlement. This chapter suggests, however, that the careful design and harmonization of standards for mutual recognition, for incidence of regulation, and for non-discriminatory allocation methods, provide the best means for avoiding WTO disputes and for protecting the integrity of the an ETS should such a dispute arise.

Two levels of emissions trading

Article 17 of the Kyoto Protocol provides that "[t]he Parties included in Annex B may participate in emissions trading for the purposes of fulfilling their commitments under Article 3." Of course, emissions themselves will never literally be traded. For the purposes of this analysis, what the Protocol describes as the trading of "emissions" has been broken down into two parallel levels. A budget or "cap" on emissions has been agreed and allocated between Parties through the sovereign obligations set out in Annex B. Annex B Parties may then engage in the acquisition and transfer of these sovereign obligations, and government-issued emissions allowances may be exchanged between private entities. While sovereign-to-sovereign trading may take place without private-sector involvement, any private-entity trading must be "shadowed" by a parallel transfer of obligations at the sovereign level.

Sovereign exchanges of parts of assigned amounts (PAAs)

Any international emissions-allowance trading system would operate within an agreed emissions budget or cap. As described earlier,

Figure 7.1   Sovereign trading: PAAs

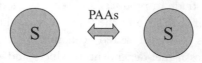

Annex I Parties to the Protocol have undertaken "quantified emission limitation and reduction commitments" which are inscribed as
"assigned amounts" in Annex B of the Protocol. Under Articles 3.10
and 3.11, and in accordance with rules to be agreed under Article
17, "parts" of these assigned amounts (PAAs) may be acquired and
transferred between Annex I Parties. This level of "emissions trading" under Article 17 involves sovereign-to-sovereign exchanges of
commitments, in which *Parties* transfer and acquire PAAs. The acquisition and transfer of assigned amounts between sovereigns does
not create a "market" in either goods or services and these PAAs
would not fall within the purview of the WTO Agreements (see fig.
7.1). Instead, this level of sovereign emission trading can be better
understood as a more dynamic version of the type of reallocation of
assigned amount contemplated under Article 4 of the Protocol,
which entitles Parties to renegotiate their assigned amount prior to
the start of the commitment period.

Entity trading of emissions allowances

A second, and parallel, level of emissions trading, which is the main
focus of this analysis, anticipates exchanges involving so-called "legal
entities." The Protocol does not mention the involvement of such
entities in any aspect of emissions trading.[5] However the majority of
Annex I Parties have indicated that "legal entities" could, at the
discretion of a Party, "be allowed to trade" or "to participate in
emissions trading".[6]

Although the details of entity participation in emissions trading
have not been put forward by either group, two basic (and non-
exclusive) options have begun to emerge. These options reflect the
possibility that some Parties will choose to establish a domestic

Figure 7.2 Domestic trading: emissions allowances

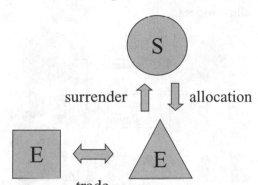

emissions-trading scheme that will then, in a building-block approach, harmonize and integrate with the domestic emissions-trading schemes established by other Parties. Some Parties may, however, wish to trade directly with entities in other Parties without first establishing a domestic emissions-trading scheme (see fig. 7.2). Parties with relatively few sources of emissions in the private sector, or that wish to maintain sovereign control over their national emissions budget, may choose to avoid the considerable investment involved in establishing the regulatory infrastructure necessary to launch domestic emissions trading.[7] These options are not mutually exclusive, as a Party may choose to allocate some part of its assigned amount through a domestic scheme and retain some part of the remainder to sell directly overseas.

This analysis focuses on the first option; however, for WTO purposes, the conclusions would be fundamentally the same. A governmental authority within each participating state would create and allocate allowances equal to some (or the entire amount) of the emissions possible within its assigned amount. Regulated entities would be required to surrender allowances equivalent to their permitted emissions and would be able to buy and sell any excess allowances domestically or internationally. Participating governments would recognize as valid, under their domestic regulatory regimes, allowances issued by other participating states. Transboundary transfers of

Figure 7.3 International trading: PAAs and emissions allowances

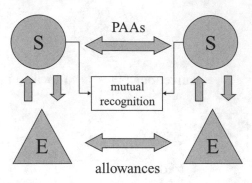

emissions allowances involving private entities would be shadowed by a parallel and equivalent transfer of sovereign obligations (PAAs) between respective Parties. The transfer of an emissions allowance and the transfer of an equivalent PAA may occur in advance or simultaneously, as the transferring Party authorizes the "export" of the allowance and the "importing" country increases its assigned amount accordingly. Participating states would then, in turn, be required to hold, at the end of the commitment period, PAAs equivalent to their assigned amount, as adjusted in accordance to whatever international transactions in emissions allowances have taken place.[8]

A private entity would not literally acquire, hold, or transfer a PAA (i.e. an international legal obligation) as such. In traditional international law, private entities are not "subjects" of that law and cannot hold international legal rights and obligations.[9] Private entities can and may acquire, hold, and transfer emissions allowances or other instruments *based* on PAAs and issued, authorized, or recognized as valid under the domestic law of one or more participating governments. The Protocol implicitly recognizes this distinction between sovereign obligations and domestic authorization, by referring to PAAs as being transferred and acquired by Parties,[10] and by providing for the involvement of legal entities as being "authorized" and acting under the responsibility of Parties[11] (fig. 7.3).

WTO coverage and rules

As has been mentioned, the WTO regime covers two general categories of trade that are relevant to a system of emission trading – trade in goods and trade in services. These are covered by distinct, but related, regimes, which bind all WTO Members.[12] Trade in goods or "products" is covered by the GATT (1994) and related agreements, for example the Agreement on Trade-Related Investment Measures (TRIMs) and the Agreement on Subsidies and Countervailing Measures (SCM). Trade in services is covered by the GATS and the various Protocols to that agreement, including, for example, the fifth protocol, on Financial Services.

In essence, WTO disciplines can be divided into *relative* standards, which require a comparison of treatment between, for example, the "like" goods and services of one or more countries, and *absolute* standards, which require an assessment of whether a particular trade-related measure meets acceptable criteria as defined within a particular agreement.

The main relative WTO standards test whether a measure, as applied to goods or services, directly or indirectly discriminates between "like" goods or services on the basis of their country of origin. The "most-favoured nation" (MFN) principle demands that each WTO Member accords to goods, services, and service suppliers of any other WTO Member treatment no less favourable than the treatment it accords to the goods or services and service suppliers of any other country (GATT 1994, Article I; GATS Article II). Under the "national treatment" principle, each WTO member must accord treatment no less favourable to the products, services, and service suppliers of any other Member than the treatment it accords to its own domestic products, services, and service suppliers (GATT 1994, Article III; GATS Article XVIII).

The WTO's "absolute" standards of treatment restrict the use of particular categories of measures because of their actual or potential impact on trade. The GATT restricts governments' use of quantitative restrictions or limitations on the number or total value of imports or exports of goods, and the GATS regulates the use of similar market-access restrictions on the "import" of services. The SCM and TRIMS agreements, for example, prohibit the use of subsidies or other forms of benefit that are designed to promote the export of domestically produced goods. The GATS requires, for example, that technical standards and licensing requirements for the provision of services are based on objective and transparent criteria and do not constitute unnecessary barriers to trade.

The GATT and the GATS differ most significantly in terms of the scope of their coverage. The GATT's absolute and relative disciplines cover all products, whether or not they are subject to specific tariff bindings. For climate-change purposes, this would include energy and energy-related products such as petroleum, coal, natural gas, and electrical energy, some or all of which may be "bound" or "unbound" within particular Members' tariff schedules.[13]

The GATS potentially covers all service sectors. However, individual WTO Members may restrict the GATS application to them in at least two different ways. With regard to the MFN obligation, individual Members have a "once only" opportunity to exempt from GATS coverage, for a limited period of time, specific measures that provide more favourable treatment to identified countries. With regard to the GATS obligations on national treatment, and on market access, each WTO Member negotiates a schedule of commitments, which indicates which service sectors it has subjected to these disciplines. In other words, through its GATS schedules a WTO Member may, in effect, specify and maintain quantitative limits on market access and maintain discriminatory conditions and reservations on its market-access and national-treatment obligations.

To encourage Members to bind as many service sectors as possible, the WTO Members have negotiated specific annexes and Protocols to the GATS to promote market access and liberalization in particular service sectors. The energy service sector, the service sector most relevant to the implementation of the Kyoto Protocol, does not yet have its own annex or Protocol. Energy-related services may be covered by the transport services (including pipelines), distribution services, environmental services, and consultancy or other business-related services enumerated in GATS schedules. Very few WTO Members have made commitments on energy-related services under these more general categories.[14] Further services provided in the context of an emissions-trading system may arise out of the trading of international emissions allowances and out of a secondary market in allowance derivatives, both of which may involve the provision of financial services.

ETS rules for the allocation and trade of emissions allowances, if designed properly, will create incentives at both the sovereign and the private-sector level for the promotion of the Kyoto Protocol. More specifically, a well-designed ETS should provide incentives for the production and trade of those goods and services that lead to emissions reductions. Rules for the allocation and trade of emission allowances may act to constrain or promote the import or export of energy or energy-related products or services. While such rules may not be discriminatory at face value, they may be discriminatory in their effect and collide with GATT or GATS disciplines that prohibit or discourage government interference with trade.

Interaction between WTO rules and ETS rules

An assessment of the potential interaction between WTO disciplines and an ETS requires an analysis of the following:

1. What rules will govern the transfer and mutual recognition of allowances?
2. What entities will be required to hold emissions allowances (the incidence of regulation)?
3. How will emissions allowances be allocated among these entities?
4. Might the trade in certain products and services be affected by these design choices in a way that may violate WTO rules?

These rules must be analysed for their impact on three different markets. Two types of markets are created by the international trade in government-issued emissions allowances, and which may be analysed in the context of WTO rules:

1. a *primary market* in the exchange of allowances by regulated sources (the so-called "end-users" of emissions allowances), brokers, or others with an interest in holding or retiring allowances, and

2. a *secondary or derivative market* in which buyers and sellers hold and exchange derivative financial instruments based upon allowances, for investment purposes.

A *third and extremely important market*, for WTO purposes, is not created by an ETS. This is the pre-existing market in the trade in goods and services that may be affected by the design of an ETS.

Primary markets: Transfer and mutual recognition of allowances

Turning first to the primary market in the allowances themselves, a threshold question for WTO purposes is whether emissions allowances can be characterized as "products" under the GATT or "services" under the GATS. The issue is of relevance because the Protocol itself – and proposals from specific Parties, including the European Union (EU) – seek to restrict the trade in emissions allowances, either quantitatively (through a "concrete ceiling"), or on the basis of "country of origin" (by prohibiting trade with, for example, non-Annex B Parties, or Parties in non-compliance).[15] If emissions allowances were considered products or services, then these restrictions on their trade would appear, prima facie, to violate WTO prohibitions on quantitative restrictions and discrimination.

It can be concluded with some confidence that internationally traded emissions allowances are themselves neither goods nor services under the WTO. They are, instead, licenses or permits issued by a

government authority and entitling (under specified conditions) the
holder to carry out a regulated activity within its territory.

However, before looking more closely at the issue, it is important
to stress that the international trade in emissions allowances, on the
scale contemplated under an ETS or under the Kyoto Protocol at
large, has never been attempted. There is, therefore, no directly relevant precedent to guide efforts to classify these instruments.

In order for international trade in allowances to take place, governments may, either unilaterally or in cooperation with other governments, agree to recognize each other's allowances as valid for offsetting emissions within their territory, and to establish procedures
for transferring PAAs equivalent to those allowances. Policy makers
may choose to design an ETS that does not recognize as valid allowances on the basis of their "country of origin." For example, they
may choose not to recognize emissions allowances that are issued by
the following:

1. countries that have chosen not to become parties to the Kyoto
   Protocol
2. countries that have joined the Kyoto Protocol but have not
   undertaken emission-reduction commitments (non Annex I
   Parties)
3. countries that have joined the Kyoto Protocol but that are in
   non-compliance with their commitments
4. countries that wish to sell emissions permits that are not clearly
   excess to their requirements, or that do not represent legitimate
   emissions reductions (described by some delegations and analysts as "hot air" permits).

Participating countries may seek to place quantitative restrictions
on the amount of emissions allowances that may be "exported" in
order to prevent, for example, imprudent "overselling" by domestic
industry. A Party may be concerned, for example, that transfers of
large parts of its assigned amount overseas may undermine its energy
independence and its economic security, as well as its ability to meet
its commitments under the Protocol. Alternatively, inspired by

either domestic or international concerns about "supplementarity" and the need to force domestic action, participating countries may restrict the quantity of emissions allowances that may be "imported."

These effective restraints on the "trade" of PAAs and emissions allowances have raised, for some analysts, the threat of a WTO challenge. If emissions allowances were characterized as "products" or "services" under the GATT or the GATS, discrimination on the basis of national origin and quantitative restrictions on their trade may be prohibited.[16] When attempting this characterization, it is important to keep in mind that the terms "product" and "service" are legal terms that take on specific meanings in the context of the GATT and the GATS, in light of the object and purposes of those agreements and the practice of Members. It would be specious to argue, for example, that anything that is tradeable and has economic value must be, simply by *analogy* to covered products and services, either a product or a service for WTO purposes.

All products traded between Members are covered by GATT disciplines, but the GATT text does not provide a definition for "a product." Guidance as to what Members understand to be products can be taken from the tariff schedules in which WTO Members include those products they have agreed will be subject to bindings, and from the internationally agreed rules on customs classifications. These lists of products – and common sense – suggest that the WTO Members understand products to be "tangible" goods, including primary goods and manufactures.[17] Because emissions allowances will be tradeable internationally, and will have a market value, they can in economic terms be characterized as "commodities." This characterization is evidence of the broadening scope of domestic and international financial markets, which now encompass a great variety of "non-tangible" financial instruments. However, there is no evidence that WTO Members have an (or will similarly expand their) understanding of what is a "product." Indeed, many forms of financial instrument, including currency, have been traded internationally for decades, but none has been considered to be a "product" for GATT purposes.[18]

The GATS does not define a service. Economic literature rather unhelpfully tends to define services in contrast to products, emphasizing their "non-durable or transitory character."[19] The GATS' potential coverage is broad, extending to trade in services in any sector except services supplied in the exercise of governmental authority.[20] Guidance on what is meant by a service can, once again, be taken from the more specific commitments Members have negotiated. As mentioned earlier, specific commitments and exemptions to GATS rules are undertaken by each Member on a sector-by-sector basis, and are set out in binding schedules. Each WTO Member's commitments within each sector may differ. Typical services sectors include financial services, transport, and telecommunications. If, as is posited in this analysis, an emissions permit is a government-issued licence, it would not, of itself, fall within the Members' understanding of a "service."

Nevertheless, the trade in emissions allowances may well indirectly be governed by the GATS. An internationally traded emissions allowance will have financial value and may well be considered a "negotiable instrument" within the meaning of the GATS agreement on financial services.[21] GATS disciplines might prohibit those WTO Members that have fully liberalized their financial-services sector from placing quantitative restrictions on the "import" of emissions allowances. For example, the GATS might prohibit such a Member from limiting access of other Members' emissions allowances to its market on the basis of "the total value of percentage assets in the form of numerical quotas."[22]

However, GATS rules would not require any Member to recognize the regulatory validity of these allowances, once they had been "imported." In other words, GATS might require that brokers and other financial-service providers within Country A be free to buy and sell the emissions allowances issued by any other WTO Member. However, Country A could, none the less, refuse to recognize these allowances as valid for the purpose of offsetting emissions within A's territory. A useful analogy is to the trade in government-issued currency. Currency is not itself a "service" or a "product," but the provision of financial services, such as currency exchange, would fall within the scope of the GATS. Depending on Country A's specific GATS commitments, it may be required to guarantee market access to bureaux de change registered in Country B, and it may be prohibited from limiting the volume of currency exchanged through these services.

Country A would not, however, under GATS rules, be required to recognize as legal tender for use within its domestic market, currency issued by Country B. Perhaps the only precedents for the international trade in government-issued environmental permits are the domestic legal regimes established to implement the "industrial rationalization" provisions of the Montreal Protocol on Ozone Depleting Substances. There is no evidence that these allowances have ever been considered to be products or services for WTO purposes. Furthermore, these regimes typically impose unilateral constraints on the trade and on the validity of production allowances, yet these practices have never attracted a WTO challenge.

For example, under the US Clean Air Act, the US Environmental Protection Agency (USEPA) is authorized to regulate the trade in ozone-depleting substances (ODS) production allowances between US-based producers and producers in other nations that are Parties to the Protocol. Entities proposing to trade must first demonstrate that the allowance being offered represents a reduction below internationally or domestically required levels, and obtain the formal approval of the government proposing to "export" the allowance.

The USEPA Administrator reserves the right to deny any international transfer from or to US sources, of production allowances for economic, trade, or environmental reasons (see fig. 7.4). The approval by each government of the transaction between producers can be seen as equivalent to the sovereign-to-sovereign transfer of PAAs that must "shadow" each transaction of emissions allowances in the climate-change context. The EC has enacted similar provisions that authorize the European Commission, together with a European Member State, to approve, on a case-by-case basis, trades in production allowances.[23]

Figure 7.4 US stratospheric ozone-production allowance-trading scheme

Under the US domestic tradeable production allowance system implementing the Montreal Protocol, a US-based producer may trade allowances only with a "nation" that is Party to the Protocol. Before acquiring a production allowance, a US-based producer company must first obtain documented authorization from the principal diplomatic representative in that Party's embassy in the United States,

> that the appropriate authority within that nation has established or revised production limits for the nation to equal the lesser of the maximum production that the nation is allowed under the Protocol minus the amount transferred, the maximum production that is allowed under the nation's applicable domestic law minus the amount transferred, or the average of the nation's actual national production level for the three years prior to the transfer minus the production allowances transferred.

Before transferring a production allowance to another Party, the US-based producer must indicate, among other things, the chemical type and level of production the allowance represents. Prior to any such trade, the US-based producer must obtain authorization from the Administrator of the USEPA:

> After receiving a transfer request that meets the requirements of Paragraph (c) (2) of this section, the Administrator may, at his discretion, consider the following factors in deciding whether to approve such a transfer:
> - possible creation of economic hardship
> - possible effects on trade
> - potential environmental implications
> - the total amount of unexpended production allowances held by US entities. (42 CFR sec 82.9(c))

No two regimes are perfectly analogous. It is likely that the market in GHG allowances will be much larger and more liquid than the ozone market and would benefit from less direct government intervention. The point illustrated here is that the fundamental legal character of the ozone and the climate-change allowances – licenses issued by a government in aid of implementing an international sovereign obligation – are essentially the same. The domestic or international tradeability of these instruments does not change them into products or services for WTO purposes.

Rather than act unilaterally, one or more Parties might agree to the harmonization of standards, or enter into mutual recognition agreements (MRAs).[24] Each government would accept as valid within its regulatory system only those allowances issued by governments that were also bound by these[25] (see fig. 7.3). This would provide a broader legal basis for refusing to recognize as valid, within domestic regulatory systems, allowances offered for sale by Parties that do not meet certain standards. It must be emphasized that the Kyoto Protocol provides that the Conference of the Parties (COP) (and not individual Parties to the Protocol) shall define the relevant principles, modalities, rules, and guidelines for emissions trading. These rules may constrain the extent to which Parties may act unilaterally or in groups to set or enforce the terms of mutual recognition. Article 17 already implicitly prevents Parties not included in Annex B from acquiring, issuing, or transferring emissions allowances under the Protocol. Parties may choose, for example (as did the Parties to the Montreal Protocol), to authorize a non-compliance procedure to suspend the ability of Parties to transfer emissions allowances under certain circumstances.[26] The Parties may choose to adopt rules based on principles provided in the Convention and similar to those of the WTO, such as non-discrimination or least trade restrictiveness.[27]

But, once again, there is neither a basis in the texts of the WTO Agreements nor a precedent from GATT/WTO practice for treating government-issued allowances themselves as either products or services. When traded internationally, emissions allowances may well be considered "negotiable instruments" for the purposes of the GATS financial-services agreement. The disciplines of this agreement may prohibit certain WTO Members from limiting the "import" of emission allowances; however, they would not prevent WTO Members from limiting the amount of imported emissions allowances they recognize as valid, or from making discriminatory distinctions as to which countries' allowances they choose to recognize as valid.

Secondary markets in allowance "derivatives"

A secondary market in the trading in financial instruments based on allowances may also develop from the introduction of an ETS. These financial instruments, such as futures contracts, may also involve the provision of financial services and may also be subject to WTO disciplines for financial services.

If the ETS is designed in a way that allows a significant number of transactions within and across borders, it will be very likely to attract the interest of service providers from the financial-services industry.[28] These services may include intermediary services, such as brokerage and agency, but also services such as banking, insurance, and the management and trade in derivatives.

If the ETS rules allow financial-service providers to buy, own, and hold allowances, the EC and its Member States may be under a GATS obligation to extend MFN and national treatment to foreign services and service suppliers. Objective "prudential," rather than nationality-based, criteria can be used to weed out any inappropriate service suppliers.[29] These might include, for example, requirements that brokers are properly licensed, or are backed by sufficient assets.

Existing markets in products and services: Incidence of regulation and allocation

The market of most concern, from a WTO perspective, is the exchange of existing products and services that may be affected by the design of rules governing an ETS. In WTO parlance, the rules governing an ETS would be considered *measures* with the potential to affect trade in products and services. Which products and services may be affected by an ETS will depend upon the scope of GHGs covered by the ETS, on which products and services generate these gases, and on the types of measures chosen by the system's designers.

The designers of an ETS will first need to determine, for example, at which point of a carbon-based fuel cycle allowances will be required. Regulators will need to choose between a more "upstream" coverage at the point of extraction, or upstream coverage at the point of processing or supply, or downstream coverage (e.g. at point of emission or end-use), or a combination of the three.[30] As will be seen, for WTO purposes, the incidence of regulation is relevant because, if the regulator moves fully upstream in the fuel cycle, it becomes more likely that constraints may be placed on the import of energy or energy sources at the border.

Once the points of regulation have been determined, emission allowances need to be allocated by an agreed mechanism or mechanisms, operating under certain principles. This allocation can be done either through the mechanism of *grandfathering*, an allocation of emission rights on the basis of historic emissions, or through the mechanism of *auctioning*, by selling emission allowances to the highest bidder. Furthermore, either of these mechanisms could be weighted by principles that favour certain types of fuel sources (such as entities that are less polluting or less carbon intensive), or certain classes of emitters (such as domestic, or domestically owned and operated entities). WTO disciplines will generally favour as open and transparent a system as possible. This analysis now turns to explore briefly the WTO implications of upstream, midstream, and downstream systems, allocated under either an open or a weighted process.

Upstream at the point of extraction

Allowances could be required not of emitters or suppliers but of "extractors" of fossil fuels, effectively limiting the quantity of fossil fuels on the market. As most countries are not energy independent, such a system might also require importers to hold and surrender allowances for fossil-fuel products as a precondition of import. Assuming that the quantity of allowances available will be limited, the importing country would, in effect, be imposing a quota on the imports of the fossil-fuel products, potentially violating Article XI of the GATT (prohibition on quantitative restrictions). Furthermore, if the delivery of energy services could be construed as falling within an importer's market-access services schedule under the GATS, limiting the delivery of energy services (such as transportation via tanker or pipeline) at the border may also violate the GATS.[31]

The issue is further complicated by proposals to "bundle" emissions allowances with energy products at the border. For example, assume that an oil producer from Country A sought to export petroleum into Country B but found that there were no allowances available for sale within Country B's market. In an upstream system, the import would be banned, unless the importer held an emissions allowance issued elsewhere that was valid within the Country B. The exporter might then seek to bundle its petroleum with allowances issued by its home Country A. If Country B's ETS did not recognize Country A's allowances as valid, Country A (if it was a WTO Member) could seek to challenge Country B's rules on the validity of allowances as a quantitative restriction.

The important distinction to keep in mind is that WTO rules apply to trade in services and products, but not to "trade" in allowances. Thus, WTO obligations would not in this circumstance require a Member to accept the foreign allowances as valid for offsetting emissions within its territory. WTO rules may, however, require a Member to allow the import of the energy-related product or service. Once it has entered the internal market, the energy-related product would be governed by domestic regulation. The fuel could not be combusted until and unless it was accompanied by a valid allowance. An analysis must then turn to assess whether importers or end-users of imported fossil fuels were allowed nondiscriminatory access to allowances that are recognized as valid within the jurisdiction of the importing country.

This raises the issue of fair allocation of allowances recognized as valid, rather than the issue of the validity of the allowances themselves. While it is difficult to predict with confidence the outcome of these challenges, it can generally be said that demanding emissions allowances at the border, in such a way as to block the import of products, would greatly increase the chances of a WTO challenge. As discussed below, if a less trade-restrictive alternative is available – such as a downstream approach – it would be more difficult for a measure to survive such a challenge through the application of a general exception to the GATT or GATS.

Upstream at the point of processing or sale

If the allowances are demanded of sellers of energy products at the point of delivery or sale, GATT and GATS rules governing National Treatment and MFN within the internal market would apply. Under the GATT (Article III: 4), imported energy products would have to be accorded treatment no less favourable than "like" energy products of domestic origin. Any system of allocation would be required to provide for "the effective equality of opportunities for imported products in respect of law, regulations, and requirements affecting the internal sale, offering for sale, purchase, transportation, distribution or use of products."[32]

Allocation of carbon-based sales allowances for fossil fuels by purely historical grandfathering would launch the market on the basis of the status quo. If the status quo was already fully liberalized, current market participants within Country A would be treated equally, whether their products derived from domestic or from imported sources. Allocation by open and transparent auction, if it is operated on a non-discriminatory basis, might favour the wealthier or the more efficient, but would not directly violate GATT national treatment or MFN obligations.

Either system would have to deal with the challenge of "new entrants," providers of domestic or imported products that wish to enter the market after the initial allocation of allowances. Rules governing allocation of allowances to new entrants would have to treat domestic and imported fuel in a non-discriminatory manner. Ensuring this non-discriminatory treatment may not be a simple or straightforward matter. WTO jurisprudence suggests that, for national-treatment purposes, the imported product must be treated in a manner equivalent to the best treatment afforded to a like domestic product. This suggests that a foreign "new entrant" must be able to compete on a level playing field with an established domestic like product, rather than a "similarly situated" domestic "new entrant."[33] If sales allowances become scarce during the commitment period, this equivalence of treatment may be difficult to ensure. If allowances are scarce, the importing government may, in effect, be required to favour foreign "new entrants" over domestic "new entrants," an outcome that may prove politically difficult to ensure.

If either the grandfathering or auctioning mechanisms were weighted to achieve other policy objectives, direct or indirect discrimination might arise. For example, Country A might wish to use its distribution or sales allowances to improve its energy independence by promoting the sale of energy products from domestic sources. This would clearly violate GATT national-treatment provisions. Favouring domestic industries in an allocation procedure might also trigger a challenge under the WTO Agreement on Subsidies and Countervailing Measures. This Agreement disciplines the use of subsidies, including the waiving of government revenue "otherwise due," which confer a benefit to a specific enterprise, industry, or group of industries operating within its jurisdiction. These benefits could enable domestically produced products to compete unfairly, in either the domestic or the international market, with products produced elsewhere. Under certain circumstances, these benefits may prove to be "actionable" subsidies that could be subject to countervailing duties imposed by an importer of the subsidized products, or to a direct challenge under the Subsidies Agreement.[34]

Emissions allowances that constrain carbon dioxide emissions inherently favour less-carbon-intensive fuels, and should increase the competitiveness of, for example, natural gas against petroleum or coal. An importing country could choose to enhance this preference by weighting its allocation to favour a particular fuel source, for environmental or other policy reasons. Although an allowance system favouring natural gas over petroleum, for example, might be (on the face of it) non-discriminatory, the trade impact might favour domestic producers or suppliers. Foreign petroleum producers or suppliers might challenge the measure as indirectly discriminatory or protectionist. A WTO analysis would turn on whether the two products – natural gas and petroleum – were "like" products.

The test for a "like product" in the context of Article III: 4 was recently articulated by a WTO panel. It calls for a case-by-case determination in which a panel should assess the following:

1. the product's properties, nature and quality
2. its end-uses in a given market
3. its tariff classification, and
4. consumers' tastes and habits.[35]

Analysis would depend, in part, on how fine a distinction the allocation system made between fuel types, and the end-uses in the markets in which the allocations were made. Broad distinctions, such as between natural gas and petroleum, would be likely to be more acceptable. These products are, for example, given distinct tariff classifications under the Harmonized Tariff System.

If the distribution or sale of energy were found to be covered by one of the importer's bound service sectors under the GATS, a similar analysis would apply, i.e. a panel would consider whether the energy services being subject to differential treatment were "like" services. Under GATS, the national-treatment provision is also broadly drafted. It provides that "formally identical or formally different treatment shall be considered to be less favourable if it modifies the conditions of competition in favour of services or service suppliers of the Member compared to like services or service suppliers of any other Member" (GATS Article XVII: 3). For the purposes of assessing the indirect discrimination arising from "formally identical" treatment, the GATS concept of "like service or service supplier" might be even broader than "like product" as the end-use customer may be interested more in the energy itself than in the carbon intensity of the source.

Downstream at the point of emission

A downstream system in which allowances are required of emitters of GHGs within the territory of the importing state is far less likely to create potential conflicts with WTO rules. In either situation, the allowances will concern only industry or emission sources *within* that state. Whether allocated by grandfathering or by auctioning, allowances will be distributed to, what for GATT purposes, are "domestic" industries based within that Member.

Allocation processes weighted against domestic firms with a majority foreign ownership would not be likely to concern the GATT, again because all the products of these firms would be considered "domestic" for GATT purposes. Such discriminatory treatment would be likely, however, to fall foul of GATS rules on treatment of foreign service suppliers. Allocation processes that favour less-polluting industries or enterprises might, however, be deemed to be subsidies by the WTO agreement on subsidies.

As has been indicated, if these preferences undermined the competitive relationship between the subsidized industries and "like" products in the international or domestic market-place, they may be subject to a direct challenge or to countervailing duties.

Electricity and other energy-intensive products

The designers of an ETS may also be tempted to discriminate between otherwise "like" products on the basis of the carbon content of the fuel used to produce those products. Allowances may be required of suppliers of fossil-fuel-intensive products such as electricity or steel.

The transboundary sale of electricity may raise particular challenges for an ETS. As the use of electricity itself does not generate emissions, participating countries might be quite happy to import electricity without adjusting their assigned amounts or requiring allowances of importers, suppliers, or end-users. Exporters of electricity may, however, feel that it should be the end-user of the electricity, rather than the generator, that should bear the responsibility for emissions. There have been suggestions, for example, that Denmark, in implementing its "CO_2 quota" regime, might require those wishing to import Danish electricity to first surrender a carbon equivalent of PAAs to Denmark, or to transfer to Denmark allowances that Denmark would recognize as valid.[36]

This requirement could act as the equivalent of an export restriction on a GATT-regulated product (electrical energy), with the importer's demand for a valid PAA or allowance acting as a precondition for an export licence. This may violate GATT Article XI disciplines on quantitative restrictions. Furthermore, by effectively allowing export only to those countries or entities capable of supplying allowances recognized as valid in Denmark, Denmark may violate GATT Article XIII, which requires that any quantitative restrictions that are in place be administered on a non-discriminatory basis. The GATS does not contain disciplines for quantitative restrictions on exports and would thus not be applicable here.

Particularly vulnerable to a WTO challenge would be any method of allocation that distinguished between otherwise like products on the basis of the way in which they are produced (so-called process and production methods – PPMs). Favouring electricity or steel produced using climate-friendly energy sources may lead to discrimination against or between imported electricity or steel produced by more carbon-intensive methods. Many trade analysts have suggested that such PPM-based distinctions, based on characteristics which are not physically embedded in the final product, are contrary to WTO principles.[37] This line of analysis argues that such distinctions would enable importing countries to use trade measures to coerce changes in environmental and other policies in their trading partners and would be open to wide abuse as means of disguised protectionism. More recent WTO jurisprudence suggests, however, that PPM-based distinctions do not inherently violate the GATT if they are applied in manner that is neither "arbitrary" nor "unjustifiable."[38] These terms arise from the application of the General Exceptions to the GATT and GATS, and are discussed below.

General exceptions

Measures that are caught by one of the GATT or GATS provisions discussed above may survive a WTO challenge on the basis of the application of the General Exceptions provided in Article XX GATT or Article XIV GATS.[39] The application of any of these exceptions is impossible in the abstract, without knowing the details of the challenged measure and the manner in which it is being applied.[40] Measures relating to the transfer and mutual recognition of allowances should not reach this stage if, as argued here, the trade in allowances does not fall directly within the WTO's coverage. Measures governing incidence of regulation and allocation of allowances that were found to violate WTO rules would be assessed for whether they were put in place to achieve certain recognized environmentally related policy objectives, and whether they were applied in a manner that would constitute a means of "arbitrary or unjustifiable discrimination between countries where the same conditions prevail" or a "disguised restriction on international trade."[41]

A WTO Member defending an ETS-related measure would have to first provide a "provisional justification" of the measure as being "necessary" for the protection of human, animal, or plant life or health (Article XX (b)), or as "relating to" the conservation of exhaustible natural resources (Article XX (g)). Thus far, provisional justification has proved easier under Article XX (g), which has been interpreted as requiring only that the measure bear a "substantial relationship" to the policy goal it purports to serve.[42] This analysis therefore focuses on Article XX (b).

In order to invoke Article XX (b), the following two criteria need to be met:

1. that the policy in respect of the measures for which the provision is invoked falls within the range of policies designed to protect human, animal, or plant life or health

2. that the inconsistent measures for which the exception is being invoked are *necessary* to fulfil the policy objective.[43]

Policies designed "to reduce air pollution resulting from the consumption of gasoline" have been recognized as "within the range of those concerning the protection of human, animal, and plant life or health mentioned in Article XX (b)."[44] It is likely that a policy to mitigate climate change would also fall within this range. The justification of the measure as "necessary" under the second criterion requires a more in-depth examination. A WTO panel has recently confirmed previous GATT jurisprudence, that a member cannot justify a measure inconsistent with another GATT provision as necessary:

... if an alternative measure which it could reasonably be expected to employ and which is not inconsistent with other GATT provisions is available to it. By the same token, in cases where a measure consistent with other GATT provisions is not reasonably available, a Member is bound to use, among the measures reasonably available to it, that which entails the least degree of inconsistency with other GATT provisions.[45]

Whether a particular measure meets this "least degree of inconsistency" test will require a highly contextual judgement by a WTO adjudicator. In the past, a WTO Panel has placed the burden of showing that there were no consistent (or less inconsistent) measures available squarely on the Member defending the measure. The test begs the question as to what rule of reason or proportionality should be used to assess the "availability" and effectiveness of the alternative measure and to balance this against the relative trade restrictiveness of the challenged measure.[46]

When assessing the range of measures available to a Member, a Panel would, no doubt, take into account any decisions of the COP that help to clarify the objectives of an ETS and that indicate agreement on the measures necessary to achieve those objectives.[47] It must be recognized, however, that Parties currently disagree on a number of objectives crucial to this analysis. Some Parties appear to believe that the Protocol would be best served by domestic measures that promoted a liberal, liquid, and non-discriminatory market in emissions allowances, and in climate-related products and services. Others may see the need for regulating one or both of these markets in order to promote domestic action, to reward trading partners that support the regime, or, perhaps, even to compensate those that are harmed by the regime's impact on the competitiveness of fossil fuels. Thus, trade restrictiveness can be seen as either central to the effectiveness of an ETS or as contrary to its fundamental objectives. This disagreement may have implications for the application of the Article XX chapeau, as well.

If a preliminary justification has been found under one of the sub-Paragraphs of Article XX, the Member defending the measure would then need to establish that it conforms to the requirements of the chapeau of Article XX. The chapeau is intended to prevent the abuse of the "limited and conditional"[48] exceptions in Article XX, and it has thus far been interpreted narrowly. It lays down three standards. The Member would need to demonstrate that the application of its measure did not constitute:

1. *arbitrary* discrimination between countries where the same conditions prevail

2. *unjustifiable* discrimination between countries where the same conditions prevail, or

3. a disguised restriction on international trade.

The application of these criteria requires the adjudicator to mark out "a line of equilibrium between the right of a Member to invoke an exception under Article XX and the rights of the other Members under varying substantive provisions," so that "neither of the competing rights will cancel out the other and thereby distort and nullify or impair the balance of rights and obligations" in the GATT.[49] The location of this line is difficult to establish *in abstracto*, as it is "not fixed and unchanging; the line moves as the kind and the shape of the measures at stake vary and as the facts making up specific cases differ."[50]

Recent WTO jurisprudence indicates that efforts to agree ETS rules multilaterally, under the auspices of COP, or through MRAs, should help guide a WTO Panel in drawing the line between the competing rights of WTO Members. The climate-change regime, with its broad participation of Parties, clearly reflects the "contemporary concerns of the community of nations about the protection and conservation of the environment" that informed the WTO Appellate Body's interpretation of the Article XX.[51] This article has, however, suggested that the COP may have difficulty in agreeing a common approach to all aspects of how parties should design their domestic ETS. In these circumstances, WTO jurisprudence indicates that Members must apply their rules in a manner that takes into account the different conditions that may occur in the territories of other Members. Members should not, for example, use their domestic rules to force other Members to adopt policies that are essentially the same as their own policies.[52] Thus, while WTO rules strongly favour multilateralism, they can also recognize that diplomatic efforts will not always succeed. Unilateral trade measures for environmental purposes, even as against non-Parties to an MEA, would be looked upon more favourably under WTO rules if the Member imposing the measure had first exhausted diplomatic efforts to agree upon common measures.

Conclusions: If and where a dispute may arise

As mentioned above, a well-designed ETS will necessarily involve the dislocation of vested interests by rewarding "climate-friendly" sovereign and private-sector behaviour. Furthermore, an international ETS, however well designed, will be untested and complex, and contain ambiguous rules. Even in good faith, conflicts may well arise:

1. In an effort to protect sovereign or commercial interests
2. in an effort to seek authoritative interpretation and clarification of ambiguous rules.

It should be the general concern of the designers of any international ETS to ensure that an effective mechanism for clarifying rules and avoiding and settling disputes is available to participants in the system. Of particular concern to the designers of the ETS will be that they ensure that disputes are resolved by a forum operating under the auspices of the Kyoto Protocol, which is most likely to resolve disputes with the objective of upholding the objects and purposes of the ETS. For reasons that have been raised, dispute resolution under WTO would probably be the least attractive forum for the ETS designers as it tends to place free-trade concerns ahead of environmental objectives.

WTO Agreements are ambiguous in many aspects, and leave broad scope for interpretation. Although the core of the GATT obligations have been in force for many countries for over 50 years, the 1994 Agreements on trade in goods and services are still relatively new and the jurisprudence interpreting them is limited. As has been suggested, what jurisprudence does exist tends to interpret the WTO's substantive rules broadly and the environmentally based exceptions to those rules narrowly.

The WTO Committee on Trade and Environment identified, in 1996, "about 20" MEAs currently in effect that contain trade provisions. Three in particular — the Montreal Protocol, the Convention on the International Trade in Endangered Species of Wild Fauna and Flora (CITES), and the Basel Convention — authorize measures that would clearly violate GATT rules, by banning the import of various substances on the basis of the status of the country of origin (e.g. countries that are not Parties to the MEA, Parties to the MEA that fall into particular categories, and Parties not in compliance with the MEA).

Despite the operation of these MEAs, there has never yet been a WTO challenge to a trade-related measure authorized by an MEA. The absence of a WTO dispute can be explained in part by the following:

1. self-restraint: WTO members that are Parties to these MEAs may have felt it appropriate to settle any differences within the context of the regime itself
2. broad participation: the main MEAs with trade-related measures have tended to attract at least as many Parties as have the GATT and now the WTO
3. narrow economic impacts: as discussed earlier, the scope of economic activity affected by previous MEAs has tended to be relatively narrow (the market in the international trade in ODS and hazardous waste, while not insignificant, is far less than the volume of trade in services in energy products and services).

It is not clear that any of these conditions will hold true for the Kyoto Protocol.

These observations, lessons from the WTO's extensive study of its relationship with MEAs, and recent WTO jurisprudence may be useful in guiding the design of an ETS under the Kyoto Protocol. Parties should:

1. make every effort to promote broad participation in the Kyoto Protocol

2. ensure that any trade-restrictive (or potentially trade-restrictive) aspects of an ETS are expressly authorized by, or are consistent with, rules on emissions trading agreed by the Convention or the Protocol institutions

3. ensure that adequate mechanisms are available within the Protocol itself to resolve any disputes that may arise between Member States and Parties to the Protocol.[53]

As with any exercise that is speculative and that is aimed at comprehensive "issue spotting," this analysis risks overplaying the potential for theoretical conflicts and the potential that theoretical conflicts might lead to actual disputes between states. The intention is precisely the opposite. Indeed, the analysis concludes that internationally traded emissions allowances are neither "products" nor "services," and thus the trade in these instruments is not directly governed by WTO disciplines. The way in which these allowances are allocated and are used to restrict emissions-related economic activity will, however, have an impact on the trade in products and services that are covered by the WTO. For these reasons, the measures chosen to implement an ETS must be designed, just as any other domestic measures that have the potential to impact trade, in a manner sensitive to WTO rules against discrimination. When rules that make legitimate distinctions between allowances, products, and services are necessary to the achievement of the Protocol's objectives, WTO exceptions should be interpreted to allow Parties to maintain these distinctions.

Notes

1. This chapter is based upon an earlier paper "WTO Issues Raised by the Design of an EC Emissions Trading System," June 1999, prepared by Jacob Werksman and Jurgen Lefevere, prepared as part of a consultancy project for the European Commission's Environment Directorate-General on "Designing Options for Implementing an Emissions Trading Regime for Greenhouse Gases in the EC." The opinions expressed in this article and in the earlier paper do not necessarily reflect those of the European Commission. Both papers benefited from comments from Eric Haites, Richard Parker, Far-hana Yamin, Fanny Missfeldt, Peter Morrison, Gary Sampson, Ned Helme, Tim Denne, Tim Hargrave, Per Schreiner, Philippe Sands, Annie Petsonk, and Richard Stewart. The views expressed are the author's.

2. United Nations Framework Convention on Climate Change, 9 May 1992 (entered into force 21 March 1994) [hereinafter UNFCCC], reprinted in 31 *International Legal Materials* (ILM) 849. As of this writing, the UNFCCC has received the ratification of 176 countries and the European Community (EC). All official documentation related to the UNFCCC can be found on the climate change regime Secretariat's website at khttp://www.unfccc.del. 1997 Kyoto Protocol to the UNFCCC, 11 December 1998 [hereinafter Kyoto Protocol]. Uncorrected text reprinted in 37 ILM 22 (1998); the corrected text and all official documentation relating to the Kyoto Protocol can be found on the climate-change regime Secretariat's website at khttp://www.unfccc.del. For general discussions of the Kyoto Protocol, see F. Yamin, "The Kyoto Protocol: Origins, Assessment and Future Challenges," 7:2 *Review of European Community and International Environmental Law* (RECIEL) 113–27 (1998); H. Ott, "The Kyoto Protocol: Unfinished Business," 40:6 Env't 16–20, 41–5 (1998); C. Breidenich *et al.*, "The Kyoto Protocol to the United Nations Framework Convention on Climate Change," *American Journal of International Law* 91(2): 315 (April 1998).

3. The rules, procedures and institutions that make up the World Trade Organization are contained in the legal texts of the Results of the Uruguay Round of Multilateral Trade Negotiations, GATT Secretariat, 1994. These texts and all official documentation related to the WTO can be found on the WTO website at http://www.wto.org.

4. WTO Agreements on the trade in goods include the GATT 1994 and the twelve other agreements contained in Annex 1A of the Marrakesh Agreement Establishing the World Trade Organization.

5. "Legal entities" may be authorized to participate in Article 6 of the Protocol (Joint Implementation) and "private and/or public" entities may be involved in activities under the Clean Development Mechanism (Article 12). Neither term is defined in the Protocol.

6. See EC submission to SB-10 (FCCC/SB/1999/MISC.3/Add.3, p. 21); Umbrella Group submission to SB-10 (FCCC/SB/1999/MISC.3/Add.1, p. 21).

7. Reference to Dutch emissions-trading scheme.

8. This Article does not address the WTO implications of project-based offsets generated under Articles 6 (Joint Implementation) and 12 (CDM).

9. According to this view, their lack of international legal "personality" means that they cannot be directly responsible for sovereign obligations that emanate from a public international legal agreement between states. Further, according to this view a private entity cannot be held directly responsible for a state's failure to comply with its sovereign obligations, nor can a private entity directly be recognized under international law as having itself "fulfilled" all or part of a sovereign obligation. This traditional view is, of course, no longer absolute. There are, for example, many cases now of private entities being able to litigate on the international plane directly against states, and the development of international agreements on the protection of foreign investors, and international human rights law, recognize that private persons can be the holders of certain rights directly under international law. But the suggestion that private entities could acquire, hold or transfer PAAs as such would extend very significantly beyond these limited developments, and states would be loath to hand over to private entities rights (and responsibilities) which historically remain within the domain of state monopoly.

10. Articles 3.10, 3.11 and Article 6.3.

11. The emissions-trading system contemplated here does not envisage the creation by an international authority of allowances, permits, or entitlements that can be directly held and traded by private entities. Early discussions of international emissions trading that pre-dated the Kyoto Protocol suggested that an international agency might be authorized to issue and allocate emissions allowances directly to states and private entities on the basis of an internationally agreed cap. See, e.g., R. Stewart, J. Weiner and P. Sands, "Legal Issues Presented by a Pilot International Greenhouse Gas Trading System," UNCTAD/GDS/GFSB/Misc.1 (1996). The Kyoto Protocol took a different approach, allocating parts of assigned amount directly to Parties, leaving it to individual governments to determine the extent to which they will trade, and involve private entities in that trade.

12. As of this writing, there are 134 members of the WTO. Countries that are Parties to the UNFCCC but are not, as yet, WTO members, include China, Russian Federation, Ukraine, Kazakstan, Saudi Arabia, and Samoa.

13. There has been some discussion as to whether electrical energy is sufficiently "tangible" to be considered a "product" for GATT purposes. State practice suggests that electrical energy would be (and, indeed, is) covered by the GATT. Electrical energy has been assigned a number under the Harmonized Tariff System (HTS). The European Court of Justice has held that, under European Community law, electricity constitutes a good, based in part on the fact that electricity is listed on its Tariff Nomenclature *Municipality of Almelo and Others v. Energie-bedrijf Ilsselmij NV*, Case C-393/92. Furthermore, for the United States, electrical energy has been "bound" at a 0 per cent tariff rate under GATT Article II. To find out whether each product is bound to a specific tariff, and at what rate it is bound, each Member's tariff schedule must be consulted. See, e.g., US 1999 Tariff Schedule http://www.dataweb.ustic.gov.

14. GATS 2000: Opening Markets for Services, European Commission DG-1, (1998), at page 57.

15. See Principles, Modalities, Rules and Guidelines for the Mechanisms under Articles 6, 12, and 17 of the Kyoto Protocol, Submissions from Parties, FCCC/SB/1999/Misc.3 [hereinafter Submissions from the Parties]; Non-Paper on Principles; Modalities; Rules and Guidelines for an International Emissions Trading Regime (In Particular for Verification, Reporting and Accountability), distributed 3 June 1998 by Australia, Canada, Iceland, Japan, New Zealand, Norway, Russian Federation, and the United States of America, on file with author [hereinafter Umbrella Group Non-Paper]; Non-Paper on Principles; Modalities; Rules and Guidelines for an International Emissions Trading Regime, distributed 5 June 1998 by the European Community and its member states, Czech Republic, Slovakia, Croatia, Latvia, Switzerland, Slovenia, Poland, and Bulgaria [hereinafter EC Non-Paper]; both on file with author.

16. See, for example, A. Petsonk, "The Kyoto Protocol and the WTO: Integrating Greenhouse Gas Emissions Allowance Trading Into the Global Marketplace," *Duke Environmental Law and Policy Forum* 10(7), (1999), pp. 185–220.

17. Most recent academic writing exploring the scope of the GATT's coverage has posited definitions of products in contrast to definitions of services, and describes products as having physical and tangible characteristics. See, for example, H. Peter Grey, "A negotiating strategy for Trade in Services," *Journal of World Trade* vol. 17, p. 378, 1997.

18. See, for example the unadopted GATT Panel Report, Canada – Measures Affecting the Sale of Gold Coins, L/5863, para. 51. Unadopted GATT Panel Reports "have no legal status in the GATT or WTO system since they have not been endorsed through decisions by the CONTRACTING PARTIES to GATT or WTO Members." However, "a [WTO] panel could nevertheless find useful guidance in the reasoning of an unadopted panel report that it considered to be relevant." Japan – Taxes on Alcoholic Beverages, WT/DS10/AB/R, 4 October 1996, p. 17.

19. Trebilcock, M. and R. Howse. *The Regulation of International Trade*, 2nd edn. (1999) New York: Routledge, at 272.

20. GATS, Article I: 3(b)

21. These are broadly defined to include "trading for own account or for account of customers, whether on an exchange, in an over-the-counter market or otherwise percentage derivative products including, but not limited to, futures and options; percentage transferable securities; percentage other negotiable instruments and financial assets." GATS, Annex on Financial Services, para 5 (x).

22. GATS, Article XVI: 2(b).

23. Council Regulation (EC) No 3093/94 of 15 December 1994 on substances that deplete the ozone layer, OJ L333, 22.12.1994, at 1.

24. Analogous Mutual Recognition Agreements are being considered between state governments along the US eastern seaboard that would allow a degree of interstate trading of NO_x emissions.

25. Such discrimination is built into both international and national tradeable allowance regimes. Internationally, under the Montreal Protocol, trading

between states through "industrial rationalization" can take place only between Parties to the Protocol. See also 42 *US Clean Air Act* sec 616. Similarly, governments participating in such schemes might wish to limit the ownership of the allowances they have issued to entities or governments within the territories of parties to the agreement. Domestically, under the US SOx Allowance Trading Regime of the *US Clean Air Act*, "persons" eligible to purchase, hold, or transfer allowances would appear to include non-US citizens and companies (even those based outside the United States) but to exclude governments other than the US federal governments, and those of the 48 contiguous US States. *US Clean Air Act* sec 403(b), 40 CFR sec 72.2. Under New Zealand's Transferable Quota System for commercial fisheries, venture with more than 25 per cent foreign ownership may not own quotas (OECD 1998).

26. Thus far, the Montreal Protocol Parties have adopted only two rules relevant to the operation of industrial rationalization, the first agreeing that "it is not possible for one country to increase its production without a corresponding reduction of production in another country." and the second authorizing the Montreal Protocol Implementation Committee, in response to the non-compliance of a Party, to recommend, "in accordance with the applicable rules of international law concerning the suspension of the operation of a treaty, of specific rights and privileges under the Protocol, whether or not subject to time limits, including those concerned with industrial rationalization." Decision 1/12D, Report of MOP-1; Annex V, Report of MOP-4.

27. UNFCCC, Article 3.5, (Principles) which provides that "[m]easures taken to combat climate change, including unilateral ones, should not constitute a means of arbitrary or unjustifiable discrimination or a disguised restriction on trade."

28. Already a number of service providers have shown an interest in their involvement with the trade in greenhouse emission allowances, such as the International Petroleum Exchange. See: International Petroleum Exchange, "*A Proposal to Reduce CO$_2$ Emissions in the European Union through the Introduction of an Emissions Trading Programme*" (undated).

29. GATS, Annex on Financial Services, Para 2.

30. "Identifying the Proper Incidence of Regulation in a European Union Greenhouse Gas Emissions Allowance Trading System." CCAP (1998). Paper prepared for the European Commission DG XI project "Designing Options for Implementing an Emissions Trading Regime for Greenhouse Gases in the EC."

31. See "Economic Instruments and the Business Use of Energy": Lord Marshall (UK Government November 1998), reaching a similar conclusion at page 13.

32. United States – Standards for Reformulated Gasoline, Report of the Panel, WT/DS2/R, 29 January 1996, para 6.10, as modified by the Appellate Body Report WT/DS2/AB/R 29, April 1996, citing United States – Section 337 of the Tariff Act or 1930, BISD 36S/386, para 5.11 (adopted on 7 November 1989) (Hereinafter US Gasoline Panel, and US Gasoline AB, respectively).

33. *Idem*, para 6.11–6.12.

34. WTO Agreement on Subsidies and Countervailing Measures, Article 1. For a detailed discussion of the relationship between an emissions-trading sys-

tem and the Subsidies Agreement, see R. Parker, "Limiting Greenhouse Gas Emissions Through Emissions Trading: An Interim Report to the H. John Heinz Center for Science, Economics and the Environment, Comments on WTO Aspects," 1999 (unpublished manuscript on file with author).
35. US Gasoline Panel, para 6.8. Essentially the same analysis was used by the WTO Appellate Body to interpret the term "like product" in the context of Article III: 2, "Japan – Taxes on Alcoholic Beverages," WT/DS8/AB/R, WT/DS10/AB/R, WT/DS11/AB/R, 4 October 1996, (AB-1996-2).
36. Purchasing Power Parity.
37. See, e.g., J. Jackson, *The World Trading System: Law and Policy of International Economic Relations*, 2nd edn, pp. 236–237, 1997.
38. United States – Import Prohibition of Certain Shrimp and Shrimp Products, WT/DS58/AB/R, para 121 (Hereinafter US-Shrimp-Turtle AB). See discussion in M. Trebilcock and R. Howse, *The Regulation of International Trade*, 2nd edn at 418–420, 1999 and J. Werksman, RECEIL 8:1 at 78, 1998.
39. As GATS Article XIV has never been invoked, and uses language similar to the GATT, this analysis concentrates on GATT Article XX.
40. GATT and WTO Panels have consistently stressed that these exceptions can only be interpreted on a highly contextual case-by-case basis. See, e.g., US Shrimp Turtle B, para 120.
41. Although it is not explicitly stated in the WTO Agreements, Article XX probably does not apply to subsidies affecting the trade in products that are challenged under the Agreement in Subsidies and Countervailing Measures. The SCM is linked to GATT 1994 (Article XVI) but it provides its own exemptions for narrow categories of environmental subsidies (SCM Art 8.2 (c)) and exceptions for subsidies with a *de minimis* impact on trade.
42. US Shrimp Turtle AB, Para 137. 42.
43. US Gasoline Panel, para 6.20.
44. US Gasoline Panel, Para 6.21
45. EFN/ "United States – Section 337 of the Tariff Act of 1930", BISD 36S/345, Para. 5.26 (adopted on 7 November 1989). A similar reasoning was followed in "Thailand – Restrictions on Importation of and Internal Taxes on Cigarettes," BISD 7S/200, Para. 75 (adopted on 7 November 1990). Both cases are quoted in Para. 6.24 of US Gasoline Panel. The Panel's interpretation of Article XX(b) was not appealed, and was thus not reviewed by the Appellate Body.
46. US Gasoline Panel, Para. 6.25–6.28. Further guidance on the interpretation of the meaning of "necessary" can be taken from the WTO Agreement on Sanitary and Phytosanitary measures (SPS Agreement), which is itself an elaboration on the provisions of Article XX (b) (see SPS Preamble, eighth tiret). Footnote to Article 5.6 of the SPS states that "[f]or the purposes of [this paragraph] a measure is not more trade restrictive than required unless there is another measure, reasonably available taking into account technical and economic feasibility, that achieves the appropriate level of sanitary or phytosanitary protection and is significantly less restrictive to trade."
47. The GATT Panel in Thailand – Restrictions on Importation of and Internal Taxes on Cigarettes – took into account the findings and decisions of the

World Health Organization (WHO) in determining the necessity of measures undertaken by Thailand in regulating the use of cigarettes. Adopted on 7 November 1990, DS10/R – 37s/200).
48. US Shrimp Turtle AB para 157.
49. US Shrimp Turtle AB para 159.
50. US Shrimp Turtle AB para 159.
51. US Shrimp Turtle AB para 129.
52. US Shrimp Turtle AB, para 163.
53. See Report of the CTE to the 1996 WTO Ministerial Conference WTE/CTE/1, para 178.

8

Investing in Sustainable Development: The Potential Interaction between the Kyoto Protocol and the Multilateral Agreement on Investment[1]

JACOB WERKSMAN AND CLAUDIA SANTORO[2]

Introduction

This chapter makes an initial attempt to assess the interaction between two, potentially revolutionary, international legal instruments, both of which attempt to influence the pattern of private-sector investment from developed to developing countries. The first is the 1997 Kyoto Protocol to the United Nations Framework Convention on Climate Change, which, when in force, will stimulate investments in the developing world in projects that reduce emissions of greenhouse gases (GHGs) through a "clean development mechanism" (CDM). The second is the draft Multilateral Agreement on Investment (MAI). If adopted and ratified, the MAI will set high global standards for the protection of investors and investments against discrimination, and against illegal expropriation. Although negotiated under the auspices of the Organization for Economic Co-operation and Development (OECD), the MAI will be open to membership of both developed and developing countries.

This discussion is necessarily speculative, as the detailed investment rules of the Kyoto Protocol's CDM have yet to be agreed. The MAI remains in draft form, and its adoption is by no means assured. Nevertheless, a study of the two instruments, even in their present forms, is of interest as it allows an exploration of the potential conflicts and synergies that may exist between efforts to use international law both to promote and to channel international investment flows. Furthermore, the greater use of market mechanisms in multilateral environmental agreements and the powerful trend towards strengthened investor protection both indicate the advisability of exploring these issues, even if neither the Kyoto Protocol nor the MAI take quite the final shapes that we presume.

While both agreements aim to promote investment flows, the MAI attempts to limit the extent to which states intervene in the market-place in order to channel such investments towards domestic policy objectives. Under the MAI, domestic regulations may not either directly or indirectly discriminate between domestic and foreign investors or investments. The Kyoto Protocol's CDM, while described as a "market mechanism," may in fact require extensive state intervention in investment decisions. The CDM does not view all categories of investor or investment equally, aiming instead to promote investments from developed into developing countries in activities that reduce GHG emissions.

The potential for conflict between economic liberalization regimes such as the MAI and the World Trade Organization (WTO) Agreements, and multilateral environmental agreements (MEAs) such as the climate-change regime, has generated volumes of academic literature. As yet, no formal disputes have arisen. There is, however, a marked trend in the regimes of MEAs to draw upon market mechanisms and market interventions to achieve policy goals. These include investment incentives, such as the CDM, tradeable allowances (also anticipated under the Kyoto Protocol), and technical barriers to trade arising from the prior informed-consent requirements under the emerging hazardous chemical and biosafety treaties.

Perceptions of the likelihood and the seriousness of the potential conflict differ widely. Hoping for synergy but seeking to avoid conflict, negotiators are increasingly looking for ways to carve out exceptions that will allow potentially competing rules to accommodate each other. However, as long as these regimes remain under the authority of distinct governance structures and dispute-settlement procedures, a risk persists that one set of objectives will have to concede to the other in an ad hoc and incoherent manner.

This chapter sketches the outlines of the CDM and the MAI, and explores the potential interaction between them.

The clean development mechanism

Under Article 12 of the Kyoto Protocol, a CDM will promote investments in climate-friendly project activities in non-Annex I Parties. The CDM will be governed by a multilaterally agreed set of rules and will operate under the supervision of the Conference of the Parties serving as the meeting of the Parties to the Protocol (COP/MOP) and an executive board. Emissions reductions accruing from the "project activities" carried out by non-Annex I Parties, once certified under agreed principles, may be acquired and used by Annex I Parties to contribute to compliance with their emissions-reductions obligations under Article 3 of the Protocol.

A well-designed CDM will have to offer positive incentives to the kind of investors and investments that will deliver "emission reductions that are additional to those that would occur in the absence" of the investment. Because CDM offsets will, in effect, allow Annex I Parties to increase their emissions above their Article 3 obligations, proof of CDM additionality is essential to ensure that overall global emissions are constrained.

Articles 12 and 3 of the Protocol leave open a number of variations on the steps in the CDM project activity cycle, i.e. the process whereby a project activity becomes a certified emissions reduction (CER) available for use as part of an Annex I Party's "assigned amount" under Article 3. It is possible to set out six essential steps in the CDM project activity cycle, as shown in table 8.1.

Table 8.1   Basic steps in the CDM[a] project activity cycle

Step	KP[b] Article	Participant(s)
1. Approval of project activity	12.5(a)	S_i and S_h[c]
2. Certification of environmental and financial additionality of project activity	12.5	Operational entity
3. Auditing and verification of emissions reductions	12.7	Independent auditor/ verifier
4. Assessment of proceeds for administrative and adaptation costs	12.8	To be determined by COP/MOP[d]
5. Transfer/acquisition of CER[e]	3.12	S_i and S_h
6. Addition of CER to assigned amount	3.12	S_i

a. CDM, clean development mechanism.

b. KP, Kyoto Protocol.

c. S_i, investor state; S_h, host state.

d. COP/MOP, Conference of the Parties/Meeting of the Parties to the Protocol.

e. CER, certified emissions reduction.

The simplest of potential CDM transactions would involve *bilateral*, project-by-project transactions between one investor and one host. These transactions may be purely intergovernmental in character or may also involve private investors and hosts.

More complex transactions are those proposed by a number of multilateral development banks and private financial service providers, which would draw together multiple investors and multiple projects, and *multilateralize* various steps in the CDM project activity cycle. Additional "service providers" may be required to pool eligible project activities into portfolios, to auction project activities or CERs to the highest bidder, or simply to match investors and project activities in a transparent manner (table 8.2).

More complex, *multilateral* arrangements are thought to achieve economies of scale, to increase the transparency and availability of

Table 8.2   Options for multilateral arrangements

Service provider (participant)	Role
Fund manager	• Pools eligible project activities into a portfolio • Attracts finance from investors • Distributes CERs[a] to investors and hosts
Auctioneer of project activities	• Collects eligible projects • Auctions project activities to the highest bidder
Auctioneer of CERs	• Collects CERs • Auctions CERs to the highest bidder
Clearing-house	• Posts information on eligible projects • Helps to match prospective investors with project activities

a. CER, certified emissions reduction.

information about transactions, to encourage the participation of smaller hosts and investors, to promote balanced bargaining positions between investors and hosts, and to spread the risk of project failure across a larger number of participants and project activities.[3]

The Multilateral Agreement on Investment

Drawing upon precedents from bilateral and plurilateral investment treaties, the MAI[4] is intended to provide a "high standard" of protection to foreign investors and investments when operating overseas. The MAI would achieve this by constraining a very broad range of government regulatory activity that might directly or indirectly harm the interests of foreign investors or that might adversely affect the value of foreign-owned investments.

Host governments would be prohibited from applying discriminatory treatment against foreign investors or investors within their
jurisdiction. National treatment (NT) and most-favoured nation
(MFN) obligations within the MAI would require governments to
extend to foreign investors and investments the same treatment that
(or better treatment than) they extend to domestic investors and
investments, and to treat foreign investors from different countries
equally. The MAI would prohibit both *de facto* and *de jure* discrimination by the host state. This means that host country regulations
that discriminate between domestic and foreign investors either expressly, or *in their effect*, would be open to challenge.

Parties to the MAI would also be prevented from forcing investors
to conform to certain types of "performance requirements." Host
governments would be prevented from conditioning the right to
invest in, for example, the use by the investor of a certain percentage
of local goods, or on the transfer of technology. This prohibition
holds even if it is applied equally on domestic or foreign investors.

Foreign investors would also be protected from illegal expropriation of their investment assets and, in circumstances in which investments were legally expropriated, would be entitled to a high
standard of compensation. Expropriation is defined broadly to include not just the direct taking of an investment but also indirect
takings including "measures having equivalent effect." The breadth
of this definition is intended to include so-called "creeping expropriation," whereby government taxation or regulations, short of a
direct taking, may diminish the value of an investment.

The level of investment protection is further strengthened by the
MAI's very broad definition of the types of "investment" that it will
protect. The MAI protects all rights acquired by foreign investors,
regardless of the inflow of capital into the host country. The term
"investment" in the MAI broadly includes every kind of asset owned
or controlled directly or indirectly by an investor; these include intangible assets, state authorizations or licences, claims to money, and
all kinds of contractual rights. A proposed interpretative note in the
MAI is expected to clarify that an "asset" must have "the characteristics of an investment, such as the commitment of capital or other

resources, the expectation of gain or profit and the assumption of risk."

Furthermore, in a provision that extends well beyond the majority of existing bilateral and plurilateral investment regimes, the MAI prohibits "pre-establishment" discrimination. This would prohibit host governments from screening foreign investors prior to their establishing an investment presence.

The MAI will take a "top-down" approach to liberalizing investment rules. In other words, countries joining the MAI that wish to preserve their sovereign discretion to make distinctions between foreign and domestic investors must specify measures or sectors of their economy that they wish to shield from MAI disciplines, and formally lodge these with the OECD secretariat as country-specific exceptions. The exceptions will then probably be subject to "stand-still" and "roll-back" requirements that discourage Parties from adding to their exceptions. It is also probable that, through negotiations, political pressure will be applied to Parties to eliminate exceptions gradually over time.

Finally, the MAI's rules would be backed by compulsory state-to-state and investor-to-state dispute-settlement procedures. These allow both private investors and their home states to enforce the MAI through the binding judgements of an international arbitral tribunal.

Potential interaction between the CDM and the MAI

By providing a stable regulatory environment for investment, the MAI would support the CDM's general objective of promoting flows of capital from developed to developing countries. However, depending on how the details of the CDM rules are designed, there is some potential for conflict between the two regimes. Reference is made here to an initial analysis of this potential undertaken by the OECD Secretariat.[5]

The broad scope of the MAI

The MAI would clearly have jurisdiction over any CDM project activity carried out in the territory of a developing country that chose to become a contracting party. Both a CDM project activity and any CER it might generate would fall within the broad scope of the MAI's definition of an *investment*. A CER has the characteristics of an investment – that is, the commitment of capital or other resources (i.e. technology transfer), the expectation of gain (i.e. the generation of profits and of CERs), and the assumption of risk (i.e. the risk that the project will not generate CERs). The CER may be a form of debt, such as a financial instrument, or a right conferred pursuant to law or contract, such as a government authorization or permit.

The MAI's broad definition of *investor* would extend rights to all private entities or state-owned enterprises involved in a CDM transaction. It would not, however, include investments made by states themselves. States are not considered to be in need of any additional protection as investors, and would avail themselves of the diplomatic channels or the state-to-state dispute-settlement or non-compliance procedures under the Protocol to defend their rights.

Non-discrimination: MFN and NT

The MAI prohibits both *de facto* and *de jure* discrimination by the host state between foreign and domestic investors (the NT standard) and between two foreign investors from different states (the MFN standard). This means that host-country regulations that discriminate between these categories of investors either expressly, or in their effect, would be open to challenge under the MAI by either states or investors.

A potential for conflict may arise if a Party hosting a CDM project is encouraged or required by the Protocol to discriminate expressly between investors on the basis of the status of their home country in at least four ways, as outlined below.

1. Annex I versus non-Annex I Parties

Although not expressly prohibited by Article 12, it is unclear whether investors from non-Annex I Parties would be entitled to participate in CDM activities. Under some conceptions of "additionality," project sponsors may be required to demonstrate North-to-South flows of financial resources before a project activity could be certified. In such a case, investors from non-Annex I Parties might be denied access either to eligible project activities or to CERs. It may be argued that a non-Annex I investor, without emissions-reduction commitments of its own, would have no incentive to invest in CDM projects. However, if CERs are designed as a tradeable commodity, it is entirely possible that an investor without commitments of its own would see the investment potential in buying and holding CERs to sell to the highest bidder should supplies become scarce.

2. Complying versus non-complying Parties

The Protocol Parties may wish to condition an investor's eligibility to participate in CDM activities on the basis of whether its home country is currently in compliance with its commitments. Article 6 of the Protocol (joint implementation; JI) sets a precedent by suspending a Party's right to add emission-reduction units (ERUs) generated by an JI project to its assigned amount if issues are raised with regard to either the investor or the host state's compliance.[6]

It may be argued that a Party to the Protocol that has authorized the use of such sanctions in general would be unlikely to invoke (or even legally estopped from invoking) the MAI to challenge such a sanction when it is applied against one of its own investors. However, the MAI's investor-state dispute-settlement procedures may allow the investor (who may care less about the niceties of international legal obligations) to challenge a measure, even if its government feels otherwise.

3. Party versus non-Party

Although this is not explicit in Article 12, most conceptions of the CDM would probably not allow investors from host countries not

Parties to the Protocol (or, at the very least, those not Party to the Convention)[7] to participate in the generation and sale of CERs. This would be justified both for enforcement reasons (as a non-Party host country could not be expected to hold its investor to comply with CDM rules) and also to give all potential host countries an incentive to join the Protocol.[8]

Indeed, the OECD Secretariat's own analysis of potential conflicts between the MAI and MEAs that used quotas and permits noted that:

> If quotas or permits are earned by enterprises as a return on participation (investment) in a pollution reducing project in a developing country, the question would arise as to whether the ineligibility for such a quota or permit (return) of enterprises of countries not Party to the system constituted a discriminatory measure of the project host. If the eligibility requirement were established by an international regime, that might be interpreted for MAI purposes to be a measure of each Party to it.

The OECD Secretariat qualifies the risk by suggesting that barring investors from non-Parties to the Protocol from eligibility may not be necessary, as a CER would have no value in the legal system of the investor's home country. This analysis is, however, based on the assumption that CERs would not have an inherent value as an investment that could be sold to investors in home countries where they did have value.

4. Foreign versus domestic investor

Under some conceptions of the CDM, a host country or its own domestic investors would be eligible to invest in CDM project activities without the involvement of any foreign investor. Foreign capital would flow only at the point when the CERs were ready to be sold. In order to promote an endogenous, climate-friendly, technology in a particular sector, a host country might decide to bar foreign investors from CDM eligible project activities in the same sector, at least until the domestic producer was prepared to compete with foreign rivals. The MAI prohibition on pre-establishment discrimination would preclude such an approach that would discriminate against foreign investors.

Performance requirements

Article 12 provides that CDM project activities should assist developing countries in achieving sustainable development, and should promote real, measurable, and long-term benefits. By some analyses, such criteria would lead a host country to require a CDM project activity to shorten the chain of production by using locally produced goods or services, to build domestic capacity by employing local citizens, or to bring about the transfer of technology to a local firm. These employment and performance requirements, even if imposed equally on domestic and foreign investors, would potentially violate the MAI.

The MAI's prohibition on performance requirements can be softened in two ways. First, the enumerated requirements may be employed in circumstances where they are conditioned on the "receipt or continued receipt of an advantage." If CERs generated by project activities are seen as being within the control and largesse of the host state, then conditioning their transfer to an investor on the basis of performance requirements may be permissible. Secondly, the MAI text has a specific environmental exception applicable to the provision on performance requirements. Modelled on Article XX of the General Agreement on Tariffs and Trade (GATT) 1994, the performance-requirement exception would allow measures that might otherwise have violated the MAI if the host country can establish that they are "necessary for the conservation of living or non-living exhaustible natural resources."

Expropriation and compensation

Direct expropriation

The transaction at the core of the CDM (Article 12 (3)) is described so ambiguously as to leave unanswered a fundamental question: who has rights to the CER, or the expectation of a CER, at what stage in the CDM cycle? This issue is of great importance from the standpoint of investor protection, in that efforts by the host state to control or retain a CER for various reasons may be characterized as an "expropriation" of the investor's "investment" as broadly defined in the MAI.

If emissions reductions resulting from a CDM project activity were treated consistently with the regime established for Annex I party emissions, they could be characterized as "belonging" to the host government. Each Annex I Party has been "assigned" emissions allowances, and will ultimately be held responsible for emissions and credited for reductions that take place within its territory. Annex I Parties may, under some proposals for emissions trading, then devolve the right to these allowances to individual domestic emitters or investors. Were a similar construct applied to the emissions reductions achieved within the territory of a CDM non-Annex I host, the disposition of CERs would lie within the power of the host government. Host government regulations affecting the validity or value of a CER might not in these circumstances be considered an "expropriation."

Alternatively, Parties may determine that host countries should be entitled to retain a share of any CERs generated within their territory. Some have argued that a host should be able to collect a "resource rent" for maintaining the regulatory framework necessary for hosting the project activity. If standard rules are not agreed among the Parties on this issue, disputes might arise over the ad hoc expropriation of all or some of the CERs expected by an investor.

CDM rules may, indeed, increase the need for selective expropriation of CERs. As part of either a domestic or an international compliance regime, a host country acting of its own volition or on instruction from a Protocol body might suspend the validity of a CER. As has been indicated, Article 6 of the Protocol (JI) sets a precedent by suspending a Party's right to add ERUs generated by an JI project to its assigned amount if issues are raised with regard to either the investor or the host states' compliance.

Indirect expropriation

The scope of the MAI's definition of expropriation would set a new global standard. Regulatory takings, or state measures such as taxation and licensing, which may affect foreign investments, do not traditionally amount to expropriation unless they are discriminatory or have the precise intent and effect of confiscation.[9] The MAI, like the North American Free Trade Agreement (NAFTA) upon which it is modelled, expands the international standard for expropriation to cover "regulatory" takings. The MAI prohibits the taking of any state action or measure that has the equivalent effect of direct or indirect nationalization or "creeping" expropriation. There is standing available to an investor concerning an alleged breach of an MAI obligation which "causes loss or damage to the investor or it investment."

Whether the MAI would require compensation for the passage of regulations that reduce the potential for generating profits, or otherwise cause loss or damage to the investment, is a matter of current debate. The experience with NAFTA to date demonstrates that the current wording of the expropriation provision would support these claims. The liberalized MAI imposes broad obligations on states and new rights for investors. Together, this increases the possibility that any state regulation will directly or indirectly discriminate against one or more investors/investments. With broader grounds for discrimination, and a high standard of compensation, investors' rights to dispute-resolution mechanisms against states will undoubtedly influence domestic policy development under an MAI regime.

This chapter now turns to two scenarios that test at a deeper level the potential relationship between the CDM and the MAI from the perspectives of a non-CDM investor and a CDM investor.

The MAI and the non-CDM investor

The CDM, as with all environmental regulatory instruments, may be vulnerable to attack under the MAI if it provides the basis for any facially neutral regulation that has a disproportionate impact on a foreign investor. In this context, CDM-related rules aimed at strengthening a host government's regulatory framework would be as vulnerable to attack as any new environmental regulation that threatened the expectations of a foreign investor.

For example, every CDM project activity must achieve environmental additionality in order to be certified. This means that the project activity must bring about overall benefits that would not have occurred in the host country in the absence of the project. A counterfactual baseline, or reference case, must therefore be constructed (on either a multilateral or bilateral basis) to describe what the host country would have done in the absence of the project activity. The counterfactual baseline must be reliable and verifiable, in order to achieve the global reduction of GHG emissions. If CDM emissions reductions that are not additional are allowed to be certified and are offset against Annex B commitments, overall global emissions will increase against a business-as-usual baseline.

The COP/MOP will probably devise a common framework for determining baselines. The framework may be prescriptive (such as the existing framework for Global Environment Facility (GEF) projects, which requires that a project baseline must reflect at least a minimal standard of "environmental reasonableness") or it may give the Parties involved in the project activity more latitude when defining the baseline on a project-by-project basis. We assume the latter for this analysis.

Once a baseline is established between the host country and the Annex I investor, and a project activity has been *certified*, the host country may choose to adopt regulations that support the baseline so that the project activity will be verified and produce CERs. In order to prevent the reductions achieved from a CDM investment to be wiped out by emissions increases in the host country, CDM rules may require the host government to demonstrate within a broad systems boundary that dirty technologies are not being introduced elsewhere.

Analogies can be drawn from the NAFTA challenge of a US-based company, Ethyl Corp. (Ethyl), against the Canadian government for enacting legislation to ban the import and interprovincial transport of the gasoline (petrol) additive methylcyclopentadienyl manganese tricarbonyl (MMT) on the grounds that it is a dangerous toxin. MMT is added to gasoline to enhance octane and to reduce engine "knocking." Ethyl is the only North American producer of MMT, and a Canadian company directly benefited from the ban on MMT. Ethyl sued the Canadian government for approximately US$250 million, arguing that MMT is safe and that Canada's ban on the additive constitutes an illegitimate expropriation of Ethyl's assets – namely, its Ontario plant, which conducted the final mixing of MMT. The Canadian government challenged the jurisdiction of the panel to hear the case, on the grounds that Ethyl followed improper procedure in bypassing their state government in initiating the claim. The panel ruled against them, finding that Ethyl had standing under NAFTA provisions, which are almost identical to those in the MAI.[10] Shortly thereafter, the claim was settled for approximately US$13 million and an apology by the Canadian government.[11]

The former Chairman of the MAI negotiations has recommended an addition to the draft MAI text of an "Interpretative Note" that would seek to prevent efforts by foreign investors to chill legislation that is facially neutral but that may have disproportionate impact. A footnote to the text would clarify that the MAI should not inhibit "normal non-discriminatory government regulatory activity." It also clarifies the presumption that it is within each Contracting Party's discretion to determine what measures "it considers appropriate" to protect health, safety, and the environment. However, the usefulness of the footnote is seriously undermined by the concluding phrase "provided such measures are consistent with this agreement," which restricts the Contracting Party's discretion to the bounds of the MAI obligations on NT, MFN, and expropriation. In other words, the paragraph does not provide an exception for environmental measures but, rather, what could, at best, be described as a clarification of burdens of proof. The burden of proof would clearly be on the complainant to establish that a facially neutral measure is inconsistent with the MAI.[12]

Similarities between the MAI and GATT principles and provisions assist understanding of this issue. The Chairman's Note includes a proposal to remove the brackets that currently appear around the phrase "in like circumstances" in the Negotiating Text of the MFN and NT provisions and to add an interpretative footnote. This proposal is in direct response to news of the Ethyl dispute.[13] This note is intended to allow a policy maker or an adjudicator of a dispute to consider "all relevant circumstances, including those related to a foreign investor and its investments, in deciding to which domestic or third country investors and investments they should appropriately be compared."

In substance, the Chairman's approach introduces a concept similar to the "like product" concept under the GATT. When an investment-related measure is challenged as discriminatory, the term "like circumstances" invites a comparison between the domestic and foreign investors/investments, or between two or more foreign investors/investments, to determine whether the "the circumstances" related to the investors/investments justifies a distinction being made between them. Should the circumstances prove to be "like," the discriminatory treatment would, presumably, violate the MAI.

The Interpretative Note anticipates two types of differential treatment that would be permissible with the introduction of the "like circumstances" language: (1) facially discriminatory measures that are justified by "legitimate policy reasons"; (2) measures that are facially neutral but that differ in their effect.

One can see emerging from the relationship between the phrase "like circumstances" and the Interpretative Note, a similar dynamic to that between the GATT's NT and MFN provisions, and the general exceptions in Article XX. Indeed, the Interpretative Note provides an example of the type of measure that, with the inclusion of the phrase "like circumstances," would be considered as justifying an exception to the MAI (i.e. one "needed to secure compliance with domestic laws that are not inconsistent with national treatment and most favoured nation treatment." In essence, this repeats the general exception in Article XX (d).[14]

Thus the Interpretative Note, in effect, introduces a very broadly worded general exception to the MAI's NT and MFN requirements. An analysis of whether the "like circumstances" exception applies, would appear to require, in the context of a facially discriminatory measure, an assessment of whether the policy reasons behind the measure are "legitimate". In the context of a facially neutral measure, a complaining party or investor could not rely solely on the effect of the measure to demonstrate a violation of the MAI.

However, unlike Article XX, there is no direct guidance in the text (other than the Article XX (d) language), as to what types of policy reasons (such as conservation of natural resources) the negotiators consider "legitimate," or by what standard they should be judged legitimate (not arbitrary or unjustifiable). Given the "package" nature of the Chairman's Note, a strong argument could be made that the provisions on labour and the environment in the preamble provide guidance as to what is "legitimate," but this is by no means clear.

Left as a footnote to the text, the Interpretative Note takes on a questionable legal character. The Interpretative Notes to the GATT 1947 have played an influential role in the interpretation of that agreement, in part because they were explicitly included, through an Annex to Article XXXIV of the GATT, as "an integral part of" the Agreement.

Generally, the breadth and vagueness of the Interpretative Note could prove attractive to environment and labour groups, as they seem to provide considerable scope to the policy maker to determine individually what types of policies are "legitimate." Presumably, measures taken in accordance with MEAs would fall within what the Interpretative Note to the NT/MFN provision describes as "legitimate," but this has not been made clear. However, in a regime that has, as its primary objective, the promotion of investor protection and liberalization, the risks are high that, in the absence of clear guidance from either the content or the legal character of the Interpretative Note, the concept of "like circumstances" will be interpreted to prevent legitimate distinctions between investors/investments. The inclusion of a positive right to protect the environment (subject to GATT-based disciplines prohibiting arbitrary, unjustifiable discrimination or disguised restrictions) is a far preferable option for allowing MAI contracting parties to pursue legitimate policy goals without being open to unrestricted challenges.[15] Potential conflicts with MEAs, such as the CDM, could be addressed more directly through a specific provision on MEAs in a General Exception clause applicable to the entire MAI.

The MAI and the CDM investor

In another scenario, the CDM project activity may itself be expropriated by a host state. A host state may decide to nationalize a major industry or natural resource for purposes of social and economic development. For example, CDM project activities may include land-use change and forestry activities undertaken to reduce carbon emissions or increase carbon sequestration.[16] Deforestation activities lead to combustion and decomposition of woody material and release carbon. Where land is purchased through a CDM project activity for the promotion of growth and regeneration in secondary forests and on pasture lands, and deforestation is prevented, the additional carbon that is sequestered may generate CERs.

A change of government and/or change in priorities or circumstance may cause a host state, after agreeing to participate in a carbon-sequestration project, to nationalize the land for other purposes. In addition to claiming expropriation of the land, an investor of a forestry CDM project will be likely to allege the expropriation of the CER certification. For the expropriation of the CER, the investor is likely to claim compensation for both the value of the land and the anticipated value of the offsets.

A host country could, therefore, face costs that include the provision of the same or similar land for a CDM project activity and compensation for present and future lost gains during the period of expropriation (or pecuniary compensation in lieu thereof). Additional benefits attached to the land itself as a CDM project activity (i.e. additional monetary investment; research for baseline; technology transfer) may also be claimed. The MAI requires compensation "equivalent to *the fair market value of the expropriated investment* immediately before the expropriation occurred." In fact, the Ethyl case demonstrates how investors consistently argue (without exception under NAFTA) that an investment had additional value, both tangible and intangible, which goes uncompensated. Ethyl had claimed that the legislative debate in the Canadian Parliament itself constituted an expropriation of Ethyl's assets because public criticism of MMT damaged the company's reputation. US trade officials responded by arguing that the ability of investors to use legal threats to influence legislative debates is a healthy innovation that will prevent governments from passing laws that violate international agreements.[17]

MAI investor-state dispute resolution

The investor-state dispute-settlement procedures in the MAI would fill a significant gap in the Protocol's institutional structure. At present, it is anticipated that only Parties to the Protocol would have the power to invoke any of the Protocol's non-compliance or dispute-settlement procedures. The MAI would be the first international agreement, open for accession to the global community, to give investors new rights and states additional obligations and to provide a mechanism for investors to enforce these rights through international arbitration.[18] In extending these rights, the MAI may shift the balance of power between investor and host government in a way that was not anticipated when the climate negotiators designed the CDM.

Each contracting Party to the MAI gives its unconditional consent to international arbitration in accordance with Article 4 upon signing the agreement. Any issue in dispute with respect to an alleged breach of an obligation (i.e. unlawful expropriation of a CER or CDM project activity) under the MAI that causes loss or damage to the investor or its investment, shall be decided in accordance with the MAI, interpreted and applied in accordance with applicable rules of international law. A Party to the MAI would further have to agree to submit any other investment dispute concerning any obligation which the host state has assumed pursuant to the agreement to enter into a CDM project activity or transfer a CER (which can be considered an investment authorization) to arbitration. In this case, the rules of law agreed to by the Parties under the agreement would prevail. Where the agreement is silent, the law of the Contracting Party and applicable rules of international law prevail. The investor may choose to submit any dispute that cannot be settled through negotiation or consultation to a number of specified forums. Only the investor has a right to withdraw a dispute once it has been initiated. In the absence of an investor's right to bring a claim directly, domestic industries or multinationals would put pressure on their home governments to bring actions to protect their commercial interests. Specious claims that may not be in the bilateral or global interest are usually filtered out by the home government. In the absence of this government filter, and on the basis of the experience of NAFTA, the MAI will be likely to increase international arbitration.

Conclusions: Regulating free markets

The agreement on Article 12 resolved a number of critical aspects of how the CDM will manage project-based JI between Annex I and non-Annex I Parties to the Protocol. However, many gaps remain to be filled, and the negotiating dynamic for the next stage of the development of the CDM remains fundamentally unchanged. This dynamic can now be characterized as pitting a market-based approach against an "interventionist approach" based on traditional public-sector development assistance. Both approaches stress the need for a system capable of generating credible CERs but differ on the best means of achieving this. The extent to which the CDM might fall foul of the MAI will depend on the level of state intervention that Parties feel will be necessary to achieve the CDM's policy goals.

A market-based approach relies upon healthy competition in a transparent market-place to provide the most efficient and effective means of encouraging hosts and investors to design credible CDM project activities. Once the intergovernmental process has set the rules on the types of project activities that will be eligible for certification, the private sector – which holds the capital and technology necessary to the CDM's success – would be entrusted with designing projects and would be entitled to hold and transfer CERs.

Interventionists are more sceptical of the private sector's ability to fulfil the CDM's stated purpose of assisting non-Annex I Parties to "achieve sustainable development." Such an approach emphasizes the need for the active involvement of public-sector institutions, including home and host governments and international development institutions, in promoting the design of projects driven by broad-based policy concerns rather than market disciplines.

The debate is further complicated by the tension between those that wish to see the CDM up-and-running quickly and with as low transaction costs as possible, and those that remain cautious and are willing to increase costs in exchange for greater accountability. Parties at both ends of this spectrum place the CDM at risk, either by undermining its credibility or by weighing it down with an over-burdensome bureaucracy.

Theoretically, conflicts between the Protocol and the MAI could be handled through a system of country reservations, whereby any Party to the Protocol that chose to accede to the MAI would "opt out" any relevant measures. If applied liberally, this could allow the Contracting Parties to the MAI to exempt from the Agreement's NT and MFN rules legitimate existing measures that facially discriminate between domestic and foreign investors, in order to achieve a variety of policy goals, including environmental protection. For example, the Parties to NAFTA, under a similar legal arrangement, have exempted their fisheries and other environmentally related sectors from that Agreement's NT obligations.

However, experience under other liberalization regimes suggests that it is difficult to draft exemptions or waivers precisely enough to avoid challenges based on such broad principles as NT and MFN. The continuing challenge to the MAI negotiators and to the designers of the CDM will be to coordinate efforts in both regimes to ensure that the potential for conflict is diminished.

Even if the MAI is never adopted, capital-exporting countries are likely to continue to exert pressure for the acceptance of high standards of investor protection in other forums, either bilaterally or multilaterally. Coming to agreement on crucial issues, such as the rules on the ownership or sharing of entitlements to CERs generated by CDM project activities, and the dispute-settlement procedures available to private entities, are likely to prove important to the CDM's stability and success.

Notes

1. The preparation of this chapter was funded in part by the United Nations University.
2. Claudia Santoro is a lawyer with the Ontario Ministry of the Environment's Legal Services Branch. The views expressed in this paper are hers and her co-author's alone and are not to be attributed to any Ontario ministry or official or to Her Majesty the Queen in Right of Ontario.
3. Yamin, Farhana, "Operational and Institutional Challenges," Chapter 5, in *Issues & Options: The Clean Development Mechanism* (UNDP 1998) [http://www.undp.org/seed/eap/Publications/1998/1998a.html]
4. The Multilateral Agreement on Investment, Negotiating Text as of 24 April 1998, http://www.oecd.org.
5. Relationships Between the MAI and selected Multilateral Agreements (MEAs), Note by the OECD Secretariat, 13 March 1998.
6. Note, however, that the suspension of this right applies to the non-complying state directly, and not to the investor. Transfers and acquisitions of ERUs can continue during the period of non-compliance, thus avoiding a direct discriminatory action by the host state against the investor.
7. This distinction may well be necessary as Article 12.10 appears to allow CDM project activities to be certifiable as early as 2000, most likely prior to the entry into force of the Protocol.
8. Note, however, that the Montreal Protocol, in order to avoid potential conflicts with WTO rules, and to encourage compliant behaviour of non-Parties, extends certain Protocol privileges to non-Parties that can demonstrate they are acting in accordance with the Protocol's provisions.
9. Ian Brownlie, *Principles of Public International Law*, 4th edn. Oxford: Clarendon Press, 1990, at 531–538.
10. Shawn McCarthy, "Trade showdown with Ethyl to rule on import ban," in the *Globe and Mail* (July 10, 1998).
11. The data in this chapter are reproduced from: Shawn McCarthy, "Gas War: The fall and rise of MMT. When the car and oil firms went to battle, Ottawa lost", in the *Globe and Mail* (July 24, 1998) ⟨http://www.theglobeandmail.com⟩. Note that the apology by the Canadian government undermined the basis for

the legislation banning MMT. The apology released by the Canadian was: "Current scientific information fails to demonstrate that MMT impairs the proper functioning of automobile on-board diagnostic systems. Furthermore, there is no new scientific evidence to modify the conclusions drawn by Health Canada in 1994 that MMT poses no health risk": see ⟨http://www.ethyl.com/news/7-20-98.html⟩.

12. Arguably, the Canadian ban on MMT should have been enacted through federal environmental legislation to better withstand a NAFTA challenge. The Canadian government did not pursue this course given what it considered a clear lack of jurisdiction, since there was no solid scientific proof of the health risks associated with MMT. The Canadian government used what it considered to be its most poignant legislative tool for a valid public purpose. It is significant to note that MMT is currently banned in California. See, Michelle Sforza and Mark Vallianatos, "Ethyl Corporation v. Government of Canada: Chemical Firm uses Trade Pact to Contest Environmental Law", Preamble Centre at ⟨http://www.preamble.org/mai/briefeth.html⟩.

13. OECD negotiators were apparently shocked by news of this dispute. See, Canadian Environmental Law Association, "The MAI and the Environment: Context and Concerns" at ⟨http://www.web.net/cela/maibrief.html⟩.

14. GATT 1994 Article XX (d) provides a general exception for measures "necessary to secure compliance with laws or regulations which are not inconsistent with the provisions of this Agreement, including those relating to customs enforcement, the enforcement of monopolies operated under paragraph 4 of Article II and Article XVII, the protection of patents, trade marks and copyrights, and the prevention of deceptive practices."

15. See also Jacob Werksman, "Is the Multilateral Agreement on Investment Sustainable?", a WWF International Discussion Paper (October, 1997).

16. Note that the absence of any mention of sinks in Article 12, in the context of their express inclusion in Article 6, provides the COP/MOP with the flexibility to exclude land-use change and forestry activities from the CDM until scientific uncertainties associated with those projects are reduced.

17. See Michelle Sforza and Mark Vallianatos, above at note 11.

18. Two major expropriation disputes between OECD member countries brought before the International Court of Justice with respect to creeping or indirect expropriation which were rejected under international law, would probably be successful under MAI. These cases concerned the terms of liquidation or refinancing of companies which had run into financial difficulties. See Electtronica Sicula case (1989) and Barcelona Traction case. In the latter case, shareholders of a company incorporated in the host country did not have standing.

9

Contractual Aspects of Implementing the Clean Development Mechanism and other Flexibility Mechanisms Under the Kyoto Protocol

IBIBIA LUCKY WORIKA AND MICHAEL BROWN
*in collaboration with Sergei Vinogradov and
under the general supervision of Thomas Walde*

Introduction

This chapter attempts to examine the types of contractual mechanisms that could be used in advancing the clean development mechanism (CDM) and other flexibility mechanisms envisioned under the Kyoto Protocol to the United Nations Framework Convention on Climate Change (UNFCCC). It attempts to distinguish the various forms of contracts that could be used to govern CDM projects, especially with reference to any United Nations Commission on International Trade Law (UNCITRAL) rules or forms.

The tentative findings are that there are a number of contractual forms for implementing long-term international commercial projects. Of these, the Intergovernmental Co-operation Framework Agreement, or that relating to a specific CDM project; the concession contracts; Build, Operate, and Transfer (BOT) project contracts;

joint venture agreements (JVAs); and the service contracts are feasible and viable contractual options because of their inherent flexibility
and adaptability in advancing the objectives of the Kyoto Protocol's
flexibility mechanisms.

However, they have to be properly drafted to reflect the substance
of the agreement and the converging (and sometimes conflicting)
interests of the major participants to these projects. To assist this
process, this chapter includes outline standardized agreements for
CDM projects and service contracts.

Background

The terms of reference for this chapter were laid down as follows:

> This [chapter] would examine the types of contracts that would
> be used between private legal entities participating in the Clean
> Development Mechanism and possibly other flexible mechanism
> schemes as envisioned under the Kyoto Protocol. The analysis
> would attempt to distinguish the types of standard forms that
> could be used to govern the transactions, particularly with ref-
> erence to any UNCITRAL rules or forms.

The Kyoto Protocol was agreed upon in December 1997 and the
CDM was created at that time as a last-minute addition to the
negotiated text. The other so-called flexible mechanisms endorsed by
the Protocol are joint implementation (JI) and emissions trading
(ET). JI exists, but only in the form of its pilot phase, activities implemented jointly (AIJ). ET is more established but, even here, there
is only one programme that could be described as actually "established," i.e. the US programme to limit sulphur dioxide (SO_2)
emissions.

In terms of contract development, there have been no instances of
standard forms developed for the CDM and only a small number for
AIJ projects. These are confidential and do not, in any event, cover
the crucial aspects relating to the crediting of emissions, since the
AIJ phase involves no crediting. None the less, for the purposes of

this chapter, some examples of formal AIJ proposals have been assessed with a view to extending some elements of this phase to the development of the CDM. Furthermore, it is hard to see what legal extrapolations pertinent to the CDM could be made to the CDM from an analysis of the US SO_2 Allowance Trading System: they are entirely different processes with dissimilar objectives and institutional frameworks.

Beyond the guidelines laid down for the CDM in the Protocol, virtually nothing has yet been agreed upon. To illustrate what an early stage we are in with regard to the CDM, it is worth pointing out that the United Nations Conference on Trade and Development/United Nations Environment Programme (UNCTAD/UNEP) International Working Group on the CDM (established with the backing of the governments of the USA, Canada, and Brazil) held its first meeting in September 1998. It was to address the following aspects of the CDM:

1. project design and implementation
2. international trading
3. financial
4. institutional.

It is clear that all aspects of the CDM relating to these four elements are still to be worked out in their entirety. This chapter attempts, therefore, to make a small contribution to the process of CDM development by:

1. analysing the background to the creation of the CDM in Kyoto
2. identifying concerns and potential problems that the CDM must overcome
3. proposing a list of the elements that should comprise, in essence, the basis of a legally binding CDM contract.

The Kyoto Protocol agreed upon in December 1997 will, if implemented, transform the way that energy is produced and used. The agreement may well turn out to be one of the most significant, in terms of impact on lifestyle, of the twentieth century. If the targets agreed upon in Kyoto are to be achieved, it is now virtually certain that the so-called flexibility mechanisms endorsed in Kyoto – ET, JI, and the CDM – will be utilized on a large and international scale involving both public and private sectors. It is conceivable, even likely, that the nature and scale of foreign energy investment will change radically.

The basis of all three flexibility mechanisms is trading. Such trading will represent transfers of credits, allowances, permits, and quotas, all of which will be linked directly to the reduction of emissions of the greenhouse gases (GHGs) stipulated in the Protocol.

In the case of JI and the CDM, the legal and contractual implications are great. Not only will it be important for contracts to protect the interests of both sides of a project or crediting deal but it will also be a requirement that the GHG credits which result from it are, as the Protocol puts it, "real, measurable, and long-term" and "additional to any that would occur in the absence of the certified project activity."

This will be of added importance for the CDM, as the credits that arise from such projects will, in total, permit Annex I countries – i.e. the industrialized countries of the Organization for Economic Co-operation and Development (OECD) that have emissions-reduction targets (ERTs) under the Protocol – to exceed their combined limits for the 2008–2012 budget period. If the CDM is abused, inaccurate, or badly designed, credits will not correspond to genuine reductions and the Annex I target will not be met. CDM contracts must therefore be watertight from both a commercial and an environmental standpoint. Indeed, the two perspectives are inextricably linked.

While it is evident that CDM contracts cannot be devised until the UN process provides a more detailed design framework, this chapter seeks to propose a standard form for the future. It is based on an analysis of the Protocol, a review of selected proposals made to the UNFCCC for AIJ project support, analysis of UNCITRAL rules – and some new thinking.

Unfortunately, it has not been possible to obtain detailed contractual information from some of the pioneering AIJ projects. Despite this, it is hoped that this chapter provides a useful contribution to the enormous amount of work that still remains to be done on these exciting and fundamentally important issues.

The UN Framework Convention on Climate Change

Since its adoption at the 1992 Earth Summit in Rio de Janeiro, the UNFCCC has been the centrepiece of the international community's effort to meet the most serious global environmental challenge. It has also become one of the most potent global forces influencing the way we live and work.

What led to the Convention? Essentially, the answer is science. Although the concept of global warming was developed in the nineteenth century, it was not until 1988 that UNEP and the World Meteorological Organization established the Intergovernmental Panel on Climate Change (IPCC). The IPCC was given the task of assessing current knowledge on these issues, predicting impacts, and proposing responses.

The first IPCC report (the First Assessment Report) confirmed the scientific basis for climate change. The report had a powerful effect on policy makers and led to calls for a climate-change treaty. A series of intergovernmental conferences was held and, in 1990, the Second World Climate Conference, involving officials from 149 countries, called for a framework treaty. In December 1990, the UN General Assembly approved the start of negotiations and a Convention was finalized on 9 May, 1992, in the short period of 15 months. The Convention was signed by 154 countries in Rio de Janeiro the following month, and has the objective of the "stabilization of greenhouse gas concentrations in the atmosphere at a level that would prevent dangerous anthropogenic interference with the climate system." Developed countries agreed in Rio to try to bring levels of emissions down to 1990 levels by the year 2000.

The Convention also stated that developed countries "may implement policies and measures jointly with other Parties." This short reference in an otherwise long document sowed seeds for the so-called "flexibility mechanisms" of JI, the CDM, and ET.

It was in the second half of the 1990s that the international response to climate change started to gather impressive momentum. In Berlin in 1995 (the first Conference of the Parties, COP 1) it was agreed that the Rio emissions targets were insufficient, that new commitments would be needed for the post-2000 period, and that these commitments should be laid down in "a protocol or another legal instrument" in Kyoto in December 1997.

In December 1995, the Second IPPC Assessment Report stated that "the balance of evidence suggests that there is a discernible human influence on global climate." In July 1996 at COP 2, negotiators agreed that the IPCC report justifies "action by Annex I countries to limit and reduce emissions of greenhouse gases." The 16 months that followed constituted a high-pressure period of intense negotiation, and the agreement was scheduled to be concluded in Kyoto in December 1997.

The Kyoto Protocol

The Kyoto COP 3 was a success for the UNFCCC process. With the agreement on the Protocol in December 1997, the UNFCCC process took another remarkable step: industrialized countries undertook obligations to reduce their collective emissions of GHGs. This is a landmark environmental agreement which, if ratified and complied with, will bring about a transformation in the way energy is produced and used and in the kind of transport systems we use, as well as the way we use them. The socio-economic impact will be great — and it will be global.

In addition, the legal implications will be vast. The issues will range from high-level diplomatic issues relating to the compliance of Parties (for example, what will happen if the EU, consisting of 15 individual Parties, does not achieve its target?) to issues pertaining to a lower level of contractual agreements between private entities in different countries.

What are the main features of the Kyoto Protocol?

1. The main significance of the Kyoto Protocol is that signatories to it have made a legally binding commitment.

2. A second feature is that the Annex I countries have each made signed commitments to emissions-limitations targets to be achieved by the years 2008–2012 (the EU, which ratified the agreement as a bloc in May 1998, is a special case). Collectively, the Protocol provides for differentiated, Annex I ERTs that amount to an average reduction of 5.2 per cent. The six gases covered are CO_2, CH_4, N_2O, hydrofluorocarbons (HFCs), perfluorocarbons (PFCs), and sulphur hexafluoride (SF_6).

3. Of especially great interest is the inclusion of the flexibility mechanisms of JI, CDM, and ET. These are market mechanisms that can be used by countries to achieve their targets. The CDM was a real surprise and emerged from the negotiations very much at the last minute.

Joint implementation (Article 6)

Annex I Parties can trade among themselves (transfer to, or acquire from) emission-reduction units (ERUs) resulting from projects aimed at reducing emissions from sources or enhancing removals by sinks in any sector of the economy. JI is subject to further guidelines for implementation.

The clean development mechanism (Article 12)

The role of the CDM was defined in the Protocol as a means of assisting non-Annex I Parties in achieving sustainable development and in contributing to the ultimate objective of the Convention, and to assist Annex I parties in achieving compliance with their ERTs.

Under the CDM:

1. non-Annex I Parties will benefit from project activities resulting in certified emission reductions (CERs)
2. Annex I Parties can use the CERs to contribute to their compliance with a part of their targets
3. CERs must be certified by operational entities to be designated
4. modalities and procedures are to be elaborated
5. participation in the CDM is voluntary and may involve public
   and private entities
6. CERs obtained during the period from the year 2000 up to
   2008 can be used towards compliance in the first commitment
   period (2008–2012).

Note that CERs will be additional to the overall assigned amount
for Annex I.

Emissions trading (Article 17)

Parties are allowed to participate in ET for the purpose of fulfilling
their commitments. The COP is required to define the relevant
principles, modalities, rules, and guidelines, in particular for verification, reporting, and accountability for ET.

It is vital to keep in mind that the new mechanisms that have
been legitimized by the Kyoto Protocol must be designed and used
to deliver emissions reductions. All three mechanisms contain issues
that still need a great deal of working out if this objective is to be
achieved. Questions that need to be answered include the following
important examples:

1. How can transparency, efficiency, and accountability be ensured?
2. To what extent can the trading of permits, ERUs, and CERs be
   used to deliver the overall Annex I commitment?
3. Who will be liable for traded units that are based on unfulfilled
   contracts (for example, if an energy-saving CDM project does
   not deliver the reductions promised)?

4. How can the major problem of assessing project baselines for CDM and JI projects be resolved?

Finally, there is one critical difference between JI and CDM that makes the unresolved issues relating to the CDM quite critical. This is, that banking of CERs is allowed from 2000, for use in the budget period. ERUs cannot be banked and thus have no commercial significance until 2008.

Implementation of the Kyoto Protocol: The CDM and other flexibility mechanisms

Why the CDM?

Two of the great debates leading up to Kyoto were related to the use of flexibility mechanisms by Annex I countries and the involvement of non-Annex I countries in the process. At Kyoto, a compromise was reached: flexible mechanisms including the CDM would be allowed, but non-Annex I country involvement was postponed, with the exception that these parties may voluntarily participate in the CDM. The CDM thus represents a central compromise that is a key to the unfolding of the Kyoto process.

It must be re-emphasized that the CDM has twin objectives: to promote sustainable development in non-Annex I countries and to assist Annex I parties to achieve their new emission-limitation and -reduction obligations. All CDM proposals, contracts, and projects must meet these objectives, and must be seen to meet them overtly, transparently, and unequivocally.

The actors

There will be two main kinds of actors in the CDM process:

1. the bodies defined by the Protocol
2. the parties to a CDM contract.

The bodies are defined by the Protocol in Article 12 (4), which states that "The Clean Development Mechanism shall be subject to the authority and guidance of the COP and be supervised by an Executive Board of the CDM."

In addition to supervising the overall operation of the CDM, the Executive Board's main order of business will be to approve and ensure certification of all relevant projects. CERs must:

1. require the approval of each Party involved
2. provide real, measurable, and long-term benefits in limiting climate change
3. demonstrably reduce emissions that are additional to any that would otherwise have occurred.

As set out in the Protocol, the CDM must be administered through three bodies:

1. the COP – authority and guidance
2. the Executive Board – supervision
3. the "operational entities" – certification; these will be designated by the COP to certify the CERs, and must therefore be backed up by independent auditing and verification bodies.

The exact roles of the three bodies, and the linkages between them, remain unclear. For example:

1. What would be the constitution of the Executive Board, who would be on it, and how would it function?
2. Who can certify CERs according to what guidelines? It would make sense for them to be appointed on the basis of expertise with project development and financing.
3. What will be the precise relationship between the three bodies?
4. Should there be internationally agreed criteria for empowering independent certification authorities, keeping in mind that the CDM is a "market mechanism" that should not be constrained by bureaucratic procedures?

These and other aspects of the design and administration of the CDM remain, by and large, unresolved. If it is to go forward in practice in the year 2000, then COP 4 in Buenos Aires will need to make significant progress in resolving these issues.

The parties to a CDM contract may be private or public. It is likely that the substance of the contract will vary according to whether the parties are both public, both private, or one of each. For the purposes of this analysis, and as laid down in the terms of reference, it is assumed that the two parties are private, but that both may also be subject in turn to legal commitments or obligations to their governments, which are Parties to the UN Convention.

The CDM contract: Starting points

It appears that the following are the central and minimal requirements for any CDM contract:

1. The CDM contract may be a commercial, quasi-commercial, or simply an intergovernmental agreement. A direct CDM Project agreement between private parties for the purpose of making profit would certainly qualify as "commercial." If it involves a sponsor and a host government with a government agreement, it would not, strictly speaking, be "commercial," because of the introduction of a "service" element, although such agreements could qualify as "quasi-commercial." However, an agreement between two governments for the carrying out of a CDM Project would be an intergovernmental agreement.

2. It envisages a long-term arrangement because it involves the execution of continuing obligations over a lengthy period of time (usually counted in years).

3. It possesses an international or foreign element, in contrast to a strictly domestic contract between citizens of one particular country.

4. It involves the transfer of appropriate technological know-how and financial resources to the host country.

5. The home country gains credits from complying with its emission-limitation or emission-reduction commitments under the Protocol.

The CERs arising from a CDM contract will have a cash value which, one assumes, makes the project viable from the donor's point of view (there may, of course, be other incentives available to either party to facilitate the project). None the less, this critical new element has significant implications for the contract.

What will be the main issues that must be covered by the contracts between the Parties involved in CDM projects? The nature of a contract between the two Parties to a CDM deal could be quite complicated. Not only will it need to satisfy as well as protect each of the Parties in the same way that any commercial contract would but also it will need to be in a form that ensures that it is consistent with the requirements of the Convention, the Kyoto Protocol, and any other subsequent agreements or requirements laid down by the COP or the Executive Board.

The consideration of the contract must also involve an assessment of the converging as well as conflicting interests of the various actors involved. The COP is the overall governor of the UN process. Its aim will be that Parties meet their obligations. It is concerned not so much as to whether there are CDM projects but rather that any that there are must deliver watertight and meaningful credits and sustainable development. Since the COP has delegated administration of the CDM to the Executive Board, which in turn will require operational entities to certify the CERs, all three have a direct and converging interest in these twin aspects. They are central to the CDM contract.

The private parties will have divergent interests that can, nevertheless, be achieved by a common project. The investor, in crude terms, wishes to minimize expenditure and maximize income while achieving a maximum number of emission credits, and is not much concerned with the delivery of sustainable development, provided that the project delivers enough emission credits to legitimize the contract.

The host wishes to maximize technological assistance, investment, and its share of any income stream. It may also be interested in the general objective of sustainable development. It will have an interest in the number of ERUs only to the extent that there should be sufficient credits to encourage the investment to take place; however, if the host is entitled to a share that can be used in due course, it will also have an interest in maximizing the number of credits and/or its share of that number.

As for the home countries (Annex I Parties), granted that they would hope to accomplish the broad objectives of achieving compliance with their quantified emission-limitation reduction (QELR) commitments in CDM projects, it is equally likely that such projects may be viewed as convenient alternatives to taking hard but realistic decisions affecting both industry and, by extension, their respective national economies back home.

The implications of all these issues and concerns are clear:

1. Particularly if credits are shared between the two parties, both will have a clear interest in maximizing (perhaps, overestimating) the number of credits available from the project. CER certifiers must be clear that the contract assesses the number of credits accurately.

2. Only the COP and Executive Board will have an interest in the promotion of sustainable development within the project contract. It remains to be determined how this should be dealt with contractually; the issue is notorious for its lack of clarity.

The CDM contract: Issues to be covered

The fundamental features of the contract will therefore be as follows:

1. a definition of the project
2. commitments by the donor in relation to financial investment, GHG reductions (see below), project performance, technology cooperation, and sustainable development

3. commitments, if appropriate, from the host in relation to site and/or project ownership, provision of goods and services in relation to effective operation of project, and sustainable development.

Specific aspects to be covered would include the following:

1. arrangements for the ownership of the project site, project, and CERs arising from the project

2. detailed identification and quantification (over the full life cycle of the project) of GHG sources and sinks at the site and which are included in emissions baseline, together with assumptions and uncertainties

3. a project schedule and timetable, including the period during which emission reductions will take place with year-by-year forecasts of reductions

4. estimated total CO_2-equivalent emissions reduction accruing to the donor investor (and host if credits are to be shared) over a specified period; note that Article 12 (5) states that emission reductions should be real, measurable, long-term, and additional

5. emissions-monitoring process and data-collection procedures

6. procedures for updating estimates of emission reductions

7. arrangements for independent auditing, external verification, and certification

8. assuming that certification takes place before the transfer of credits, enforcement mechanisms will need to be laid down in the event of non-compliance

9. penalty arrangements in the event of non-compliance by either party, in particular in the event of emission reductions being lower than estimated

10. commitments relating to Article 12 (2), that the CDM should help developing countries to achieve sustainable development; all non-GHG environmental impacts of the project should therefore be detailed

11. commitments relating to Article 12 (8): the contract should determine what share of the proceeds are allocated to cover administrative expenses and/or assistance to Parties for adaptation to climate change.

An illustration

An illustration of a CDM project might be as follows. The investor or donor might be a European electricity company which is participating in a domestic ET system applied by its government as a means of achieving its Kyoto target. The electricity company comes to the conclusion, after allocation of permits by the government or regulatory body, that it would be more cost-effective to invest in a CDM project than to undertake mitigation efforts domestically.

It identifies a major opportunity for an industrial co-generation project in Asia. This project is not economic because of the artificially low price of industrial power in the country (this raises other CDM issues: if the host country liberalized its power market, the co-generation project could become economic without credits), but the European company estimates that the project would save about 100 kT CO_2 over a 10-year period and it could therefore acquire a corresponding amount of CERs. Given its forecast of the value of credits, it decides that the project would now be profitable. It opens talks with the domestic power monopoly and they agree to proceed with a CDM agreement on a BOT 10-year basis.

The project is certified by an operational entity and the CDM Executive Board endorses the estimate of credits. The project proceeds and the European company derives its credits over a 10-year period. At the end of the period, it makes its credits available for sale within the domestic trading market, or in the international trading market, to offset some or all of its own excess emissions.

Sustainable development is promoted through the replacement, by the co-generation plant, of the host industry's brown-coal boilers and the financial resources flowing into the host country's national economy.

Other mechanisms of implementation: ET and JI

ET and JI already exist. ET is taking place within the US SO_2 Allowance Trading System to combat acid rain and there are other, more minor, examples. In addition, BP and other global companies are introducing internal trading trials. JI is taking place within the framework of the AIJ programme in the form of a series of pilot JI projects, under the supervision of the Convention.

As far as both ET and JI are concerned, the Protocol makes it clear that all the rules and guidelines for their operation have yet to be decided. Much of this will need to be done at COP 4 in Buenos Aires.

Standardization and CDM projects

A standardized contract for the CDM?

Is it possible to have a standardized CDM Project Agreement? The question of standardization has elicited much controversy in contract law. In relation to a CDM project, the main argument against a standardized agreement would be that not all CDM projects will be exactly alike and so standardization could undermine the potential for flexibility and dynamism in achieving contract objectives. Given widely varying cultural and commercial circumstances in different countries, a case-by-case approach seems legitimate.

None the less, it is likely that the Executive Board of the CDM will lay down a series of contract guidelines that will need to be met in order to secure the achievement of the goals of the Protocol. Some of the advantages of standardization include the following:

1. standardization facilitates the conduct of commercial/investment transactions, thus saving costs and time
2. it facilitates the comparison and evaluation of contractual responsibilities and associated risks, if these are based on the same well-known contractual terms

3. it makes financing easier, since financiers would be familiar with contractual terms

4. it enables the parties to plan ahead and to have effective control, monitoring, and supervision of projects

5. it reduces the tendency for the private sector to exploit its financial and technical advantage in the course of negotiations with national or local authorities

6. it may facilitate subcontracting and negotiating of other project-related contracts

7. standardized project agreements are more carefully drafted and, as such, are usually of a higher quality

8. standardization does not necessarily preclude introducing special conditions if needed, thus ensuring flexibility and dynamism.

It could be contended, however, that standardization is not very common or appropriate in long-term contracts; rather, it is an instrument for short-term, immediately consumable transactions.[1] There is, however, a growing trend to standardize long-term agreements, even in the natural resources sector, as evidenced by the tendency of host countries to draw up similar model contracts to govern such transactions. This is equally true at the international level, where the United Nations Industrial Development Organization (UNIDO), the International Chamber of Commerce (ICC), the Association of International Petroleum Negotiators (AIPN), as well as the World Bank, have been working on (and have even published) some standard terms.

Then, even if standardization of CDM project contracts were preferable, the issue arises as to the type of contract to be adopted. Do the UNCITRAL practices or laws provide any guidance?

UNCITRAL was created in 1966 in order to enable the United Nations to play a more active role in reducing or removing legal complications in the free flow of international trade. It has accordingly produced a continuous flow of studies, standard terms (for documentary credit) and model rules or laws (for arbitration and procurement) in areas of international trade law for national enactment.

So far, however, there are no particular UNCITRAL rules or forms for CDM project contracts. This is understandable, as this mechanism was invented after UNCITRAL and could not have been contemplated by UNCITRAL rules or forms. In the circumstances described in the scenario above, recourse would have to be had elsewhere for any further analysis on the possible types of contracts for CDM Projects. It is pertinent to stress, however, that whichever type of contract is eventually adopted, a conciliation, mediation, and/or arbitration clause should be mandatory for every such contract.

Possible contract types for CDM projects

Generally speaking, there are already a number of example contracts that have been negotiated since the Kyoto Protocol was agreed upon, most of which would not squarely fit into the CDM Project framework because these later projects were obviously not originally contemplated by such contractual arrangements. However, considering the substance of CDM projects, other examples of intergovernmental agreements (such as intergovernmental co-operation agreements, concession contracts, BOT project contracts, and joint venture and service contracts) deserve closer analysis because they have certain features that make them more easily amenable to the kinds of agreements envisioned under the CDM.

Intergovernmental cooperation agreements

Intergovernmental cooperation agreements are agreements entered into by governments for, and on behalf of, their respective sovereign states and can be of a general, framework nature or relate to a specific CDM project. They usually provide, among other things, procedures and joint institutions for cooperation programming, for project preparation and evaluation, as well as for implementing projects and monitoring their performance.[2] These ongoing efforts to develop suitable intergovernmental cooperation contracts can be complemented by the further deliberations of the COP under the Kyoto Protocol. Intergovernmental agreements relating to specific CDM project(s) could contain provisions relating to the following:

1. The partial, or full assumption of risk of non-performance of such projects by their respective home countries. Where projects are initiated by private legal entities, the home states should bear partial assumption of risk. However, full assumption of risks should be borne by home states if projects are initiated by their respective public sectors.

2. Provisions regarding financing and market-access conditions to enable the proper and effective implementation of the CDM.

3. Host-state guarantees regarding stability of the enabling regulatory regime, including the terms of the CDM agreement.

4. Host-state guarantees relating to the uninterrupted supply of energy and natural resources, where these are applicable to the CDM Project.

Some of the advantages of intergovernmental cooperation agreements include the following:

1. this type of agreement seeks to link project contracts with international law through home-state commitments to assume performance responsibility[3]

2. it provides a convenient framework for project agreements on the enterprise level by shielding such enterprises from the vagaries of host country regulatory regimes

3. the reduced number of participants allows commitments to be more concrete and precise in terms of specific sustainable development goals and strategies or quantified emission limitation and reduction objectives (QUELROs)

4. as this type of agreement can take a variety of forms, it is flexible enough to reflect correctly the degree of state intervention in concrete cases of cooperation at the project level

5. the rules or terms of the agreement may be bilaterally negotiated, thus allowing innovative solutions and a gradual evolution of the entire process.

The main disadvantage of these types of agreements stems from the assumption of the equal bargaining power of the respective parties, which is not usually the case. Indeed, it is not unlikely that the unequal bargaining power and the inadequacy or absence of experience on the part of developing countries will result in an agreement that reflects this lopsided relationship in favour of the industrialized country. The solution lies in drafting such agreements to meet the differing, legitimate expectations of the parties. This would imply, *inter alia*, that:

1. the agreements should not be exclusively reflective of the defensive interest of the investing or exporting countries
2. they should equally reflect elements of the collective interests of developing countries and actions in keeping with those interests, such as technological cooperation, financial resources, and respect for sovereignty over natural wealth and resources
3. they should contain concrete commitments from the parties aimed at creating a package of mutually beneficial interdependence.

Concession contract

The term "concession," connotes "ownership," or what in common-law systems is described as a "freehold interest." It is an arrangement whereby the private sector is granted the right to develop a public infrastructure project. The concession system has become transformed in the light of the exigencies of modern international commercial transactions. The following are some of the features of the modern concession contract:

1. it gives exclusive right to the concessionaire to undertake its operations in a given area, including other ancillary operations within a certain duration with the possibility of renewal
2. the concessionaire has exclusive rights to manage its operations without undue interference from the host government
3. it sets out clear commencement, work, and other obligations, which may include the filing of work reports
4. it involves a simplified tax system that enables the concessionaire effectively to amortize its investments within a reasonable period of time

5. pricing is always set by the concessionaire, but with government supervision

6. dispute settlement is usually by ad hoc arbitration with the laws of the host country and international law as the choice of law clause

7. there is a possibility for revocation in exceptional circumstances.

The concession system has been modified in recent times to accommodate various other types of projects, with a considerable reduction in host-government participation and control. It is possibly one of the most attractive options for CDM projects, as it enables the private sector to exercise a free hand in developing and managing the project, with minimal host-government interference. Innovative contractual clauses can be drafted to synchronize with the objectives of the CDM.

It is important to note that, in all contract types, the problematic issues are always in investment guarantees: non-expropriation, repatriation of investment/revenues, stabilization clauses and duty-free imports, to mention just a few. These issues deserve much more than a mere mention here. Although, in theory, the foreign private investor can obtain maximum government guarantees for the security of investments by very clear contractual provisions, in practice the government has some shrewd ways of bringing about tangible changes or the termination of an agreement.

Non-consensual modifications of economic development agreements may arise outside the realms of clear cases of breach of contract or *force majeure* from:

1. government's unilateral action taken on the ground of public purpose

2. a fundamental change of circumstances rendering the performance of the agreement unduly onerous or wholly or partially fruitless.

Traditionally, foreign private investors have tended to protect themselves by contractual devices such as inserting stabilizing clauses, choice of law clauses, and arbitration clauses. The stabilization clause aims to protect the original contractual terms from future legislative changes of the host state, which may have negative repercussions in terms of taxation, environmental controls, and other regulatory matters. The choice of law clause is usually aimed at subjecting the agreement to some other law (usually international law or general principles of law) besides the laws of the host state, which could be changed at will. The arbitration clause is usually aimed at choosing a neutral forum for settling disputes that may arise from the agreement. The combined effect of these clauses is to internationalize the contract.

Although there have been a number of very persuasive objections to the theory of internationalization, current trends appear to favour a delicate balancing of the often-conflicting interests of foreign private investors on the one hand and host governments on the other. This approach involves the recognition that no sovereign state can divest itself of its primary responsibilities of protecting public interests and promoting sustainable economic development on the one hand, and ensuring some adequate guarantees against the consequences of unilateral government action on the other. These responsibilities may involve an obligation to renegotiate contracts if and when the original contractual equilibrium has been modified by a fundamental change of circumstance. Such a clause affords the possibility for the "dynamic stability" of the original contractual terms.

BOT project contracts

According to the UNCITRAL:

> BOT is conceived as a way to reduce pressure on the use of public funds for project financing and to promote the transfer of technology through the involvement of the private sector in financing, building and operating infrastructure projects. In its most basic form, a BOT project is where the Government grants a concession for a period of time to a consortium for the devel-

opment of a project. The consortium finances or arranges for financing for the project, constructs the project, and operates and maintains the facility during the life of the concession. Meanwhile, through sale or charge for the use of the facility or its products, the consortium recovers returns on its equity and pays off its debts. At the end of the concession period the project is transferred to the Government.[4]

The potential advantages of using the BOT Project contractual approach to both the private and public sector are illustrated in table 9.1.

BOT project agreements may be said to be modified versions of the concession contract. There can be considerable diversity in their form and content, ranging from "huge, complex contracts, tailor-made for a particular infrastructure project to straightforward and to some extent standardised contracts for each infrastructure sector, as in China's BOT programme."[5] To this extent, they can be said to be as flexible and dynamic as concession contracts. Again, in view of the fact that in the construction, implementation, and maintenance of some CDM projects (like their AIJ counterparts), science, engineering, and construction works would play a considerable role, the attractiveness of BOT project agreements cannot be overemphasized.

However, they have to be specially and carefully drafted to fit into the legal systems within which they are to operate. Legal systems that are less supportive of, or less transparent to, the BOT approach may require far more comprehensive provisions in BOT agreements than those that are more supportive or transparent.[6]

Joint venture agreements (JVA)

The "joint venture" (JV) is "a business arrangement in which two or more parties undertake a specific economic activity together." Although there are different variants of JVs, they are generally a popular way of pooling scarce financial and technical resources for the purpose of carrying out a commercial undertaking. The JV contract spells out the terms of the JV, especially the financial commitments of each partner and the modalities for sharing of profit, which

Table 9.1   Potential advantages to both private and public sectors of using the BOT[a] approach for infrastructure development

Private sector	*Public sector*
• Gives private sector a free hand to finance the project, rather than depend on contribution from host government, which may cripple project because of government's other commitments	• Use of private-sector financing to provide new sources of capital, which reduces public borrowing and direct spending and which may improve host government's credit rating
• Ability to accelerate the development of projects that would otherwise have to wait for, and compete for, scarce sovereign resources	• Ability to accelerate the development of projects that would otherwise have to wait for, and compete for, scarce sovereign resources
• Use of private-sector initiative and know-how to reduce project construction costs, shorten schedules, and improve operating efficiency	• Use of private-sector initiative and know-how to reduce project construction costs, shorten schedules, and improve operating efficiency
• Private sector is responsible for the operation, maintenance, and output of the project for an extended period (normally the government would receive protection only for the normal construction and equipment warranty period)	• Allocation to the private sector of project risk and burden that would otherwise have been borne by an already encumbered public sector
• Involvement of private sponsors and experienced commercial lenders, which ensures an in-depth review and is an additional sign of project feasibility	• Gives government a breathing space to source indigenous and skilled manpower comparable to the private sector
• Able to recoup the costs of technology transfer, training of local personnel, and the development of national capital markets towards the transfer of the project	• Public gains from technology transfer, the training of local personnel, and the development of a national capital market
• Private sector establishes a benchmark, against which the efficiency of similar public sector projects can be measured, and the associated opportunity to enhance management of infrastructure facilities	• Public sector can measure its efficiency against the benchmark established by the private sector in respect of similar projects and associated opportunities to enhance management of infrastructure facilities

Source: Adapted by authors from *UNIDO BOT Guidelines* (Vienna: UNIDO, 1996), p. 7.

a. BOT, Build, operate and transfer.

need not necessarily be in equal proportion. In the energy sector, host governments see JVs as an effective way of participating in the development of their natural resources, with the concomitant prospect of technology transfer.

The CDM will involve an arrangement between non-Annex 1 and Annex 1 Parties, by which the former benefits from project activities resulting in CERs and the latter may use the CERs accruing from such project activities to contribute to compliance with part of their quantified emission-limitation and -reduction commitment. In practice, though, both industrialized and developing countries could use private and public entities to undertake CDM joint ventures (CDMJVs). Clearly, a CDM joint venture agreement (CDMJVA) would be the most appropriate framework to guide the commercial and legal relationship between such entities. A standardized CDMJVA can be adapted to take care of the special requirements or substance of the CDM. Table 9.2 is an attempt to summarize some common advantages and disadvantages of the JVA.

Two observations should be made here. The first relates to the varying objectives of the JV partners (investor on the one hand and host government on the other). Whereas the host government would be more interested in attaining sustainable development, including technology transfer for the benefit of the national economy, the investor would be more interested in making a profitable return on its investment. The second relates to the host government's ability to meet its cash-call obligations (in practice, usually the responsibility of the appointed government agency, or public enterprise). Many feel that cash-strapped non-Annex I countries can hardly be expected to meet their financial commitments under the JVA.

However, in no contractual arrangement is an investor's objective identical to that of the host government. Furthermore, fears about the host government's inability to meet its cash call obligations under the CDMJVA would be arrested by Article 12 (6) of the Protocol. Furthermore, even if the CDMJVA is not a favoured option because of host-government involvement, it is, none the less, an attractive option for several companies willing and able to pool their resources to undertake a CDM project in a non-Annex I country.

Table 9.2   Some common advantages and disadvantages of the JVA[a]

Project developer's viewpoint	Host government's viewpoint
Advantages	
• Moulding a project in a form compatible with government policies	• Maximizing national sovereignty
• Minimizing political risk	• Receiving subsidized or risk-free participation
• Improving predictability and stability of operational conditions	• Sharing in the rewards of value added
• Providing a communication channel to the government	• Influencing training, education, labour recruitment, and labour policies
• Availability of tax or other investment incentives	• Influencing decisions on sourcing and pricing of plant, equipment, production inputs, and services
	• Influencing destination and pricing of products
	• Minimizing any perceived adverse effects of FDI[b]
Disadvantages	
• "Soft" value of host country's capital contributions	• Need to contribute capital or other assets
• Less efficient decision-making and financing structures	• Need to offer tax incentives
• Exposure to risk of loss of confidential commercial information and know-how	• Exposure to business risks
• Exposure to risk of incompatibility with government bureaucrats	• Exposure to risk of incompatibility with foreign partner

Source: Adapted from R. Pritchard *et al.*, "The Use of Joint Ventures in FDI", in R. Pritchard ed., *Economic Development, Foreign Investment and the Law: Issues in Private Sector Involvement and the Rule of Law in a New Era* (London: Kluwer Academic Publishers, 1996), p. 178.

a. JVA, joint venture agreement.

b. FDI, foreign direct investment.

Risk service contracts

Risk service contracts are usually a camouflaged concession, BOT, or JV arrangement. In risk service contracts, the services of an investor, who assumes the legal status of "contractor," are hired by the sponsoring (hiring) state. In the case of a CDM arrangement, the task of the contractor would be the construction, maintenance, and implementation of the CDM project, or the training of personnel for the purposes of managing any such project. After successful execution of the contract, the contractor is reimbursed for its costs and investments and paid for its services by the sponsoring state. The contractor bears the entire financial risks and is reimbursed only after successful execution of the undertaking. This explains why it is referred to as a "risk service contract."

The main distinction between a risk service contract and the JV or sole-investor arrangement is that, in the former, the contractor provides a service and gets its payment from the sponsor whereas, in the latter, the investor puts up risk capital and gets its return from an expected flow of profits from the venture (usually shared in the case of a JV).

A further distinction should be made between a risk service contract and a real service contract: whereas, in the former, the host or sponsoring state pays for the services of the risk service contractor, in the latter, someone else pays. The latter situation may arise where, for example, a home country or international agency hires the services of an independent contractor (service contractor) to undertake certain services for the benefit of a third-party beneficiary which is also a host country. In this situation, there is no contractual relationship in the legal sense of the term (privity of contract) between the host country and the service contractor as such, since the service contractor receives payment from the sponsoring home state or international agency. Exceptionally, there could be a subcontract between the service contractor and the host country for the rendering of the particular service it has been hired to perform, even when the sponsor is not the host country. Even in this latter situation, the service contractor is paid by the sponsoring agency rather than by the host country. An example of the real service contract is the Phare/Tacis

Multi-country Project.[7] In that project, for instance, the contracting authority – the European Community (EC) – hires a consortium (service contractor) comprising two or more partners with a view to providing, among other things, training and a good level of understanding of the Energy Charter Treaty and the Protocol on the part of selected key personnel of each of the Phare partner countries. This is done with a view to bringing their legislation in line with ECT requirements and harmonizing their legal, policy, and institutional framework with the EC.[8] The consortium (service contractor) is not paid by the beneficiary countries – Central and Eastern European Countries (CEEC) – but by the sponsor or contracting authority – the EC. Similarly, the COP could, in addition to arranging funding for CDM Projects, hire a private or public entity as service contractor to construct and implement a CDM mechanism in a non-Annex I country. While this would be with the consent of the parties, the service contractor would not be paid by the host country but by the COP. Details regarding quantification and allocation of credits can be worked out within the framework of the service contract.

As in every other contractual arrangement, the potential for conflict always exists in the real service contract because of its peculiar arrangement. The real service contractor may be bound under the real service agreement not to indulge corrupt officials of, for example, the host country or to abide by certain standards. This may, however, pose practical difficulties, as the host country may set its own agenda in the "national interest," including the imposition of import duties and levying of taxes. These are undoubtedly very thorny issues in practice, as poor governments cannot easily refrain from either levying taxes or imposing duties on imports. If these difficulties are not anticipated and an amicable resolution properly provided for, the effective execution of the real service contract is bound to be prejudiced.

Possible contract types for other flexibility mechanisms

The contract forms for ET and JI are simpler than those for the CDM in the sense that there are already a number of pilot projects implementing the former mechanisms. Since emissions, or emissions reductions, amount to tradeable commodities in the ET mechanism, a simple standardized contract for the buying and selling of "permits," "allowances," or "emissions reductions" by which one Party agrees to sell and the other agrees to buy such tradeable commodities could be drafted. Besides, precedents already exist in the United States, where ET has been successfully employed in limiting emissions of sulphur dioxide (SO_2). However, considering that assigned amounts, defined by Article 3 of the Protocol, may be traded, an emissions-trading contract (ETC) within an umbrella or framework intergovernmental agreement is possible.

Also, since JI envisages Annex I countries undertaking GHG-reduction projects within other Annex I countries, by means of which reductions are credited to the country financing the project while debiting the excess reductions of the host country, an intergovernmental agreement that defines the framework for this JV relationship between the home country and host country is appropriate as a necessary starting point. However, considering that countries can authorize private companies to develop JI projects (while reserving the powers of approval, certification of emissions reductions, and/or monitoring and verification, for themselves), the option of using either an intergovernmental framework agreement or an intergovernmental agreement relating to a specific JI Project is not a *sine qua non*. On the contrary, the JV, BOT, or even service contract are equally feasible and viable options. Whatever contract form is employed for JI, it is the substance of the contract that really matters. Such a contract has to state very clearly, *inter alia*:

1. how to establish a baseline for the calculation of real emissions reductions of projects

2. how to monitor, verify, and certify real emissions reductions

3. how to scale down the administrative and transaction costs of projects.

At the risk of repetition, it must be reiterated that a big issue will be investment guarantees, in particular tax and import duty issues. A review of intergovernmental and interorganizational/government agreements such as Tacis EC and United Nations Development

Programme (UNDP) agreements indicates that there is always a promise by the beneficiary host government to provide import duty exemptions and to impose no taxes. However, these promises would be difficult, if not impossible, to adhere to in practice, since developing-country governments are urgently in need of revenue for the development of their national economies. The prudent approach seems to be to anticipate these potentially disruptive tendencies in an investment regime and to provide adequate safeguards that would not only minimize the damage to investment but also enable both parties to renegotiate the original terms of the contract where a fundamental change of circumstance so dictates.

Conclusions and recommendations

This chapter attempts to examine the use of contracts for achieving the CDM and other flexibility mechanisms envisioned under the Kyoto Protocol ("the Protocol"). It takes the view that, although intergovernmental cooperation agreements, the concession contract, the BOT project contracts, JVA and the service contract are preferable because of their inherent flexibility and adaptability in advancing the objectives of these flexibility mechanisms, in practice it is the substance of the agreements in question rather than the form that matters most in terms of effectiveness. It is also necessary to add that these distinct forms can be used for, perhaps, three broad scenarios:

1. an intergovernmental agreement (either a framework agreement or one relating to a specific project) between two or more Annex I countries for ET, which may be accompanied by a specific standardized ET agreement
2. an intergovernmental agreement between two or more Annex I countries, which may be followed by a specific concession, BOT, JVA, or service contract in respect of a JI project
3. an intergovernmental agreement between an Annex I and a non-Annex I country, followed by a specific concession, BOT, JVA, or service contract in respect of a CDM project in a non-Annex I country.

However, certain general principles are fundamental for any contract to be effective both in terms of the relationship between the Parties to the agreement and in terms of achieving general contract objectives. These include (but are not limited to) the following principles:

1. Full conformity to the requirements of the UNFCCC, the Kyoto Protocol, and any subsequent agreement relating to the CDM. In particular, the contract should define the following: the emissions reduced (CERs) and how they should be measured, verified, certified, and shared between the contract Parties; how the project stimulates sustainable development; liability arrangements in the event that the project fails to deliver the contracted CERs.

2. Equity or fairness and transparency in apportioning rights and obligations between the Parties. This may involve "affirmative action" to counteract unequal development and compensate for the structural weaknesses of the developing-country Party.

3. Cost-effectiveness in the pursuit of contract objectives.

4. Unambiguous stating of terms, which should include *modi operandi* for implementation and enforcement, financial mechanism, dispute settlement, liability, and compensation for damages or failure of the undertaking.

5. The principle of both host and home state co-responsibility for international economic and environmental cooperation.

Appendix 1 attempts to fashion a table of contents for a standard CDM Project contract as well as a summary explanation of what the various subheadings should include. However, these should not be taken as sacrosanct, considering that different local conditions and project types or objectives could dictate justifiable modifications to this model.

Notes

1. T.W. Walde, Modellvertraege unde zwischenstaatliche Kooperationsabkommen: Formen der verflechtung zwischen Recht und Wirtschaft. *Jahrbuch fuer Rechtssoziologie und Rechtstheorie* 1982, p. 372.

2. T.W. Walde, "Methods and Mechanisms for International Industrial Co-operation." *UNIDO Industry 2000 – New Perspectives Collected Background Papers*, Vol. 2, UNIDO/IOD.325 19 December 1979, p. 40.

3. T.W. Walde, "North/South Economic Cooperation and International Economic Development Law: Legal Process and Institutional Considerations," *German Yearbook of International Law* (GYIL) (1980), 23: 79.

4. See Netscape – [United Nations Commission on International Trade Law, Twenty-sixth session Vienna, 5–23 July 1993], "Possible Future Work: Note by the Secretariat", Website: ⟨http://www.his.com/~pildb/acn9-378.htm⟩, (visited 08/03/98), p. 5 of 7, para. 3.

5. UNIDO, Table 1, at p. 226.

6. A supportive regulatory framework could contain, for example, a Law, Regulation or Code like the Indiana code 22-3-2-15 Enacted 1929, Amended 1991, where "BOT agreement" was defined as "any agreement between the state or a political subdivision and an operator to construct, operate, and maintain a public facility and to transfer the public facility back to the state or political subdivision at an established future date." See Netscape – [IC Title 36, Article 1, Chapter 14.3, Section 4], Website: ⟨http://www.law.indiana.edu/codes/in/36/36-1-14.3-4.html⟩ (visited 08/03/98), p. 1 of 2; A supportive legal framework could also contain and publish general project eligibility criteria and national rules, which are not incompatible with the provisions of the Kyoto Protocol as the Czech Republic already has done for JI development projects. See Netscape – [JI Project development in the Czech Republic], Website: ⟨http://www.vol.cz/nondek/jicz/websi2.htm⟩ (visited 08/06/98), p. 1 of 2.

7. Energy Charter Treaty Project III, Phare Multi-country Project No. B5-97-042.

8. "Phare" means "European Community assistance programme for the reconstruction of the economies of Central and Eastern Europe." "Tacis" means European Community assistance programme for Technical Assistance to the Commonwealth of Independent States and Mongolia."

Appendix 1: Summary explanation of a standardized agreement for a clean development mechanism (CDM) project.[1]

Commencement

This is the beginning of the agreement, which details the date of commencement as well as the names of the relevant Parties. The host government or its appointed representative or agency should be one Party, while the concessionaire(s) or a company that has been formed for the purposes of the project (CDM project company) should be the other Party.

Recital

This is the section that begins with "Whereas," and often provides background information regarding the project and the context in which subsequent sections of the agreement become necessary. Although, *strictu sensu*, the recital does not form part of the agreed terms, it may be admissible in evidence to prove the contextual framework of the agreement.

Chapter I: Purpose of the CDM project agreement

1. Interpretation

This should provide definitions of the key terms employed in the CDM project agreement. It should include terms such as "CDM project," "project company," "associated company," "Minister," "Secretary," "principal," "exceptional circumstances," "concession-aire," "documents," "maître d'oeuvre," "national defence," "safety," "security," "Conference of the Parties," or "international agencies."

2. The CDM project and its characteristics

This should describe in some detail the CDM project, its characteristics or what it would comprise, including how it intends to operate. It might be necessary to include details of scientific specifications in an Annex.

3. Coming into operation and duration

This should set out the conditions preceding the coming into operation of the CDM Project, as well as the time when it is expected to lapse. These may, perhaps, be without prejudice to other subsequent provisions relating to renewal and transfer of the CDM project.

4. Acquisition of land and ownership of the CDM project

This should state the availability of land for the project and the ownership of the project. The state or its agency might have to undertake to make land easily available for the project and stipulate that, for a certain duration, ownership of the project shall vest in the project company or concessionaire.

5. Financial requirements

This section might require considerable flexibility and dynamism, as financial requirements may differ from one project to the other. Nevertheless, it might be necessary for the concessionaire to guarantee the availability of funds for the completion of the project and implementation thereof. Conversely, the concessionaire may wish to disclaim liability in the unlikely event that finances are inadequate to complete or implement the project. In the latter case, the provisions regarding termination of the project would become applicable.

Chapter II: Construction of the CDM project

6. Independent project managers (maîtres d'oeuvre)

The parties to the CDM project contract may wish to spell out how to appoint one or more persons (nationals of either or both parties) as project managers, and to whom the project managers should be responsible.

7. Monitoring of the design phase

The concessionaire should be required to submit details of the CDM project design to the Conference of the Parties (COP), which may wish to confirm that the project is fit for its purpose. In case of differences of opinion between the COP and the concessionaires, it may be necessary to state how this is to be resolved, preferably amicably by amendment of the design and technical specifications.

8. Contract procedures

It might be necessary to set out contract procedures if there are no such procedures to be followed by the concessionaire. Such contract procedures might form other annexes to this agreement, and should be scrupulously followed by the concessionaire and subcontractors. Issues such as tenders, supply of spare parts or procurement, and discrimination against nationals of either parties, should be spelt out in the contract procedure.

9. Monitoring of construction works

This would require the concessionaire to provide the COP with periodic reports with a view to establishing that the construction works are in compliance with the project design and cost estimates.

10. Timetable

This should state when preparatory works are to be carried out from the date of commencement of this agreement and the date of probable completion of the project.

11. Inspection and bringing into operation

The relevant government ministry or agency may have to inspect the project upon completion and submit its inspection report to the COP, which may wish to verify that all technical specifications have been met and give approval for the commencement of operations.

Chapter III: Operational phase

12. Commercial policy

The concessionaires should have a free hand in price determination irrespective of domestic laws relating to price control and tariffs. It should undertake to treat its customers, consumers or end-users, including third parties, without discrimination on grounds of nationality or user status. This should not preclude the concessionaire from adjusting its price or tariff in accordance with commercial exigencies. The concessionaire should also undertake to make public its prices and/or tariffs in the manner agreed upon between itself and the government agency or ministry.

13. Environmental policy

Provisions should state the general environmental policy of the concessionaires in terms of reducing greenhouse gas emissions (GHGs), but should stipulate that this would be accomplished without deteriorating environmental quality of the other environmental media, such as land and water.

14. Public order and operating rules

This should state not only that regulations relating to public order will be prescribed by the competent organs of the host country, but also that the concessionaire shall submit the operating rules of the CDM project to the COP, which may approve the same within a specified period of time; otherwise, the operating rules shall be deemed to have been approved.

15. Maintenance and continuity of the CDM project

This should require the concessionaire to maintain the CDM project in good condition and repair as would be necessary for it to be used for the purpose for which it is designed and constructed. The concessionaire should have the right to bring the project into temporary closure for the purpose of carrying out maintenance works, provided that adequate notice has been given to the competent authorities (governmental departments, general public, and COP).

16. Safety, security, and control

The Parties to this agreement should undertake to ensure the safety and security of the project. In particular, the concessionaire should undertake to abide by all regulations relating to safety and security, which are binding on it through the principals, or by the COP in relation to the project. Control of the project shall vest in the concessionaires at all times until ownership or control is transferred in the manner specified under this agreement.

17. Subcontracts relating to ancillary facilities

The concessionaire may freely enter into any contracts for the operation of any ancillary facilities that may be open to the public or of benefit to users or customers of the CDM project, provided that such ancillary facilities would be necessary in achieving the purpose of the project.

Chapter IV: Common provisions

18. Rights and obligations of the government

The government should have right of access to the project facility, collect samples of product or emissions for testing and verifications, and the right to request further and better particulars in relation to any matter it deems necessary to appraise the continued viability of the project. The obligations should include, at the minimum, provisions protecting the project or concessionaire against the adverse consequences of laws and regulations. The government should also facilitate the project company in obtaining necessary permits and approvals and streamline the bureaucratic process associated with the project's implementation. Other general obligations may extend to import and export permits, tax and duty incentives, employment permits, access to public utilities, performance guarantees for public-sector entities associated with the project operation, and protection from competition.

19. Rights and obligations of the concessionaire

The project company or concessionaire should have the right to operate the facility with minimum interference from government or its agency and the right to set its own prices or tariff and to petition the government or its agency in respect of any matter it deems contradicts the letter or spirit of this agreement. Minimum obligations of the concessionaire should include such issues as undertaking to comply with the laws and regulations of the host country during project implementation; environmental protection; safety standards; use of competitive national constructors, goods, and services; and protection of labour rights, employment, and training of nationals.

21. Common obligations

Provisions that require joint commitment of the Parties to this agreement include those on *force majeure* and rights in relation to project documents, including ownership and design of drawings, confidentiality as to information and documents obtained, obligation to cooperate, and warranty against improper payment.

22. Sharing of costs and revenues

Again, these provisions should be flexible, allowing the Parties to specify how they intend to share certain specified costs and revenues from the project. However, this should be without prejudice to the fact that the concessionaire should, by and large, have a free hand as the principal cost bearer and revenue collector, at least until such a time when the project is transferred.

23. Joint and several liability of the concessionaires to the principals

This may simply state that the obligations of the concessionaires to the principals under this agreement shall be joint and several.

24. Liability with respect to consumers/users and third parties

It may be necessary to state clearly, as between the concessionaires and principals, who is liable for damages to third parties or users (which should, ideally, be the concessionaires). Although the concessionaires may wish to indemnify the principals from any claim from a third party or user, this should not extend to those damages that can be attributable to default of the principal.

25. Insurance obligations

It may be necessary to spell out these obligations in a more detailed annex. In general, the concessionaire should have insurance coverage and maintain it throughout the duration of the project. Copies of such insurance coverage shall be submitted to the COP, who shall ensure conformity of the insurance with the specific details that would be laid out in the annex mentioned above.

26. Exceptional circumstances and *force majeure*

Provisions should set out the circumstances to be regarded as exceptional – such as war, invasion, riot, nuclear explosion, radioactive or chemical contamination or ionizing radiation, effect on the natural elements (including geological conditions such as earthquakes that it was impossible to foresee), strike of exceptional importance and duration, or the behaviour of one Party causing serious and certain damage to the other Party. These should be without prejudice to the right of either Party to contest the grounds of exceptional circumstances by arbitration.

27. Interruption of construction or operation by order of the principals

It would be necessary to state that the construction or operation of the project shall not be interrupted except in such circumstances as have been stated in this agreement. This should be without prejudice to compensation to be paid to the concessionaire, as would be determined by the competent arbitrage body.

28. Penalties for breach

This should enable the principals to levy a penalty for breaching the obligations under this agreement, provided that the concessionaire has been given an opportunity to remedy the breach in question within a definite time frame.

29. Relations with the COP and other international agencies

There should be a provision incorporating article 12 (3) (b), (4)–(8) of the Kyoto Protocol, which stipulates the functions of the COP serving as the meeting of the Parties to the Protocol under the supervision of the executive board of the CDM.

30. Free access for supervisory personnel

This should authorize personnel of the COP, as well as other authorized personnel of the host government, to have access to all parts of the CDM project for the purpose of carrying out any of their functions or to inspect and investigate any matters relating to its construction or operation. The concessionaires should undertake to cooperate with such persons, provided that there is minimum disruption to the construction and operation of the project.

31. Duties, charges, and taxes

All duties, charges, and taxes levied or to be levied shall be the liabilities of the concessionaire and shall be in accordance with national law. However, such duties, charges, and taxes shall not either expressly or by implication amount to a creeping expropriation of the project.

32. Transfers of funds and financial settlements

This should permit the transfer of any funds, subject to any applicable procedures required under the national laws. It might be necessary to ensure that such transfers are facilitated and not unduly encumbered by bureaucratic procedures.

33. Assignment and security

The concessionaire may assign its interest in the undertaking or create any form of security over this agreement or its rights thereunder, provided that the consent of the principals has been first obtained, with the understanding that such consent shall not be unreasonably withheld.

34. Provisions relating to lenders and principals

This provision should enable lenders and principals to exercise their rights to substitute the original concessionaires in the event that the latter are unable to perform their obligations under this agreement. The substituted entities should, however, have financial and technical competence to continue and operate the CDM project but this must be with reference to the COP. Details of the grounds for substitution and resolution of conflicts can be spelled out in an additional annex to this hypothetical agreement.

35. Intellectual property and confidentiality

This provision should require the concessionaire to undertake to make all documents in respect of the project available to the principals, COP and other competent authorities designated by them. The latter Parties should equally undertake to hold such documents in strict confidence and not to disclose same unless for the purposes of the project.

Chapter V: Renewal and/or transfer issues

36. Conditions for renewal or transfer and timing

This may provide that, at a reasonable time before actual transfer or renewal, the Parties to this agreement will confer to elucidate the modalities for such transfer arrangements, including the conditions preceding or subsequent to such transfer or renewal and timing. This may include, *inter alia*, the scope of transfer of such elements as improvements, buildings, machinery, equipment, fixtures, fittings, and spare parts. In order to ensure that the host government does not inherit a "shell" (as opposed to a viable project), it may be necessary to include clauses on adequate maintenance of project assets to be in good working order, usual wear and tear excepted, but up to a minimum standard of quality of fitness.

37. Transfer of insurance and concessionaire's warranties

This may require the concessionaire to provide warranties to the host government with respect to the project assets to be transferred, including unexpired warranties available to the concessionaire either by contract or by law. Perhaps the concessionaire's contractors and suppliers should be made to consent to such an assignment as part of the original contractual documentation, or to enter into a subcontract with the host government guaranteeing their continued commitment to the original contract.

38. Technology transfer

Under this provision, it may be necessary to specify that an appropriate number of copies of plans, drawings, blueprints, operating manuals, instructions, and computer programs (including licences to operate such programs, where applicable) be turned over to the host government at the time of the transfer. Transfer provisions should include the training of local personnel during the original duration of the contract in order to assist operation and maintenance of the project facilities.

39. Definition and allocation of transfer costs

Although there can no hard-and-fast rules about this, it is important to specify what direct and indirect costs are associated with any transfer and how to allocate this cost between the concessionaire and the host government. These should include, for instance, such costs as the transfer or stamp duties, recording costs and notarial fees, fees for new permits and approvals, employees' termination costs, costs of training local personnel, and fees to third parties.

40. Transfer or renewal procedure

This is set out quite clearly in the procedure to be followed for transfer or renewal. Such a procedure should be as simple as possible and avoid unnecessary bureaucratic bottlenecks.

Chapter VI: Termination of the concession period

41. Termination by reason of exceptional circumstances or other events

In this event, any of the Parties should apply to the arbitral tribunal to terminate the project agreement formally. In that case, no compensation may be paid (except to those principals who have received net financial benefits, in which case a nominal sum could be paid to the concessionaire).

42. Termination on grounds of national defence or war

In this case, the principals should pay the concessionaire compensation to be determined by the arbitral tribunal.

43. Termination by reason of the fault of the concessionaires

Here, the principals should give notice of the breach and a specified time within which the concessionaire should rectify the breach. Where this fails, the principals should give notice to the lenders, who may wish to exercise their right of substitution. Where this happens, the project shall be deemed to be continuing.

44. Compensation for termination

The principals should undertake not to terminate the project agreement except in such circumstances as specified in this agreement. Otherwise, the concessionaire shall be entitled to compensation which should include both *damnum emergence* and *lucrum cessans*, account being taken of any mitigation of loss, which the concessionaire should have undertaken.

45. Consequences of the concession period terminating

This should state that this agreement shall cease to have any effect upon such termination of the concession period. This should be without prejudice to any rights and obligations that may have accrued prior to such cessation.

Chapter VII: Disputes, laws, and rules

46. Settlement of disputes

Any disputes between the concessionaire and the government agency or any of the principals shall be submitted to international arbitration at the request of any of the Parties. The arbitration shall be conducted in accordance with the UNCITRAL Rules of International Commercial Arbitration.

Note to Appendix 1

1. The compilation of this table of content and the accompanying explanations of its content, has been adapted from two principal sources: Niclisch (Hrsg.), *Rechtsfragen privatfinanzierter Projekte: National und international BOT-Projekte* (Heidelberg: Muller, Jur. Verl., 1994), pp. 93–117 and UNIDO, *UNIDO BOT Guidelines* (Vienna: UNIDO, 1994).

Contributors

Michael Brown is a private consultant on environment/energy-related issues.

Laura B. Campbell, JD, is a lawyer and the former Director of the Environmental Law and Institutions Programme at UNEP. She is currently an Abe Fellow, Director of Environmental Law International and professorial lecturer at the George Washington University Law School, Washington, DC.

W. Bradnee Chambers MA, LLM is a Fellow and Coordinator of the Multilateralism and Sustainable Development Programme (MSD) of the Institute of Advanced Studies, United Nations University, Tokyo, Japan. Mr Chambers specializes in public international law and works on environmental treaty and international economic legal issues.

Joanna Depledge is a former Programme Officer, Science and Technology for the United Nations Framework Convention on Climate Change (UNFCCC) Secretariat. She has recently left this position to complete a PhD at University College, London, England.

Catherine Redgwell BA, LLB, MSc is a barrister and solicitor (British Columbia, Canada) and a Senior Lecturer in Law at the University of Nottingham, England. Ms Redgwell has published widely on international law and energy law.

Gary P. Sampson PhD Econ, is a Visiting Academic at the London School of Economics and Professor of International Economic Governance at the Institute of Advanced Studies, United Nations University, Tokyo. Until early 1999, Professor Sampson was director of a number of divisions of the GATT and WTO, most recently the Trade and Environment Division.

Claudia Santoro BA, LLB is a lawyer with the Ontario, Canada, Ministry of the Environment's Legal Services Branch.

Sergei Vinogradov LLB, PhD is a Senior Research Fellow at the Centre for Energy, Petroleum, and Mineral Law and Policy (CEPMLP), University of Dundee, Scotland. His current research interests are in the areas of environmental regulation of offshore petroleum activities, transboundary water resources, legal status and regime of the Caspian Sea, and shared petroleum resources.

Thomas Walde is Professor of International Economic, Natural Resources & Energy Law; Professor of International Investment, Petroleum and Mineral Law; and Jean Monnet Professor of European Economic and Energy Law (1995–99), University of Dundee, Scotland. Professor Walde is also the Executive Director of the Centre for Energy, Petroleum and Mineral Law and Policy (CEPMLP).

Jacob Werksman BA, JD is a Senior Lawyer at FIELD (Foundation for International Environmental Law and Development) and Lecturer in Law, School of Oriental and African Studies, University of London. He has published widely on international environmental and economic law.

Ibibia Lucky Worika LLB, LLM is a Commonwealth Academic Staff PhD Research Scholar at the Centre for Energy, Petroleum and Mineral Law and Policy (CEPMLP), University of Dundee, Scotland. Mr Worika specializes on international environment and energy law.

Zhong Xiang Zhang PhD is a Senior Fellow at the Department of Economics and Public Finance, University of Groningen, The Netherlands. Dr Zhang also lectures part-time as a Professor of Economics at the Centre for Environment and Development, Chinese Academy of Social Sciences, Beijing, PR of China, and has published widely on economics and the environment.

Index

BP Amoco: intra-firm emissions
trading scheme 28–29
Britain: meat and poultry importation ban (1981) 92–93
Brittan, Sir Leon 72
brokering of ERUs 28, 33
Buenos Aires Plan of Action 8,
14–16
Build, Operate, and Transfer
(BOT) project contracts
215, 237–38, 243
Burkina Faso: and AIJ programmes
37

Canada
and emissions trading 132
Ethyl dispute 205, 206
and Kyoto Protocol 110
carbon dioxide emissions 74, 77,
119–20, 128, 130–31,
175, 228
carbon taxes 81, 121–23, 128,
130–31, 143–44
carbon-sequestration projects 29
Center for Clear Air Policy (CCAP)
141
Central and Eastern European
Countries (CEEC) 242
certified emission reductions
(CERs) 194–95, 198, 211,
222, 228, 245
China
BOT programme 237
and emissions trading 132, 137
and JI concept 142
CITES see Convention on
International Trade in
Endangered Species of
Wild Fauna and Flora
clean air: as a natural resource
96–7

Clean Air Act (US) 168
clean development mechanism
(CDM) 10, 11, 12, 18,
25–26, 32, 52, 53–54,
221–30
administration 224–25
and certified emission reductions
(CERs) 194–95, 198, 211,
222, 224, 228, 245
contracts 216, 218, 225–44
BOT project contracts
235–37, 238, 244
concession contracts 234–36,
244
intergovernmental cooperation
agreements 232–34, 244
joint venture agreements
(JVAs) 237–39, 240, 244
risk service contracts 241–42,
244
standardized agreement
summary (Appendix 1)
247–59
and ERUs schemes 82, 90, 226,
227
expropriation and compensation
201–03
implementation 215–45
joint venture agreements
(CDMJVAs) 239, 240, 241
and MAI interaction 197–203
and MEAs 192
options for multilateral
arrangements 195
project activity cycle 194
projects/investment 37, 191,
194–95, 200–201, 218,
226, 229
quantified emission limitation
and reduction objectives
(QUELROs) 99, 233